Tales until Dawn

The World of a Cape Bretoi

Joe Neil MacNeil holds in his memory a wealth of Gaelic folktales, learned in his youth in Cape Breton. For over a decade, he has told his tales to John Shaw, a specialist in Celtic folklore and fluent speaker of Gaelic. And Shaw has recorded, transcribed, edited, and translated the tales and folklore into English. This rich and entertaining collection is the result of their collaboration. Folktales, anecdotes, proverbs, expressions, rhymes, superstitions, and games are presented; included are a fragment from the Ulster cycle, some items from the Fenian cycle, hero and wonder tales, fairy and witch lore, romantic tales, tales of the exemplum type, tales of cleverness, "numbskull" stories, animal tales, and tall tales.

MacNeil also describes his early years growing up in a Gaelic-speaking rural community, where story-telling was a basic element of the community life. He explains how he learned the tales and the customs and practices associated with telling them. He also introduces us to the families and individuals who were custodians of the tales. John Shaw's introduction outlines the informant's tradition and its place in the world of the European Gaelic story-teller.

The commentaries by MacNeil and Shaw, the tales, the games, and the other folk material offer a rich and unique perspective on the Gaelic culture generally, and as it developed on Cape Breton in particular. The specialist will find it fascinating; the general reader will be equally enthralled. A cloth-bound edition that includes the original Gaelic as well as the English is also available.

JOE NEIL MACNEIL lives in Big Pond, Cape Breton County, Nova Scotia, and continues to tell folktales. JOHN SHAW is compiling a collection of Gaelic songs and folktales from an Inverness County, Cape Breton Gaelic reciter.

Tales until Dawn

The World of a Cape Breton
Gaelic Story-Teller

Joe Neil MacNeil

Translated and edited by
JOHN SHAW

This edition first published in 2005 by
Birlinn Limited
West Newington House
10 Newington Road
Edinburgh EH9 1QS

www.birlinn.co.uk

First published in 1987 by McGill-Queen's University Press

ISBN10: 1 84158 333 2
ISBN13: 978 1 84158 333 4

British Library Cataloguing-in-Publication Data
A catalogue record for this book is available from the British Library

Printed and bound by Antony Rowe Ltd, Chippenham

Contents

viii   Contents

Author's Preface

Dear Readers

A thing has happened which I thought would never come to
pass – that the folk tales and the items of Gaelic tradition that
are in this book should be published. But first I must tell you
that this work could never have been realized were it not for
the encouragement and the constant help which I got from
my friend of long standing, John Shaw. It was he who saw it
fitting and important that this sort of publication be prepared
and who gave me all the help that was necessary.

Every story and item from our tradition here has come from
wonderful and kind people who are no longer living today. It
is my hope that you will share with me in remembering them
with great warmth and in respecting their achievements.
Please do not regard me as deserving of any special praise but
see this book as a tribute to those living in times past who
were gifted, kindly and sensible, and generous with their store
of tales. I wish also to remember those people who were
kind to me in the progress of this effort and who gave me the
courage to do it, as well as those who helped me in ways or
with things too numerous to name at this time. It is my wish
that you will all enjoy this book and derive great pleasure
from it, for that is what will give me the greatest happiness.

Joe Neil MacNeil

Acknowledgments

My grateful thanks are extended to the individuals and in-stitutions who have contributed towards the preparation of this work: Joe Neil MacNeil for his generosity, his patience, and his faith in his tradition; Professor Charles Dunn of Harvard University for many helpful comments and constant encouragement; James Watson for help in correcting the Gaelic proofs and suggestions regarding the manuscript; Sister Margaret MacDonell of St Francis Xavier University for her advice; my wife Jill Shaw for her help in compiling the maps and correcting the English proofs; the Multiculturalism Directorate of the Department of State, Ottawa, for funding received towards research; St Francis Xavier University for the use of its research and office facilities; the Harvard University Library; Allan J. MacEachen; Lawrence O'Neil, MP; Irene Campbell for typing the manuscript; Malcolm MacLean, Mrs Dan Neil MacNeil and Mrs Michael MacLean, all of Sydney, for their helpful generosity; and the many Gaelic-speaking story-tellers in Cape Breton, living and dead, for learning and passing on the tales.

John Shaw, Glendale, Cape Breton

Introduction

This collection of Gaelic oral tradition from the Middle Cape and Big Pond area of Cape Breton County on Cape Breton Island, Nova Scotia, has been transcribed and translated from tape recordings made by the editor of Joe Neil MacNeil (Eòs Nìll Bhig) of Middle Cape, the most remarkable Gaelic reciter to emerge in Cape Breton since the 1960s. Born in 1908, Joe Neil, unlike most Gaelic-speaking folklore informants on the island, has achieved literacy in Gaelic, largely through his own efforts, but the Gaelic text is based on the unlettered tradition of his people and has been transcribed as told.[1] It is not our task here to attempt a comprehensive account of the culture of this Gaelic-speaking community as it existed in Joe Neil's youth.[2] Instead, we have endeavoured to portray in part the intellectual life of a once vigorous Gaelic area as seen through the eyes and heart of a traditional story-teller living in our own time.

Joe Neil's fund of *sgeulachdan*, or narrative tales, is what is most remarkable in his repertoire and forms the major part of this collection. The tales have been ordered according to their sources – and where possible according to families of reciters – to provide a partial record of the groups of story-tellers who flourished in the parish some sixty years ago. Until the middle of this century – and the final decades of the story-telling tradition in Scottish Gaelic – little attention had been given to that important element of oral transmission, the tradition-bearer. Hence the character and family background of the many story-tellers, wits, and musicians who so willingly passed on their learning to Joe Neil have been described and the glimpses given of these learned Gaels permit some comparison with story-telling counterparts in neighbouring cultures and else-

where.[3] Family information about the story-telling sources is
included in part because there are no written genealogies for
the people of Middle Cape and Big Pond, most of whom claim
Barra and South Uist descent. Perhaps later study of these
genealogies may one day reveal more concerning the proven-
ance of the region's Gaelic culture and the processes of oral
transmission in small rural communities.

Because of the island's isolation and lack of convenient
internal transport well into the twentieth century, Gaelic
folktale research in Cape Breton, compared to that of Scotland,
was begun at a late stage in the life of the culture and has
enjoyed at best sporadic progress, mostly through the efforts of
outsiders. In 1937 John Lorne Campbell of Canna and his wife
Margaret Fay Shaw made the first organized recording expedition to the island to collect songs from the descendants of
settlers from Barra and South Uist living near Boisdale, Cape
Breton County, and Iona, Victoria County. Although no tales
were recorded on this pioneering expedition, the collectors
cannot have been unaware that there were competent reciters
in the neighbourhood.[4] Four years later, Charles Dunn of Harvard University travelled the island extensively in search of
Gaelic material and recorded a number of folktales on a portable
dictaphone.[5] During the same year the Reverend Malcolm
MacDonell of Hillsdale, Inverness County, while a student at
St Francis Xavier University, Antigonish, transcribed a tale
from a neighbour, Hector Campbell, which was subsequently
published.[6] Tales from the same reciter were written down by
Kenneth Jackson of Harvard University and the University of
Edinburgh in 1946 and published a few years later.[7] More of
Hector Campbell's tales were tape-recorded in 1952 by collector
MacEdward Leach. In 1964 Kathleen MacKinnon, a Scottish
student from Tiree, recorded and published an excellent version
of Cath nan Eun "The Battle of the Birds" from Hughie Dan
MacDonnell of Deepdale, Inverness County.[8] Some five years
later, C.I.N. MacLeod, then professor of Celtic studies at St
Francis Xavier University, published a collection of Cape
Breton Gaelic stories from both written and oral sources which
included one full-length hero-tale taken from the lips of a

Benacadie reciter on his death-bed (see "The Man in the Light Grey Coat" in Part 2). Additional recordings of Hector Campbell were made by Sister Margaret MacDonell of St Francis Xavier University and Dr Gordon MacLennan of University College, Dublin, and Ottawa University in the late sixties. During the first half of the seventies various collectors contributed tape-recorded folktales to the archives at the College of Cape Breton, and a few Gaelic folktales from collectors were made more widely available in *Cape Breton's Magazine.*[9] Between 1977 and 1983 the Gaelic Language and Folklore Project at St Francis Xavier University, funded by the federal Multiculturalism Directorate, was engaged in a concentrated effort to record Gaelic material in Cape Breton, including folktales and the lore associated with story-telling. It has recently published a collection of tales from the late Hector Campbell.[10]

On the basis of the number and quality of the folktales recorded or alluded to in the course of our field-work since 1977, it is clear that had a collector of like talents and dedication been active in Cape Breton during the 1850s and 1860s, the results would have rivalled those contained in the manuscripts and published collections of John Francis Campbell (of Islay), which today form the basis for Scottish Gaelic folktale scholarship. The striking degree of cultural conservatism among Cape Breton Gaels is certainly a result of geographical isolation. Yet, for items in the oral tradition such as the Ulster Cycle or Fenian material which can be termed particularly ancient, there is a further cause: Cape Breton is the most recent and far-flung outpost of the Scottish *Gàidhealtachd* (Gaelic-speaking region), and it is a well-documented phenomenon that archaic survivals of social and cultural institutions are most likely to be found at the periphery of a given cultural area.[11]

My acquaintance with Joe Neil MacNeil began during a routine perusal of Gaelic tapes while I was working as a researcher in Gaelic folklore at the archives of the College of Cape Breton in Sydney during the summer of 1975. A recording that immediately caught my attention was a version of *Nighean Rìgh na h-Éipheit* (Part 2, no 34 below), delivered with a sureness of detail and a command of Gaelic that I recognized as the work of a master story-teller. The same command of the language – without apparent effort or limitations – impressed me again when I met Joe Neil some weeks later. Over the following months my task of designing a Gaelic language course for the island based on local traditional materials and methods and incorporating tradition-bearers in their former, time-honoured role as teachers, brought us together frequently. Over the winter months, what had begun as an effort to introduce Joe Neil's lore into a language program grew into a more detailed study of his tradition and an effort to recover as many as possible of the apparently endless stock of tales that he recalled from his youth. In February we began noting down scattered details from some thirty separate tales, adding to the notes gradually as Joe Neil recalled additional events. The process of remembering was reinforced by a visit we made over a number of days to another accomplished story-teller, Lauchie MacLellan of Dunvegan, Inverness County. I knew Joe Neil was looking forward to exchanging stories with another reciter, but I did not fully realize how seriously he took our expedition until I became aware in the car on our way to Dunvegan that in a barely audible whisper he was going over the difficult parts of the tales he had prepared for the occasion.

By April we were able to record versions of seventeen of the thirty tales, including a number of the more important ones in the present collection: *Fear a' Chòta Liathghlais, Iagan 's a Mhaighstir, Mac Duine Làidir na Coilleadh*, and fragments of further Fenian material. Versions of *Brìd Mhór Each* and *Bàs Chù Chulainn* were also recovered but were not recorded until 1977. In addition, Joe Neil was able to deliver an excellent version of a long hero-tale, *Iain Mac an Iasgair Mhóir* (AT 300), along with extensive fragments of other tales.[12] Our practice of keeping notes and reviewing them as details were added allowed us to check internal consistency, though such checks became superfluous as Joe Neil's own penchant for accuracy in his recitations began to assert itself. The same attention to faithful reproduction of detail extended to the sources of the tales, and at this point Joe Neil first pointed to the Kennedy family of Middle Cape as coming from a line of story-telling specialists. Although literate in Gaelic, he always took care in our conversations to distinguish between the oral and written sources of his tales.

While literacy in Gaelic has provided Joe Neil with a welcome access to material in the Gaelic books and papers available locally, the oral tradition of his own area has remained the touchstone. As has been noted in reciters elsewhere in the Gaelic world, Joe Neil's conversation is replete with the expressions, proverbs, and anecdotes that enlivened the ordinary speech of the previous generation of tradition-bearers of Middle Cape and its environs. Also characteristic of outstanding Gaelic informants is their willingness to record for the serious collector.[13] Once the informant's confidence is gained, such a task is perceived as a duty growing out of their unspoken role as the guardians of their people's tradition. Such a sense of responsibility was apparent during a marathon two-week recording session with Joe Neil in the autumn of 1978. Our recording began in the morning and frequently finished in the early hours of the following morning; yet Joe Neil's energy and enthusiasm never flagged. The material from this session, filling overy fifty half-hour tapes, was by no means the end: a good informant will always have recalled additional important items for the next session.[14] Since that time Joe Neil has recorded hundreds more of these, among them further accounts of the lengendary carpenter *Boban Saor* and the miraculous physician *An Dotair Bàn* (see Part 2, nos 15, 16, 35, 45–9) which only came to light in late 1981.

It is revealing in terms of cultural change in Cape Breton's Gaelic-speaking areas that the informants themselves possess a greater understanding of the importance of collecting their oral literature than is evidenced by their adult offspring who, as a rule, are non-Gaelic-speaking, have had more formal education, and have a more cosmopolitan cultural outlook. Here, as in so many other Celtic areas, the older informants

often express their regret that systematic folklore collecting
was not begun earlier.[15]

To this day, Joe Neil's social contacts are within the Gaelic-
speaking world or around the area where he was raised. Gaelic
is and always has been his preferred language; Joe Neil is one
of the few Gaels living in Cape Breton today who is satisfied
to use his language in public, or indeed within the hearing of
non–Gaelic-speakers. Perhaps more unusual in a person of his
generation – and those following – is his refusal to accept the
often proffered dictum that the living language and the Gaelic
world have no place in our times. Joe Neil's relationship to
the modern world follows a theme of adapting present realities
to suit older priorities that are well known in Gaelic culture.
His wide range of skills as a carpenter, plumber, mechanic,
electrician, and sawmill operator have provided him with an
adequate livelihood in an economy increasingly dominated by
technology and money, while allowing him to maintain the
centuries-old pattern of the itinerant versatile journeyman.
He keeps well informed of events outside the island through
the media, yet does not hesitate to express his view that the
social benefits of the media have definite limitations compared
with the neighbourhood gatherings of his youth.

It came as a surprise to me that a person of Joe Neil's gifts of
memory and narration would have so little to say concerning
his own life. The reason for this apparent reticence is best
expressed in the reciter's own words: *chaidh mi thro shaoghal
cumanta gu leòr* "my own experience was ordinary enough."
Like the famous Irish story-teller Peig Sayers, who required
lengthy coaxing before she saw the importance of dictating
her autobiography, Joe Neil views his own personal story as
relatively insignificant next to the tradition of which he is an
active part.[16] Many of the finer exponents among the older
people in Cape Breton – singers, bards, reciters, fiddlers, pipers,
and step-dancers – are inclined to regard performing gifts
as a part of the shared cultural store, rather than the exclu-
sive property of gifted individuals. When asked whether
such a communal concept of traditional performances was
prevalent in Gaelic areas in the past, Joe Neil's unhesitating

answer was, *Nach eil fhios agaibh gu robh* "Don't you know it was."

The accounts given in Parts 1 and 2 of the house gatherings in the Middle Cape district, where the stage was set for stories, songs, and other lore, as well as those of the practice of story-telling itself, provide us with an indication of the extent to which the practices surrounding oral transmission in Old World Gaelic areas were retained in Cape Breton well into this century. Here, as in the rest of Gaeldom, the main occasions for the recitation of tales were reserved for the long winter nights.[17] The description of those present quietly engaged in their evening tasks of sewing, knitting, repairing equipment, and so on, could come from any of the *céilidh* settings of the nineteenth century published by collectors visiting the Outer Isles. The customary *céilidh* sequence given here, starting with a detailed discussion – with full commentary – of the local news and progressing to the recitation of tales, was well known elsewhere.[18] As in all Gaelic communities, the *taigh-faire* or wake-house was a favourite venue for story-tellers, who often performed until daylight. In his district, as in Western Scotland and Ireland, Joe Neil recalls that tales helped to pass the time as fishermen waited to haul in their nets, but story-telling in Cape Breton was no longer associated with other work places such as kilns.[19]

The rules of etiquette surrounding the recitation of tales in Cape Breton have been relaxed since the beginning of the century. John MacLean's account of an invitation from Donald Kennedy (Part 2) to listen to his rendition of a substantial hero-tale during school hours shows that the prohibition against reciting hero-tales and wonder-tales during daylight hours was not in effect in Cape Breton as it was in Ireland until recent times.[20] The custom of direct criticism, in company, of a reciter's performance among Hebridean story-tellers is not known to have existed here.[21] Occasional corrections from the audience have been observed, often as not from a spouse or sister of a passive tradition-bearer during recent sessions. As a rule, local listeners expressed their appreciation of reciters' gifts through the frequency of their requests for tales and the numbers who gathered to listen. Although some highly regarded women story-tellers were always active in Scotland's *Gàidhealtachd*, there, as in Ireland, they were subject to certain traditional constraints.[22] The longer, more elaborate wonder- and hero-tales including Fenian tales were regarded as the preserve of male reciters; occasionally women recited from the body of historical and legendary lore (*seanchas*) and more frequently they were the custodians of songs (with their associated stories), musical traditions, charms and various other branches of the oral tradition. Joe Neil does not recall any instances of Fenian tales being recited by women in his own district, though the area boasted a large number of good women story-tellers.[23] Throughout the island, constraints on women's story-telling repertoires seem to have been relaxed compared to Scotland and Ireland: in 1978 a lengthy introduction to an elaborate romantic tale, *Conall Ruadh nan Car* "Red Conall of the Tricks" (AT 953), was recorded from Mrs Peggy Smith (Bean Sheumais Alasdair Pheadair) of Deepdale, Inverness County,[24] and a Mrs Sarah (Mór) Gillis who lived in the same locality some sixty years ago was well known for her rendition of the Fenian tale *Fear a' Chòta Shliobaistich Liathghlais* "The Man in the Slovenly Grey Coat" (see Part 2, no 1).[25]

On the rare occasions when a practised reciter is available, folktales are still valued by Cape Breton's remaining Gaelic-speakers as an enjoyable and absorbing pastime. When word was passed around the parish of Glendale, Inverness County, in the autumn of 1978 that Joe Neil would furnish an evening's entertainment of long tales, my house was filled with neighbours who listened raptly to the three-hour session. The role of master story-teller won him the instant respect of his audience, as did his comical turn of phrase. The tendency of both reciter and audience to become completely immersed in a story is well documented for Scottish Gaels; Michael MacLean's lapse of attention with the stove covers so clearly remembered by Joe Neil (page 20) recalls accounts from nineteenth-century Scotland where whole groups sent out to perform heavy labour were known to pass an entire day sitting at the work-site listening to stories.[26] Joe Neil's remarks concerning the feeling of oneness within the audience during the performance of stories and other forms of traditional entertainment (page 10) point to the unifying effect of tales produced through a literature of shared internal experience. For children in traditional Gaelic society, the didactic function of many of the tales, along with riddles, is easily appreciated.[27] Equally noteworthy, as pointed out by the Dunvegan, Inverness County, story-teller Lauchie MacLellan, is the profound dramatic effect of a well-told tale which recruits the imagination of its listener.[28] Among Gaels and other story-telling cultures, the tales formed a "bridge from reality to illusion, from the state of wakefulness to that of the dream, as many folklorists have pointed out."[29]

In the repertoires of present-day island story-tellers, wonder-tales and romantic tales are now rare. Our attempt over four years to compile a list of tales known to have been current in Cape Breton, however, offers substantial evidence that these more elaborate and demanding tales were more plentiful around 1860, during the days when reciters of the caliber of Archie Kennedy of Middle Cape first heard stories as children. Wonder-tales and hero-tales have suffered erosion here, as they evidently also have in Ireland.[30]

The selection of tales transcribed here has tended to emphasize the lengthier tales. However a wide range of shorter tales, both international and regional, have been recorded during the past decade. These include a surprising number of religious tales of the *exemplum* type; occasional simple tales (animal tales and formula tales); jokes and anecdotes, which, together with stories of witchcraft and second sight, are the most plentiful variety now remembered. Tales of cleverness, in keeping with the popular proverb, *théid seòltachd thar spionnadh* "cleverness will prevail over physical strength," are highly regarded.[31] That part of the narrative tradition termed *seanchas* by Delargy incorporating local historical legend, not surprisingly, has been most reduced by the effects of relocation, but some interesting though isolated examples have been recovered.[32] One such is a version of the Morar legend *Cù Glas Mheòbail* "The Grey Hound of Meoble"

briefly referred to by Calum Maclean in his accounts of collecting in that area.[33] Another, also summarized by Maclean,
concerns the pact made by the Black Captain with the devil and
the catastrophe that resulted when the devil returned to claim
his own.[34] Survivals of fairy-lore, three of which are in this
collection, have been recorded in numerous island localities.
Interestingly, the Hebridean legend of the origin of the fairies
has been preserved by a family of Morar origin in the parish of
Broadcove, Inverness County.[35] Narrative tales were not
strictly confined to transmitted stories; many locales boasted
reciters who, like Sandy MacIsaac (Sandaidh "Illeasbu" Mhóir)
of Big Pond (see Part 2, nos 32, 33), took pleasure in relating
their own compositions. Locally composed stories, as Bruford
notes for their Irish Gaelic counterparts, did not travel far
or become permanently established in the general repertoire
of tales; yet memories of tales (now lost) composed by the
widely admired Southwest Margaree bard Donald (Dòmhnall
Thormaid) MacDonald still persist in his native area.[36] Recently
a full-length wonder-tale was composed by Lauchie MacLellan
of nearby Dunvegan which equals the standard set by the best
traditional examples recorded.[37]

Joe Neil's recorded tales are rarely longer than forty-five
minutes (about twenty double-spaced, typewritten pages).
This seems to be the maximum length for tales recorded from
Cape Breton reciters and agrees well with the accounts of
twentieth-century Irish story-tellers cited by Delargy.[38] The
longest tale Joe Neil remembers hearing was Archie Kennedy's
version of the hero-tale *Leigheas Coise Céin* "The healing of
Cian's Leg" (see Part 2, no 2) which lasted for a little over two
hours, approximately half the length of that told by Islayman
Lachlann MacNeill and written down in the early 1870s
by Hector MacLean.[39] Further nineteenth-century sources
mention tales of greater length: J.F. Campbell refers to a four-
hour version of *An Ceatharnach Caol Riabhach* "The Slim
Swarthy Champion" and a rendition of *Conall Gulban*
extending through three evenings.[40] Angus (Aonghus Barrach)
MacMillan, a Benbecula reciter and the son of one of
Carmichael's informants, dictated *Alasdair Mac a' Cheird*, a

tale lasting some nine hours, to Calum Maclean in the early 1950s, as well as forty-three other tales that each lasted over three hours.[41] Such gleanings from oral sources have led Delargy and Gerard Murphy to observe that the stories in medieval manuscripts served only as condensations of the oral versions which were originally one to several hours in length.[42] The labour and interruptions involved in written transcriptions from reciters would offer an explanation for the brevity of many of the tales in J.F. Campbell's published collections; the original oral renditions would more likely be along the lines of Lachlann MacNeill's *Leigheas Coise Céin* or K.C. Craig's transcriptions of the tales of Duncan (Dunnchadh Clachair) MacDonald of South Uist.[43]

The traditional favourites of the story-teller's audience in the cultural unit formed by the *Gàidhealtachds* of Scotland and Ireland were the Fenian tales recounting the adventures of the legendary warrior Fionn mac Cumhail and his band of followers. These formed the chief epic of Gaelic culture since the Middle Ages and were equal in importance to the Kalevala in Finland.[44] Such was the Highland Gaels' reverence towards the Fenian tales that men often removed their bonnets during their recitation. It is therefore not entirely surprising that Fenian lore should have been given the position of precedence by rural Cape Breton audiences in Middle Cape.[45] In Scottish Gaelic areas, if not beyond, stories of Fionn were considered to be the domain of story-telling specialists, an office that in Middle Cape was filled by the family of Archie Kennedy.[46] Fenian material in Scotland, as J.F. Campbell remarks in the introduction to the first volume of his published collection, was most plentiful in the Hebridean Isles of Barra and South Uist, and it is among the communities of Middle Cape and Christmas Island, both with populations primarily of Barra and South Uist extraction, that the greatest amount of such material has been retained.[47] Nevertheless, there is ample evidence of an active Fenian tradition among people of mainland or Inner Hebridean origin elsewhere on the island and on the Nova Scotia mainland. A fragment of a Fenian dialogue was recorded in 1946 from a Harbourview, Inverness

County, informant; Sarah (Mór) Gillis of Deepdale, Inverness
County, was reputed to have recited a popular Fenian hero-
tale in the 1920s; a version of *Teanndachd Mhór na Féinneadh*
was mentioned as being in the repertoire of an Antigonish
County native in the early 1950s; and a *Ceudach* tale was
recorded from Hector Campbell of Hillsdale, Inverness County,
in 1964.[48]

The singing of Fenian lays (*duain*), which disappeared in
Ireland sometime during the last century, can still be heard
among the older people in isolated communities of the
Western Isles, and until quite recently survived in the memory
of Joe Allan MacLean (1892–1984), a native of Rear Christmas
Island, Cape Breton County. Joe Neil's account suggests that
the singing of the lays, as well as the recitation of Fenian tales,
was considered the task of specialists in Cape Breton, as it was
in Scotland.

The next forms of narrative preferred by Joe Neil, the full-
length wonder-tales (including hero-tales) and the romantic
tales, have clearly declined within the story-telling tradition
since the time Cape Breton was settled, and many are known
to have been lost. Archie Kennedy's rendition of *An Tuairisgeal
Mór*, an important hero-tale which was well known in Cape
Breton but never recovered, took two nights of telling, and
similar though less spectacular instances of attrition can be
found in most localities where tales are told.[49] Within tales of
this kind, the fixed descriptive passages couched in colourful
language termed "runs" have in only one case been recorded
in Cape Breton in more than fragmentary form.[50] In-tales are
likewise rare, having been so far encountered only in two fine
versions of a romantic tale (given in the Aarne-Thomson
classification of tale-types as AT 953 "The Master Thief
Recounts his Adventures"), *An Gadaiche Dubh* "The Black
Thief" from Lauchie MacLellan and *Conall Ruadh nan Car*
"Red Conall of the Tricks" from Hughie Dan MacDonnell;
and in the version of *Leigheas Coise Céin* in this collection.[51]
In Cape Breton, this class of tale is to be found in the Catholic
areas only, though tales of a less elaborate variety, particularly
humorous stories, are common in the Presbyterian areas. The

absence of longer tales outside the Catholic areas can be directly attributed to their condemnation by the fundamentalist clergy at least from the sixteenth century and Bishop Carswell, himself no stranger to the Gaelic oral tradition of his time, whose single sentence of invective rivals in its narrative power the descriptive passages from the older tales.[52] The results of the suppression of extended story-telling in the reformed districts were described by J.F. Campbell and Alexander Carmichael as both thorough and extensive.[53] Yet some of the lighter tales noted down in 1978 from Angus MacKinnon, a native of the isolated Gaelic community of Black Point, Victoria County, settled by Protestant families from Skye and the adjacent mainland, indicate that story-telling among these people remained in a fairly highly evolved form until the 1920s and was not, in J.F. Campbell's words, entirely "buried alive" before the time of immigration.[54]

The same Angus MacKinnon was able to give successful summaries of his tales in English for the entertainment of eight of his seventeen children during my visit, but with few exceptions Gaelic stories have not crossed over into English.[55] The occasional tales in Cape Breton that have weathered the language change are of the "numbskull" or humorous variety, or, like *The Golden Arm*, turn on a trick that is external to the bounds of the narrative.

If the clergy's disapproval of story-telling was confined to specific Gaelic-speaking regions, the advent of formal education, with its insistence on the English language and literacy, has taken a universal toll on the tradition throughout Gaeldom. The best reciters encountered during this century, though learned men in their own terms, possess few or none of the benefits of *sgoil na Beurla* "English-language education." In the case of Benbecula reciter Angus MacMillan, described so compellingly by Calum Maclean, Gaels' reaction to the enforced demise of their own learned tradition was not always passive; Angus MacMillan never bothered to learn English and terminated his own formal education by thrashing the schoolmaster.[56] A combination of selective censure and indirect institutional pressure has driven the practice of story-telling in Scottish Gaelic-speaking districts underground, or towards the social periphery. In Cape Breton the vestiges of a vast store of tales are still remembered, but folktales are easily the most difficult items to record of all folklore items. In Scotland it is revealing that such an acute observer as Calum Maclean, born into a family of noted Raasay and Skye tradition-bearers, did not encounter a practised story-teller among his own countrymen until 1946.[57]

The earliest descriptions of Scottish Gaelic reciters date from the era of collecting activity in the Outer Hebrides during the second half of the last century. In his introduction to *Popular Tales of the West Highlands*, J.F. Campbell furnishes a brief sketch of Donald MacPhie of Iochdar, reputed to be the outstanding reciter in South Uist in his time; in his journals Campbell has left a more detailed portrait of another exceptional performer, Lachlann MacNeill of Islay.[58] Alexander Carmichael, while staying with Campbell on Mingulay, near Barra, in 1871, made the acquaintance of Roderick Mac-Neill (Ruairidh mac Dhòmhnaill), whom he later described.[59]

Until very recently not even the most cursory description of Cape Breton story-tellers has been attempted. Among Scottish researchers, however, increased attention has been paid to the story-tellers themselves, beginning with Calum Maclean's innovative article "Hebridean Storytellers" (1952) together with "Aonghus agus Donnchadh" (1954), his contrastive study of the two greatest Scottish Gaelic story-tellers living at that time, Angus MacMillan of Benbecula and Duncan MacDonald of South Uist. Further valuable studies of Duncan MacDonald have been published by Maartje Draak in 1958 and William Matheson in 1977. The first autobiography of a Hebridean story-teller, Angus (Aonghus Beag) MacLellan of South Uist, appeared in 1964, to be followed by a short study of another South Uist reciter, Donald Alasdair Johnson and a full-length collection of tales and other material from Pàdraig Moireasdan of North Uist.[60]

These published sources together with experience drawn from work in the field make it clear that story-telling is a rural occupation for Scottish Gaels, and story-tellers in Cape Breton,

as in Scotland and Ireland, are not exclusively identified with
any particular profession within rural society.[61] Of the story-
tellers included in this study, Archie Kennedy was a subsistence
farmer and part-time labourer, while his neighbour Michael
MacLean spent much of his working life fishing off the Grand
Banks, and Michael's nephew Donald worked as an inspector
for the railways. Joe Allan MacLean of Rear Christmas Island,
Cape Breton County, made his living as a blacksmith and
Hughie Dan MacDonnell from an early age worked underground in the coal mines a short distance from the farm where
he was born in Deepdale, Inverness County. The tradition of
the intinerant story-teller continued among those without
property or a profession.[62] Whether by choice or circumstance,
wandering story-tellers like Anna MacNeil, travelling a well-
defined circuit through the countryside, were commonplace
until the early 1900s; some, like Joe Neil and the Stewart
Clan of Scotland, have maintained their way of life into the
1980s.[63] The many travelling tailors and shoemakers among
reciters in Scotland mentioned by J.F. Campbell have left no
record in Cape Breton.[64]

Joe Neil is one of a few remaining story-tellers in Cape
Breton who could be termed an active tradition-bearer, and
the skills of most of these have declined through lack of
opportunity to perform. There is no doubt that the demand on
the talents of these few occasioned by the interest of collectors
has provided a welcome challenge and a source of encouragement.[65] However long a time has passed since they practised
their art, all good active story-tellers share an unusual degree
of expressiveness and skill with their native tongue in ordinary
conversation. Joe Neil's use of Gaelic recalls Delargy's remarks
concerning Irish story-teller Michael Turraoin, a "master of
idiom, phrase and linguistic nuance."[66] A frequent device of
Joe Neil's is to use his skill with expressions, usually with
underlying humour, as a means of putting new acquaintances
at their ease. William Matheson in his tribute to Duncan
MacDonald, remarked that the old man's "command of the
language was consummate: the elegance of his phrasing was
noticeable even in the most ordinary conversation."[67] Equally

characteristic of active reciters is their concern for their language and the total lack of concern for English as evidenced by Angus MacMillan of Benbecula.[68] One need only read Pàdraig Ó Siochfhradha's moving description of the Kerryman Micheàl ("Mici na gCloch") Ó Súilleabháin, "the king of all the storytellers," standing on the steps of the church and announcing with great excitement the impending restoration of the Irish language to understand the degree to which such men have been the true champions of the Gaelic language.[69]

The training of story-tellers in Cape Breton, though never formal, began early in childhood. Joe Neil recalls listening carefully to tales at the age of eight or nine.[70] Hughie Dan MacDonnell by the age of ten had begun to acquire a repertoire. Similarly, Duncan MacDonald of South Uist began his career by making a conscious effort as a child to learn and to recite tales.[71] As a rule, Irish reciters also began as young boys, showing a fondness for tales and an affection for the old people who used to tell them. While evidence of any formal instruction in acquiring tales in Cape Breton is lacking, Calum Maclean mentions that young lads in the Outer Hebrides were enrolled in schools of story-telling in learning heroic lays from the older tradition-bearers to chant on New Year's Eve.[72]

Story-telling throughout Gaeldom, particularly of long, elaborate tales, tended to be transmitted through families. This has been demonstrated for the traditions of Duncan MacDonald (back three generations and possibly more) and Angus MacMillan, and, according to Joe Neil, is true for the Kennedy and MacLean families of Middle Cape.[73] Nevertheless, transmission through the family *bho ghlùin gu glùn* "from generation to generation" is by no means a fast rule even among the most accomplished reciters. Seumas MacKinnon of Barra learned all of his stories from one man who was not a member of his family, and Seán Ó Conaill of Kerry, much like Joe Neil, names twenty-seven sources for his tales.[74] The Kennedys of Middle Cape were, to my knowledge, unique in the island in being regarded as specialists in Fenian and romantic tales. Unlike Hungary, for instance, where certain tales became the "property of an established story-teller," there was no formal "ownership" of specific tales among local reciters, though one person's version of a tale might be requested most frequently.[75] Nor is there evidence of overt competition between reciters here, as has been recorded in Hungary and Ireland, though the absence of visible rivalries does not preclude considerable respect being accorded a skilful narrator.

From the picture given here by Joe Neil of his own parish, along with the large number of active reciters that he can recall living in the Benacadie–Christmas Island district of Cape Breton County, it is more than likely that there was an abundance of active tradition-carriers in many of the local rural communities. Similarly, in Scotland at the turn of the century, the North Uist reciter Pàdruig Moireasdan was well acquainted with twenty competent reciters in his own small neighbourhood.[76]

The extraordinary memory possessed by story-tellers has been remarked upon by collectors since the time of Alexander Carmichael.[77] In Cape Breton, Neil Gillis of Jamesville, Victoria County, by his own admission a passive tradition-bearer, was able to recite a lengthy and detailed version of a romantic tale which he had heard some fifty-five years earlier from Charles (Tearlach Pheadair Ruaidh) MacInnis, a well-known reciter in nearby Christmas Island; the performance was the more remarkable since Neil Gillis had not used Gaelic in his daily life for the previous twenty-five years.[78]

The size of present-day Cape Breton reciters' repertoires does not compare with the examples given by Delargy for Irish informants but approaches more closely those contained in recent collections from Scottish reciters.[79] Informants assure us, however, that repertoires of reciters from the previous generation when regular story-telling flourished, those of men like Archie Kennedy and Michael MacLean, were considerably larger. As for the retentive abilities of individuals, Maartje Draak has made a detailed comparison of two separate renditions (1944 and 1950) of the lengthy hero-tale *Fear na h-Eabaid* from Duncan MacDonald of South Uist.[80] The results show a surprising degree of accuracy where the story-line is concerned (the two renditions differed in only one minor detail); differences in the choice of words are present only to the extent of demonstrating that the tale is not couched in rigid or mechanical language. Similar feats of memory were commonplace among modern Irish reciters, many of whom needed to hear a tale only once or twice in order to acquire it.[81] Especially striking is Delargy's anecdote concerning a Valentia Island story-teller named Lynch who managed to "steal" a long, jealously guarded tale, *Fáilte Úi Chealla* "O'Kelly's Welcome," from an itinerant beggar by concealing himself in a loft at night while the tale was being told.[82]

Comparisons of the processes of tale transmission in Ireland and Scotland suggest that Scottish story-tellers take more pride in accurate transmission of stories.[83] If this is so it could stem from what Douglas Hyde already recognized at the beginning of this century as the relatively slight influence exerted by the manuscript tradition on oral transmission in Scotland from at least the eighteenth century.[84] Literacy in rural Gaelic communities, although not unknown in Cape Breton, has been relatively rare; in Middle Cape during Joe Neil's youth, Hector MacMullin and James Smith were the only other residents able to read the language. Moreover, most Scottish reciters distrusted the quality and accuracy of printed versions and did not hesitate to express their reservations to the most illustrious collectors in the field.[85] In Ireland, as in Joe Neil's Middle Cape, a good memory was a consciously cultivated, highly prized asset, and literacy was regarded as an obstacle to a good story-telling memory; one man's failure to retain a story was (doubtless correctly) attributed to his having read too many books.[86] There are scattered indications, neverthe-less, that some manuscripts were in circulation in Scotland at least until the eighteenth century. The MacNabs of Dalmally were reputed to be in possession of a manuscript containing Fenian material; the famous MacMhuirich family, hereditary bards to Clanranald, were also said to possess manuscripts, one of which may have contained romantic tales; Edward Lhuyd in his notes on the contents of manuscripts belonging to the Reverend John Beaton of Mull, the last learned member

of a famous family of leeches and scholars, lists manuscript
versions of the story of the death of Cù Chulainn, along with a
number of long romantic tales.[87]

Whatever influence such manuscripts, both of native and
Irish origin, had on the fund of tales in the Scottish *Gàidhealtachd*, written materials have exerted a decidedly limited
influence on the story-telling tradition in Cape Breton. There is
only one fragmentary written transcription of a tale surviving,
taken down some time before 1911 from the dictation of an
unknown informant in the Middle Cape district.[88] Printed
versions left some traces in many Gaelic-speaking areas. The
memories of the generally unlettered listeners allowed these
to pass into the oral tradition easily; in some instances
the known printed texts were reproduced with astounding
accuracy.[89] J.F. Campbell was aware of the currency of the
Arabian Nights stories in the Outer Isles in the nineteenth
century and a version of *Sgeulachd a' Lampa Dhuibh* "The
Story of the Black Lamp" entered the repertoire of Archie
Kennedy of Middle Cape, probably through a version printed
in the Gaelic newspaper *Mac-Talla*.[90] Many long romantic
tales in Ireland, which could be repeated by some almost as
heard from two readings of the manuscript, were improved by
being absorbed into the stock of orally transmitted tales; in
1978 Joe Neil with no apparent effort recited a Gaelic version
of an Irish tale printed in English which is superior to the
original.[91]

Regardless of their origin, once absorbed into the Gaelic
folk repertoire, stories are passed on with close attention to
the plot or narrative framework. Yet no two reciters tell the
same wonder-tale alike. Douglas Hyde, in attempting to
account for the differences between Scottish and Irish versions
of "alliterative passages" (runs), speculated that the incidents
rather than the language were passed on.[92] Delargy explains
the process in greater detail.

> The old-time Gaelic story-teller was a conscious literary artist,
> proud of his art, jealous of his rivals, eager to pass on the
> tradition as it had come to him, intolerant of change, conser-

vative as to form and order and plot; but the style and the language are stamped with his own personality, and, as he had an eye for the symmetry of the spoken word, he felt at liberty — true artist that he was — to elaborate inside the traditional framework of the narrative events of the story, and to clothe the commonplaces of fiction with the rich garment of poetic prose.[93]

Certainly in their efforts toward "the ideal of a story well and truly retold," Gaelic story-tellers were allowed considerably less latitude with regard to plot and order of events than their counterparts in the equally active story-telling communities of Hungary, where the overall length and contents of a tale, especially the beginning and the end, were habitually altered to suit the immediate wishes of the audience.[94] In Cape Breton it is the story-teller's selection of the tale to suit the listeners that is regarded as crucial and determines as much as anything else his success in pleasing them.

Within the carefully transmitted framework of the tale, the story-teller was an active, frequently vigorous "shaper of tradition" whose personal, creative role in telling the story was known to Middle Cape story-tellers as *Éideadh na Sgeulachd* "The Raiment of the Tale."[95] The devices used to achieve this differed from person to person, depending on a narrator's ingenuity and talents. The range of such narrative devices is impressive: in his remarks contrasting the narrative techniques of the South Uist reciter of wonder-tales Duncan MacDonald with his contemporary Angus MacMillan, Calum Maclean notes Duncan's reliance on his consummate skill with language and style; Angus MacMillan, on the other hand, was given to elaborate detail in the story-line, with a talent for conjuring up visual images, and took great delight in extensive *oratio recte* dialogue.[96] Joe Neil's technique incorporates elements characteristic of both great reciters, yet his main concern is with the psychology of the story, using the relations between events to elicit the pathos or humour from the characters' situations with a frequent emphasis on the moral implications of the tale. This is all expressed through language which, although not ornate, is slightly formal and reminiscent of the wording used by the Islay story-teller Lachlann MacNeill in his version of *Leigheas Coise Céin.*[97] Joe Neil understands the meaning of every word in his tales. There is none of the purposely obscure or elaborate rhetoric, termed in Scottish Gaelic *a' chruaidh-Ghàidhlig dhomhain* "deep, hard Gaelic," which was an attractive feature for Irish audiences of the romances read from post-medieval manuscripts.[98] A more formal narrative style can also be seen in the South Uist reciter Angus MacLellan's fondness for impersonal forms in his tales.[99] Characteristic individual styles in Cape Breton are the rapid and dramatic speech of Hughie Dan MacDonnell of Deepdale, Inverness County, and the slow, understated, and often laconic presentation of Hector Campbell. The use of gestures among Irish reciters, and some Scottish reciters, was important in their dramatic presentation.[100] Although Joe Neil's observation that gestures played no part in the story-telling of his district seems to be borne out in other parts of the island, he remarks later that the narrative techniques of John MacIsaac, his neighbour in Big Pond, extended to acting out the roles of his characters.[101]

Most accomplished Scottish reciters possess unusually strong and resonant speaking-voices. Calum Maclean noted this of Barra reciter James (Seumas Iain Ghrunnaraidh) MacKinnon, and we have observed the same to be true of Joe Neil, Lauchie MacLellan, Hughie Dan MacDonnell and Angus MacLellan.[102]

A final dramatic technique, one that Lauchie MacLellan inherited from his grandfather Neil MacLellan, born in 1826 of recent Morar immigrants, consists of creating suspense by shifting the scene of the narrative at a crucial point in the story and picking up the thread later on.

Good Gaelic reciters everywhere, though they may be regarded by their audiences as specialists in wonder-tales or *seanchas*, invariably have command of wide-ranging repertoires. Material recorded by the School of Scottish Studies, University of Edinburgh, Scotland, from Duncan MacDonald

of South Uist, in addition to his famous hero-tales, included
Fenian tales, Fenian lays (duain), historical legends, religious
lore, and fairy lore; an additional 1500 pages of material were
transcribed from him by his son, Donald (Dòmhnall Iain
Dhunnchaidh) over a winter and given to the school.[103] The
contribution of his fellow Uistman Angus MacLellan is no
less impressive.[104] A similar degree of versatility among Irish
reciters is apparent from the collection of the Kerry story-
teller Seán Ó Conaill, along with other examples cited by
Delargy.[105]

The art of humorous repartee, although among the types of
least published material in Scottish Gaelic tradition, furnishes
the most enduring variety of short anecdote in the Cape Breton
communities. The best examples have rapidly passed into the
local repertoire where they have been enjoyed for many
decades. One MacInnis family (Clann Eoghainn Duinn) of
Judique, Inverness County, achieved such a renown for their
ability that a whole series of anecdotes has survived in popular
memory a half-century later. It is clear that many such friendly
exchanges amounted to a sport and may be a continuation of a
much older tradition.[106] The tendency to answer using
various kinds of word-play could explain why repartee only
occasionally crosses over into English.

Joe Neil's speech, like that of many story-tellers, often
incorporates proverbs, both for the humour they contain and
as a type of linguistic shorthand, as well as expressions to
characterize the complex situations encountered in daily life.
Although some fairly rigorous attempts have been made to
describe the proverb, Joe Neil and Gaels in general do not
distinguish between proverbs (seanfhacail) and expressions
(gnàth-fhacail).[107] The list of proverbs and expressions given
here resembles strongly those collected by Neil Sinclair on
the Isle of Barra beginning in the 1930s.[108]

Accounts of traditional children's games are widespread in
Cape Breton, both in Protestant and Catholic communities.
Although some clear descriptions, such as those below,
have been recorded recently, most memories of these, like
the duain, are vague enough to indicate that the practice

was declining when the present older generation was in its youth.

Of the various kinds of marriage divination practised on the island, the most popular survival is the ring in the bowl of *fuarag* (a kind of whipped-cream dish) eaten on Halloween night (*Oidhche-Shamhna*). All of the examples described here by Joe Neil involve performing acts that give rise to the interpretation of omens and can thus be classed as "active divination."[109] The interpretation of *frith* "augury" and the various other omens in the following section are largely forms of "passive divination," being based on conditions independent of the seer. Clearly, in the case of the items concerning death divination, birds, and people encountered on journeys, we are dealing with the remnants of a larger body of omen-reading tradition still current in Gaelic Scotland at the time of Alexander Carmichael and described by him in *Carmina Gadelica*.[110] The ability to read omens, to Joe Neil's mind, is closely associated with the faculty of *beachd* "keen observation of everyday matters," which remains a strong cultural characteristic among present-day Gaelic-speakers as their conversation and humour often make clear.

Short tales of ghosts and spectres were a mainstay of the story-telling sessions in Cape Breton and were particularly enjoyed by children; a common expression from children so affected was *tha an t-eagal 'gam mharbhadh* "I'm dying of fear."[111] Numerous versions survive of ghost and spectre stories that arrived from Western Scotland with the settlers, for example, *Colunn gun Cheann* and *Eoghann a' Chinn Bhig*.[112] A few Inverness County informants claimed in 1978 to have seen Eoghann riding by on his horse. Local ghost stories similar to those told here are found in every Gaelic-speaking district of the island. These have crossed over effortlessly into English and have become the most popular part of genuine Gaelic tradition for English-speakers.

The nature and extent of Gaelic music and dance in Cape Breton before 1900 have only recently been investigated. While it is understandable that instrumental music was more prevalent in the Catholic areas since the time of settlement,

the importance that violin music held in the Big Pond and
Middle Cape areas, by Joe Neil's accounts, would seem to
indicate that Inverness County was not the only home of a
vigorous Gaelic violin-playing tradition.[113] The number of
active players, along with the survival of the Gaelic words to
many dance tunes of undoubted Highland origin, suggests the
existence of a considerable tradition of violin-playing in South
Uist and Barra at the time of the clearances which was
subsequently lost on those islands. There is also strong
evidence of a rich folk tradition of piping for dances as well as
for listening, and possibly extending to the small pipes, which
continued into recent times through the teaching and playing
of Neil MacIsaac of Big Pond. A study of the dances of Gaelic
origin on the island, particularly the regional square sets, the
older dances of the *Cailleach an Dùdain* type described by
Flett and Flett, and the origin of the scores of steps known to
step-dancers on the island, would yield interesting results.[114]

The Gaelic text has been selected from over four hundred
items recorded between February 1976 and October 1980. Part
1, which consists of Joe Neil's reminiscences of Middle Cape
and of the stories and story-tellers, contains the greatest
number of collations. Tape numbers and dates are given in the
notes. The tales in Part 2 have not required collating; the only
changes made are in the rare instances where Joe Neil has
corrected himself, and this was usually a matter of one or two
words. The first five sections of Part 3, those dealing with
repartee, proverbs, expressions, children's rhymes, and games,
contain the greater part of Joe Neil's recordings on these topics.
The sections on marriage divination, signs, superstitions and
second sight, and apparitions comprise only a small number
of selections from Joe Neil's contributions. The concluding
section on music and dance, except for traditions associated
with particular tunes, comprises everything recorded from Joe
Neil on these topics.

In my translation I have endeavoured to provide an idiomatic
rendering into standard English both readable enough to
convey the sense of entertainment so natural to the Gaelic

story-teller and accurate enough to be of use to scholars in folklore and Celtic studies. Because of the recent expansion in English of the semantic range of Gaelic *céilidh* to cover any group activity of a Celtic nature, actual or purported, I have chosen, with Calum Maclean, to translate the Gaelic word by "house-visit."[115] Joe Neil, with his thorough knowledge of English, has supplied many helpful and illuminating suggestions in the translation; the final responsibility, however, rests with the translator.

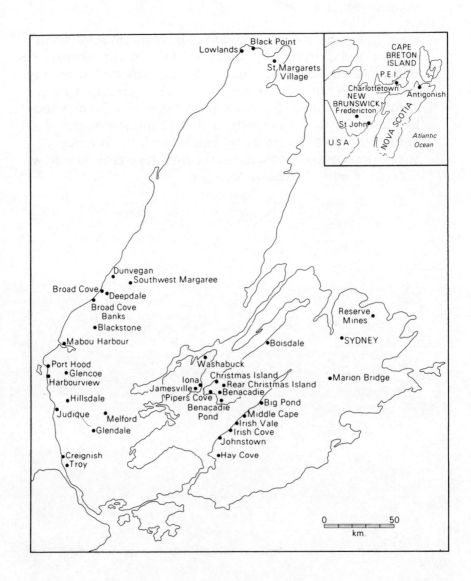

Cape Breton Island

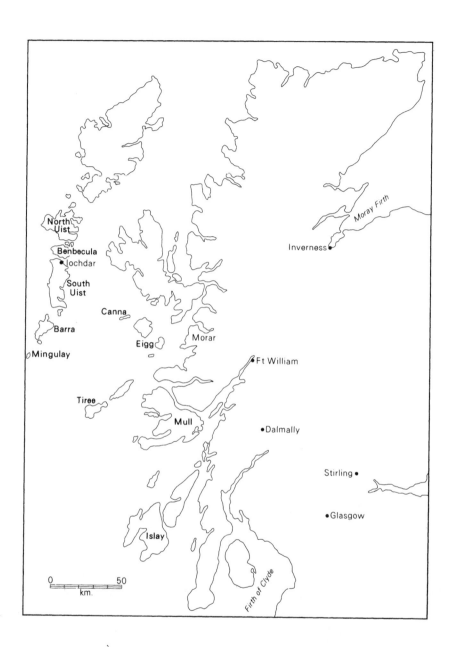

The Western Highlands and Islands of Scotland

Part One

THE WORLD OF THE STORY-TELLER

An nì nach cluinn cluas
cha ghluais cridhe

What the ear does not hear
will not move the heart

Middle Cape

They call me Joseph MacNeil. I came to Middle Cape, Cape Breton County at the age of six months. I was raised by an old couple there – they were elderly by the time I joined them – and grew up in that parish.[1] Gaelic was the first language that I spoke for there was no English used in the home. Even if people came to the house the woman of the house could not speak English to them; she had no English. The man of the house could speak a little English but Gaelic was what we used, and if a stranger or a travelling man arrived – what we would call a pack-merchant, or as they say in English "a peddler" – he would be told that they spoke no English and that they were just getting along that way.

I said that I spoke only Gaelic when I was young, but I used to make some effort to pick up a bit of English here and there, though I only spoke the odd word. There was one man, now no longer living, who worked as a cobbler – repairing shoes – and, since he had a few words of English, when I was around him I used to ask him the English names for various things: I would ask him in Gaelic what the English for a certain word was. I remember asking him one day what the English was for the glasses that covered his eyes when he was at his cobbler-work and I managed to learn the word for them somehow and *glasses* was what he said. Another day I asked him the name for the shoe last – they had lasts made of iron, the kind of last they would put into shoes when they were putting in the nails to attach the soles – and he said that *last* was the English word. They had three of these and a stand on which you could put each one as you needed it while you were working. There was a big one and a middle-sized one and a small one. In those days some people in the country used to have them and people would borrow them from each other along with everything else. One day a young man came to the house; he was older than myself perhaps by three years. He spoke no Gaelic at all and the man of the house was not home at the time; only the wife was in. The young man asked for the iron shoe lasts and the woman of the house who spoke no English did not understand what he was saying. She asked him if he saw the object he required around and he understood what she was saying but he shook his head and he said that he did not see it. And so it went on. But as was their usual custom in the countryside at that time, anyone who came to the house would be given tea and something – perhaps a sweet biscuit – with it. This was offered to the young man as it had been to others before and he was asked once or twice whether he saw the thing he required and he didn't. But what he had said was *lasts* and that put me wrong; I was uncertain because I had only ever heard *last* from the late cobbler; he had never said *lasts*, only *last* because he was just referring to a single one. But however many of them there were the young man wanted them. Finally he went on his way; as he was leaving I said to the old lady that it must have been the last that he was looking for.

"And why," said she, "didn't you say so before?" And she called to him to come back and went over to where the iron lasts were kept in a box: they were in a cubbyhole beside the stairs. She brought over one of them and asked him whether this was it and he said that it was. And that was the first time in my life that I ever attempted translating.

Around the age of seven I began going to school. I should have attended when I was six years old but I took a bad infection in my hand during the summer and I was in such distress with a sore hand well into the fall that they agreed not to send me that fall. And since I did not go there early on they decided not to let me go for the rest of the school year; particularly when the cold season came they wouldn't let me go. So that left me even poorer in English; I had to go another year without learning English at all, so the language came to me very, very slowly until I finally attended school. And I am sure that that is the reason even until today that I have such an interest in Gaelic, for Gaelic is my first language and it is still the language that I prefer.

So when I began to go to school I had no English at all except a few words here and there – perhaps they were so far over there that people here didn't know what was going on. They taught me what to say when they asked my name; that was taught to me in English and I was able to remember it. But when they went further I didn't have many answers. That didn't mean that I couldn't read a little. That's what was strange. How could a person read English without speaking it? But I hope this will make something clear to people today who think that they can learn the beautiful Gaelic language by reading from books; they won't do as well as they expect. But people used to come visiting at the house and someone got hold of a small book somewhere with a few English words in it. I could recognize them and the spelling; I knew the whole alphabet. And that's all the English I knew when I went to school and I had to begin acquiring it from there.

At school we didn't use Gaelic except when we were outside playing. At that time most spoke Gaelic and English because their parents spoke both. The oldest children in the families at home had learned a good deal of English in school so that the younger ones picked it up and could speak it, but most of them also spoke Gaelic well. When I began to go to school I can't think of any who spoke no Gaelic. There may have been some who didn't speak Gaelic well – perhaps two. In fact there were two who could not speak Gaelic but still knew some words; I believe that their Gaelic was about as scarce as my own English. But there was enough so that when we were outside we could converse and anyway there was so much English spoken in the schoolhouse. So little by little I learned English, but it took a long time before I learned the better part of it.[2]

For writing we had slates with a thin piece of slate for a pen. It was a stick of the same sort of material as slate but not as hard as the writing slate. You copied down every letter or figure or whatever on the slate, formed the way they put them on the blackboard with chalk. When this was looked over and corrected or accepted as correct you could erase it from the slate: you put a little drop of water on it and wiped it off with a rag and it was ready for the next part.

And things would become silent in the one-room school-house and those who were not in our own class – say those in grades two or three and those in grades six and seven – were concentrating, quietly working on their slates and they would stay quiet and orderly at their study.

Not every schoolmistress who taught us would put us through this kind of work. There were some who did not attend to us that much. But here I'll mention the best of them, and the reason is that I realized when I came of age that there was one schoolmistress who was the best I ever saw or heard of. I used to think very often and reflect on the various ways that she had of driving some education into our heads, however hard the shell. In additon to everything else, that teacher was never, never still. When spring came she used to ask each pupil, "Have you heard a frog croaking yet?" And nobody would move, but after perhaps a day or two, "Have any of you heard a frog croaking yet?" And one or two would raise a hand that pupil's name was put down on the calendar – there was a calendar on the wall – or else she would put it in the book; she would keep track of when you heard a frog. Another day we would be asked, "Who has seen a snake?" The first person who had seen a snake then would raise his hand and that was noted down. And as far as birds were concerned, there was not a bird around but (she would ask), "Who saw a robin?" and "Who saw a butterfly?" As for daisies and all the small flowers that grew in the meadows or the woods and everywhere else, as well as mayflowers and the like, the children used to gather them and bring them to school every day they could find them. If somebody found a bird's nest before the school closed, that was a special event. Every single thing had to be observed and maintained. She was keeping us aware of the ways of the world around us in a special way and I feel that was as good a way to teach children as any ever practised.

When I went to school I can say that Gaelic was as good as forbidden there; we were not allowed to use it at all except outside. When we were playing in the playground we used to speak Gaelic together, and there was no way on earth to control us then. I had to speak to somebody in Gaelic or I couldn't talk at all; and somebody had to speak to me in Gaelic or I wouldn't know that they were addressing me. But I remember the day that the dog followed me to the schoolhouse when I was only very young. The schoolmistress who was teaching us at the time could understand Gaelic; she spoke a few words of the language too. But the dog entered the schoolhouse after me, and people began to try to put the dog out of the school. And one of the young boys said in Gaelic, "Out you go!" or "Put him out." And I believe from the few words of English that I was able to understand vaguely, that the lad was spoken to – was censured – for speaking Gaelic. That's what I understood from it anyway. But we suffered no punishment or restraints or anything for speaking Gaelic outside the schoolhouse. To be sure, we would sometimes speak it among ourselves outside although a lot of English was being promoted. And that was the situation of Gaelic; I am sure that with the insignificant activity going on outside the classroom nothing more was said about the games we played around the school.[3]

I think it would be in order now to make clear how poor my memory was when I went to school. In the short time that I did attend, I barely got as far as the fifth book and I was only promoted to that at the end of the year. I attended for a few weeks into the next school term and was beginning on the fifth book. But after a month and a half or so I left school and didn't return again for instruction. And soon I had to start making my choices little by little through the world. But I became aware around that time that there were older people who were extremely precise and learned without being able to read or write; and that their memory of things was what had brought them so far. I made a great effort then to see if I could develop a retentive memory, and that was how I came by an ability to recall events.

My own experience was ordinary enough, I feel, similar to that of the other young country people at the time, but since there were no young lads or girls at home except myself I used to spend most of my time in the company of older people. When people would come for a house-visit I would show more interest than most, I believe, in their conversations and goings-on. When young people, two or three or four of them, were together they would spend more time in their own company and socialize more among themselves. But that was not the way it was for me; instead I frequented the older people. In that way I developed a great attachment to them and was attentive to their conversation and stories.

No people in particular were invited to a house-visit, nor were people expected to pay admission to go to one; but they were happily welcomed when they came to visit and were extended hospitality.[4] It didn't matter who came to visit, whether it was one person or a number of people. Whether six or eight or more came they would receive the same warm reception. And the first thing a person was asked when he came to the house was how he and his family were. And the next thing that he was asked was if there was anything new. People often used the expressions, "Is there any recent news?" or "Is there anything new?" And that's how news was circulated.

Today things are fast and easy for us. We have the daily newspaper and the telephone and the electronic gadget known as television as well as the other one – I'm sure in real Gaelic it would be called *craolan* but, these days at least, it is always called the radio in Gaelic. In the countryside in its own place and time, the *céilidh* or house-visit was a fitting and suitable thing, and in its own way it accomplished things that the various electronic gadgets do today and more. Yes, we can say more, although it didn't act so swiftly.

These days we get news in the newspapers; we get the news about the world situation. We get a little more breadth – more scope – than the old fashioned house-visit could supply, but the house-visit offered the same things, perhaps on a smaller scale: all the bits of news and the various stories from the surrounding area were told. There was talk of marriage and weddings and births and deaths and many such things; there were stories of gladness and stories of sorrow, just as we find them today in the newspapers.

But perhaps now I should start with the telephone, as it is
called today. Such a thing is extremely easy to use, swift,
suitable and quite useful today to people, especially to those
living out in the countryside some distance apart. But in
times past the house-visit fulfilled its function. You could
find out what was happening: whether the smith was active
and whether the merchant had received the load of goods he
expected from the boat. The steamboat used to bring wares to
the merchant, delivering his merchandise to the pier. And
people would ask whether he had his winter stock yet of such
things as flour and meal – the kind of winter merchandise
that was brought in to be sold to the country people when the
coldest season came. They would ask one another whether
the boat had come to the wharf yet so that they could go down
to fetch the things that they required. People also would ask
whether the miller had begun to grind the grain, whether he
had begun carding or whether he finished grinding, and so on.
Just as they gave out information about events they might
also mention that there was extremely good flour at the
merchant Murdock's place and people would be very happy to
find out that kind of thing. There would be times when not all
the flour coming to the stores was considered good. And they
would also describe the wonderful, fine cloth that such and
such a merchant was carrying; it would be good for suits,
tweed of the very best quality or good cloth. And they used to
discuss the linen and the thick drugget cloth and calico and so
on. That subject was discussed very often in the old gatherings.

People would mention those they had met as they went to
the mill or the blacksmith's or the merchant's. Whatever their
destination, they would pick up a lot of news on their way
down and back, and this was shared so that people were kept
informed in every way. When a certain fish started coming up
the river people would know about it from time to time from
the social gatherings, where people were extremely good about
circulating news.[5] To be sure there may have been a few with
a little too much to say concerning various things, but
generally folk were good in those times about minding their
own business. There was not much idle talk – what we would

term gossip – going between houses; most people had no interest in that at all.[6]

But perhaps now I should leave the telephone and pass on to the other two devices known in English as radio and television. Today everything is available on these two devices – music and news and so on – but in those days the people had entertainment that was really fine. There were those who excelled at singing songs and people who excelled at reciting poems and people who were outstanding story-tellers as well as those who were good musicians and dancers. So they had what I consider to be the very best of entertainment. I mentioned before that they used to have everything that these electronic devices supply us with today and more. And in my view the extra was that when you were listening to the people who were entertaining you there – whether it was playing music or singing or rhymes that they were reciting or songs, or whether they were doing a dance for you to watch – you were alive with them there in the flesh and participating in the whole event. You could talk to them right there, but if you ever chose to address the gadgets that I mentioned they could never answer you. So there was that pleasure and a sense of unity. I think that people felt very united, united physically and united in spirit.

And then there was the generous hospitality as a part of the gatherings, which can still be found today, at least in the countryside. This code of hospitality dictated that food – something small – must be given to visitors. On some occasions they were to be given a dram, if it was plentiful, or at the very least they were given a drink of milk or buttermilk, and frequently tea. But some small meal was given to them – whether large or small it was offered. It seems from the way things were then as I saw them, that even in times of scarcity people felt that there was an abundance and they all derived full enjoyment from whatever there was. And I still maintain that the house-visits were good for bringing people together and keeping them happy and that they kept them close to each other and in harmony physically and spiritually; I see it as a great loss that so much of this has declined and grown so rare.

There was one man living further on by the name of Hector MacMullin.[7] He used to come to visit us in Middle Cape very frequently and could read Gaelic. If there was a piece of paper with a little bit of Gaelic around we used to keep that until he came. And it occurred to me about that time that I would like to begin to read Gaelic. So I got a copy of *Mac-Talla*, an old paper which had gone out of print before my time but contained stories and various items.[8] But it was the ads from the merchants – merchandise that they were selling like hardware and flour and meal and tea and suits and things of that kind – that (helped) my progress bit by bit. Of course I had some idea what merchants should be selling and thanks to that I was able to understand and make some progress with reading, because I spoke Gaelic as my first language.

I also came by a copy of *Sàr-Obair nam Bard*.[9] I used to try to read it but I found it very difficult. There were a large number of words there which were far beyond me – hard to get around. I got a loan of *Clàrsach na Coille* and used to try to read the songs from it; some of the songs I had heard before and learned from hearing them passed on orally and that was a great help to me.[10] There was also a paper printed in Sydney at that time called *Teachdaire nan Gàidheal* and I used to get a copy of that from a friend in the area who himself had begun to read Gaelic; he was extremely diligent in his efforts although he didn't speak Gaelic in his early childhood.[11] His name was James Smith and he made a remarkable effort to read and write Gaelic.

From that time on I used to get the loan of books and all the Gaelic that was printed in papers such as the *Casket*, published in Antigonish.[12] There was a section there called *Achadh nan Gàidheal*, which consisted mostly of songs or a short story or letters sent to them and so on. And the newspaper that they printed in Sydney – the *Post* – used to come out and there was a little bit of Gaelic in it once each week. And with everything that appeared I managed to keep up with Gaelic. After that I eagerly graduated to books and finally I got a dictionary so that I could find nearly all the words I was looking for. And that is how I was able to start and make some headway in reading Gaelic.

I was young when I had to start working – working hard – for a living. We were kept busy working hard when we hired out to a farmer to make some money, and the wage that we got was very small indeed. I'm sure I worked some hard days for a wage as small as ten cents an hour and sometimes less than that. And when I reached the age of fifteen or sixteen I worked a little at farming, but that was a kind of work I always disliked and I still do to this day. So I began trying to learn a few skills; I used to work at carpentry. Although I still kept on initially working with the farmers on their holdings cutting hay and putting it in the mow and putting grain under a shelter and so on, when I began to do a little bit of carpentry the farming went by the board altogether and I wasn't sorry. I spent some time repairing cars; I did a little bit of work as a mechanic and after that back to the carpentry and occasionally installing electricity in houses – wiring for lights. And I continued on with that work. I never went to work for a big company such as the steel works or coal-mining or for a big project lumbering in the woods or for any big concern. Instead I used to saw lumber for people, hiring out to one man at a time. And that is how I passed my time. Now I have reached an age where I don't do much work at all except on my own time – a little bit of carpentry and such like. And that is how things stand for me now.

A big change has come over Middle Cape since I was there at an early age; from the time that I was five or six and my memory was clear about the way things were, there have been changes. Today there is no farming at all, no agricultural activity at all at Middle Cape although they did a great deal of that when I was in my youth. There aren't many living there. There is only one family remaining at Middle Cape of those who lived there in the old days. Other people came there and built houses and lived there and worked at the steel-plant and at fishing and so on. And that is what happened at Middle Cape.

Stories and Story-Tellers

I used to hear stories frequently from the time I was a young boy; I was quite young when I first heard stories being told. I am sure I was as young as I could be and still remember – perhaps I might be able to remember back to when I was four years old and people were telling stories. And as far as singing songs goes, I could remember that from the time that memory came to me; I wasn't a year old when I used to hear songs and mouth-music.

I remember the first story that I ever heard, told by a woman who used to visit around in the houses. She recited the story and the story I remember her telling was *Biorachan Beag agus Biorachan Mór*.[1] I remember another story I heard a man telling – I was then around five years old – actually he told two stories at the house. And I recall reading the same story in a book a good many years later, perhaps more than forty years after hearing it for the first time. As for the story-tellers, the woman from whom I heard *Biorachan Beag agus Biorachan Mór* was called Anna MacNeil. I can't style her altogether accurately unless she was the daughter of Rory Bàn's son; anyway she was a woman who never married. It was the poor woman's habit to circulate throughout the district, where she would spend time at various houses and do a good amount of work such as the washing and scrubbing and the like. She could tell short stories but she wouldn't tell them at all when company came to visit; but if she was at home with children – the young ones – she would tell little stories. But most often she preferred to sing songs. There wasn't a single song made locally throughout the whole countryside that she didn't know if she had heard it once, and there were a good number of songs made at the time in those parts. She would learn them and sing them in the homes, and many years after the poor woman's death when people were singing songs they would say that they had heard them from Anna and that she had a marvellous repertoire. And that was the way with the wonderful old women who used to wander through the countryside giving entertainment and pleasure to people. People didn't find it a burden at all to feed them. Although there was scarcity at times, there was plenty to go around; people always gave them food and shelter and warmth. And that was the way in that contented world.[2]

There were some outstanding story-tellers that I don't remember at all. When we were out visiting the conversation would turn to good story-tellers, and I think one was called Donald Bàn who was considered as good a story-teller as lived in the country. There was another story-teller whom I saw; I never talked to him or heard him telling stories, but I did see him on various occasions and I knew some of his family. The man's name was Michael MacDonald (Mìcheal Iain Bhàin na Banndraich), and he was considered by people who knew about story-telling to be extremely accomplished. Perhaps he was not as good as Donald Bàn MacNeil mentioned above, and perhaps he was, but he was considered to be among the extremely accomplished story-tellers.

Long tales were most often recited on occasions when people called in at the houses and there was some encouragement. People would make small conversation at first, inquiring about happenings in the vicinity and whether there was any news. Perhaps someone there would then be asked whether he could still recite a story, and the person would admit that he still told a few; or perhaps people might be visiting at the house of one of the great story-tellers, one who could tell the long, elaborate tales. As the proverb had it, "It's not every day MacIntosh has a mod."[3] And there was another proverb that people quoted: "It's not every day MacNeil goes on horse-back." There were some reciters who were especially adept at telling tales and who knew some that were extremely long; these tales were not heard very frequently. Most people told items that were shorter than the big, long tales when they

went out visiting; for that reason there were some who perhaps
had not heard any of the long tales recited by an accomplished
local story-teller. But when people who were good at circulating
around and acquiring tales visited, they would tell these
wherever they were and they were always encouraged.

It was mostly during the long winter months that people
engaged in this kind of activity. The nights were so long.
Nightfall would come early on and the day's work would be
done. People would finish their work just as it grew dark.
They weren't accustomed to doing anything except by daylight
when they could see what they were doing – they didn't do
much work by lantern light or anything; they just had candles
and lamps for light in the houses. But they were ready to go
out for a house-visit as soon as they had finished their evening
meal and night had grown dark. There were so many people
living in the country then and the young people at least – the
young lads and the young girls – would be going out visiting.
So during the nights time was long and, on the long winter
nights especially, perhaps two people would pass the time by
telling a fine, long tale.

People didn't come just from one house or two houses for a
house-visit; people would come from perhaps three or four
houses, and some people would come over a distance as great
as three miles.

Generally the long tales were the ones that most pleased
people. It did not matter whether it was a man or a woman
who was a good story-teller. When she or he began, the tale
was so enjoyable and would please you so well as it progressed
that you would find yourself hoping that it would not end for
a long time, that there would be a great amount of working
around it so that the story-teller could make it very, very long
before he arrived at the end of the tale. You would have some
idea of what was going to happen, but it was as if you did not
understand and you were only seeing in your mind how the
story was unfolding and you didn't think about how it was
going to end at all. The long tales were preferred, but there
were also a large number of short tales and often a story which
was too long would not be suitable. Everyone used to spend a

short while in conversation; people would have short little stories, little rhymes and funny stories and the like, and for that reason the long tales were not recited so often.

Now when there was somebody who could recite the Fenian tales, those were indeed long. They were exceedingly lengthy tales and their subject matter was so strange. In a way they were just as strange as some things that could happen today, but at the same time so understandable; you could understand everything that was there – every misfortune and hardship that they encountered.[4] I think that the Fenian stories were people's favourites, but there also were other tales as well, some of which were fairly lengthy. Some of the many tales concerning giants were extremely long; tales of battles and other things were not altogether as long as giant tales or as the Fenian tales.

There was a man from the same area as myself who, although he had none of the Fenian tales, could sing the lays. He could put an air to the lay and sing it. If we happened to be visiting this man Michael who was good at the Fenian tales – Michael MacLean (Mìcheal Iain Chaluim Òig 'ic Iain 'ic Lachlainn Ghobha) – he would recite [the lays]. And if we were visiting Archie Kennedy (Gilleasbu' Mhurchaidh), Michael would say, when he had recited or sung the lay, "I'm through now and you'll get the rest from Archie. He's the one who knows the tales." And perhaps then Archie Kennedy would begin and tell a very pleasing story about the Fenians. And in one part of the lay, Fionn's men would be gathered about him. There was a great deal that was mentioned but I remember none of it except for a reference to "Galleys under Lords": it seems the lords were going to arrive in boats.[5] And there was another lay in which the "Bald, Red Muilgheartach" was mentioned, when the four strongest men of the Fenians would go out to battle.

> Who would battle against the beast
> And she was dealing with them one after the other
> As snow would melt before the flame[6]

I don't remember any more of it except for this.

There were special houses for story-telling. Most of the visiting houses were good enough. Any of a number of nice homes could be visited, but people were more willing and eager to go to some houses in particular because there were more people frequenting these. There were also houses where people went expressly to hear tales, but on a night when a lot of people would go to the house it was not so good because there was so much conversation before each new arrival was heard from that there was no time for a long tale. Therefore it was very lucky if you were fortunate enough to come to a suitable house. Perhaps no one would go there but yourself or one other person, and after a little bit of conversation great, long tales were told. They always would gather in a place where there was a lot of oral tradition, and, in the neighbourhood where I was, it was Michael MacLean's house that was the best for lore and songs. And when people wanted to hear tales, it was Archie Kennedy's house; that was the house for tales, for if there was any entertainment at all there the tales would prevail. To be sure, if people came visiting who were good singers they would certainly sing songs at Kennedy's and tales would not be so well represented; and so if we were looking for a tale, we would be somewhat disappointed if many people came to the house and there was a lot of conversation and songs.

And on the subject of tales, the wake-house was an especially good setting for story-telling. As was often the case, there would be a number of people staying at the wake-house throughout the night and, if there were no old people there who could tell tales, there were young people who would pass time telling stories they heard when they were going around visiting houses. There was one particular man whom I got to know, John MacIsaac, the son of Big Archie (Gilleasbu' Mór) MacIsaac, who excelled at story-telling. He would be in a wake-house and when things quieted down, when those who were coming and going the first part of the night settled down and the hurrying and the going around – the bustle as they would say – stopped, things would become quiet and the long tales would begin. Although there were a large number of people inside, they would gather around listening to the tales and passing the night in this manner.

Now there were some people in the country who were slightly better story-tellers than others. I mentioned MacIsaac; he was a particularly distinguished story-teller. As far as people quieting down is concerned, a wake-house was no different than a dwelling-house. Things were going on but nothing was happening which would hinder or interfere with the story-teller. Perhaps the woman of the house would be knitting socks or mittens; people would be working with knitting needles at the same time and twisting yarn, and the story was in no way interfered with by that. But as for carding, they might not be so set on doing that for fear that they wouldn't hear what was happening; they would lose the gist of the story. As for the spinning wheel, nothing was done with it when tales were being recited although they would work with the wheel and other implements when a house-visit or *céilidh* was going on; it didn't interfere with people then. Among the especially good story-tellers were some older people. To my memory Michael MacLean and Archie Kennedy were the two oldest and I'm sure they were the ones who had the best backgrounds. There was a Finlay MacDonald who was as old as they, or perhaps a little older, but had tales of a different kind which he knew by memory very well. These people had had a chance to hear tales, especially long tales. I believe it was mostly from their fathers and uncles and close relations that they learned their tales, so they didn't have to do as much travelling around to hear stories as did some of the younger people. I believe that is one reason that the real old-timers had such good memories and recited their tales in such a pure form. To be sure, people who circulated through the countryside had a chance to pick up more of the short stories – short anecdotes – and songs, because travelling from house to house gave them that opportunity. I think that those who were working in the houses – working around – learned a large number of stories and songs and rhymes and things of that kind from being on that circuit. I don't remember any of them well except for Anna MacNeil who used to travel through the

country passing time among the folk and indeed she was
always welcomed.

Very often when someone would tell a great, long tale, and
particularly if it was one that someone had heard part of,
perhaps from his grandfather's sister or somebody far back,
they would say, "God's blessing be with you, my man. Isn't it
a long time since I last heard part of that tale." Then most of
the people there would say, "Many thanks to you, many
thanks to you. That was certainly a wonderful story to listen
to." And then they might ask the story-teller whether he
remembered a particular man who lived many years ago,
whether he had heard him reciting tales, and the person might
reply that he had, saying, "I heard him telling tales." "Did
you learn any from him?" "Oh, I think that I came away with
one of them," he might say, "but it's such a long one." "Oh
well, then we'll go over to visit you some evening and we will
hear it from you." "Very well then. Come over some night to
visit and I will give you that tale." And that is how the long
tales were shared.

Once when I had begun to attempt to recite a few stories I
remember going one Sunday evening on a house-visit – it was
in the winter – and I told three short stories that evening
before I left. I believe that the woman of the house also told a
short story which was very enjoyable. And that is how the
stories were told; the people who were sitting listening to the
tales being told certainly heard a lot, and I feel after all that
they used to get pleasure from sitting and listening to tales.
People were so united; they were like one person – one being –
inside. And that was the kind of entertainment they derived
from tales and rhymes and songs and poems of every sort.

I was once asked whether it was the practice of story-tellers –
the great story-tellers like Michael MacLean and Archie
Kennedy – when they were telling tales to perform movements
or particular gestures with their hands, and I don't remember
that they used to do much of that. I remember Michael
MacLean stretched out on a sort of a bench in the kitchen
telling us a story, and a nice one too. And I also remember
well one night when my good friend Archie Kennedy lay

stretched out in bed in a room while I was at the door of the room; he was quietly and comfortably reclining on the bed reciting the tale for me and there was not much gesturing or anything to be seen with his hands. I wouldn't have seen; I wasn't looking anyway. The room was dark except for a light shining through the doorway. So I don't believe that they did much of that at all. Nonetheless I was told of an accomplished story-teller whom people went to hear recite and when he came to an awesome tale – the terrible feats that a hero performed which surpassed the valour of many – he would have to stand up and raise his hands and introduce some of his own embellishments; he might add some words of English to the tale. But it was not at all usual in company for the people that I often saw telling tales to do much of this, and if you find one of the old people who can still recite a tale you will see that they stay very still; they don't make much of a commotion at all about it.[7] But now I am going to introduce a short humorous item. One night we were visiting Michael MacLean and he was telling us a story. It was a cold night in the winter and he didn't think at the time that the fire was catching briskly and giving us enough heat, and so he got up to poke the wood that was in the stove. He took the covers off the top of the stove one after the other, and then he put back the one on the west as it were on the east and put the one on the east on the west and got confused because he was so busy telling us the story and keeping the fire going at the same time. And that is what I remember hearing and seeing of the people who moved or gestured as they recited tales.

Part Two

THE RECITERS AND
THE TALES

The Kennedys

The Kennedys were descended from Murdock Kennedy. I would guess that Murdock Kennedy came over from Scotland when he was young, for he was married to a woman known as Janet Johnston and the Johnstons lived over in a place known as Red Islands or Hay Cove or around there.[1] For that reason I have supposed that he married over here in Cape Breton.

To my knowledge Murdock had three sons: James, Donald, and Archie. Now there was a Michael Kennedy among them, and Alexander, but I never heard anything about these two; they were just mentioned. James and Archie and Donald had three sisters: Sarah, Anna, and Catherine, or Ceit Mhór ("Big Kate") as we used to call her. And she was a big strong woman indeed – an amusing, cheerful woman and one who had, as they would say, both big and small tales. And she was more than willing to tell them. Now Sarah was married to one of the MacPhersons, Hector, son of Murdock MacPherson. And Anna was married to Neil MacPherson. I did not hear her telling any tales – I did not know her well – yet she may have also been a good story-teller.

To return to the others, I did not know James; he died before I could remember. Nor did I know Donald; I remember hearing he left early, before I was born. But there was a friend of mine by the name of John MacLean (Mac Chaluim Iain Chaluim Òig 'ic Iain 'ic Lachlainn Ghobha), the brother of Donald MacLean from whom I got tales, and John told me about one day when he went to school and something was wrong in the schoolhouse. They had no way of heating it – it may have been the pipe that took out the smoke that broke and fell – and he had to return home. And as he was on his way home

Donald Kennedy was out working near the house and he
called him up to the house.

"'Come on up, boy,' said he, 'and have some tea and I will
tell you a tale.'

"And I went up to the Kennedys' house and got a cup of tea
from Peggy, and Donald told me the story. That was Donald
Murdock Kennedy. And it was a while before I reached home.
When I arrived my father asked me what had happened that I
had arrived home earlier than usual from school. So I told him
there was no school taught today and related to him what had
happened.

"'And what,' said he, 'kept you so long from coming home
since there was no school taught today?'

"'It happened,' said I, 'that Donald Murdock called me up
to the house for cup of tea and told me a tale.'

"'And what tale did he tell for you?' said my father.

"'He told me the tale of the Man in the Light Grey Coat,' I
answered. My father laughed and said, 'It's strange,' said he,
'that you should be home so early if that's the tale that you
heard.'"

I also knew the children of James Kennedy. I was acquainted
with the oldest of his daughters and one of the sons by the
name of Murdock. I got a tale or two from him and I knew him
very well. We used to have a lot of fun together.

Of all of the Kennedys I was best acquainted with Archie
and it was from him that I got the most tales.[2] He was an
outstanding reciter of Fenian tales and everything that had to
do with them. But, unfortunately for me, when he was around
seventy years of age they moved from the district where they
were living – Irish Vale it was called – and they went down to
East Bay and spent about seven years there. Whether or not he
frequently recited tales there I do not know, but I believe that
there was not really much going on, and when he returned
after seven years the poor man had grown forgetful.[3] He was
very much up in years by that time. It was a great loss to me
that he was not in the community for those seven years so
that I could have learned tales from him. I realize today what a
great personal loss this was.

And, since I am on the subject of Archie, he was a big, rugged man – a strong man, light-hearted and funny. I would often go to visit. He lived about a mile and a quarter from the place where I lived. I lived in the lower place – perhaps you might call it a small glen – and he was living up on a higher property on a sort of a hill which was fairly steep. There was a little valley down in front of their property but he was up high above this valley. The place they had was not well suited to farming but I believe that at that time they did their best to do a little bit of farming to sustain themselves. And when I went over to the Scottish Highlands I understood that it was a natural enough thing for Gaels to make their living this way for I saw that there were many places that I would consider ill suited for farming where they did not have many nice, wide, level pieces of land. For that reason I believe people were used to making the best of the worst, as they would say.

I knew Archie Kennedy's family. The two youngest sons and the youngest daughter went to school when I was going. Indeed I learned from the sons some of the riddles and the stories and the other things with which I credit the Kennedys today. And I must say here that I have a great regard for the Kennedys; particularly because they were so good when it came to tales. I understand from what was passed on that James himself was very good at this and that Donald was an especially good story-teller.

As for Archie's livelihood, it came through a little farming that they did on the property. They were comfortable, and in no great need as far as I knew. In his youth, I believe, he was out on various jobs; he worked for some time for a company that was putting up the big poles for installations to send messages from one end of the country to the other. I believe that they were working for the telegraph at that time.

And now I am going to give a short account of something I heard which is true enough. When they were working on the job there were people who kept giving the impression that they were very rugged and strong; and since Archie took a dim view of what was going on they wanted very much to find a way to get the upper hand on him. But it was silly for them to

imagine that they could do that. One day Archie Kennedy was
not pleased with the way things were going and to show them
that he might be capable of holding his own he grasped a big
telegraph pole. To be sure, the wood in it was not terribly
heavy and the hole was already in the ground for the pole.
Usually two or three men would be around the pole setting it
up, but Archie went over to the telegraph pole and put it on
his shoulder. He walked over with it and lifted the end up as if
he were going to toss the caber and lowered the butt into the
ground. I find it very easy to believe that from that day on the
others stayed on the safe side of him, that they didn't go too
close to him for fear they would be in danger. I believe easily
enough that this happened because I was used to seeing the
man. I saw a picture of him taken as a young man and he was a
fine-looking powerful man then with a handsomely shaped
face. He was indeed a fine-looking man.

1   *The Man in the Light Grey Coat*

This is quite a long story; this afternoon I can only record a
little of it because it is so long and I have forgotten a large part
of it. I heard the story from a fine old man out in the country
many years ago. It is more than forty years since I heard it.

The story is about the Fenians – Fionn and the lads out
hunting. At that time it seemed that game was becoming
quite scarce for the Fenians; it had failed on their expeditions to
the hunting-mountain. When they arrived out on the hunting-
mountain, as they would say, the men would sit on the Hillock
of the Men and the lads would sit on the Hillock of the Lads,
and though they would remain all day there was no game to
be found. As time passed things were getting very scarce, but
one day when they were out they saw in the breeze before the
shower the Man in the Light Grey Coat coming from the west
and approaching them very rapidly. And just as he reached
them they saw a deer up on a hillside, so they sent Caoilte
after the deer, and off went Caoilte. But as he did, the deer
took off. In spite of Caoilte's fleetness it seems that the deer

was swifter and after a while the Man in the Light Grey Coat said to Fionn, "Put your finger under your tooth of knowledge to see if you can determine how things are going."[1]

Fionn did so and said, "They are a mountain and a glen and a summer sitting-place away from us now, and Caoilte is no closer to the deer than when you saw it up there."[2]

"Indeed," said the Man in the Light Grey Coat.

They spent another while sitting on the hillocks and then the Man in the Light Grey Coat said to Fionn, "Put your finger under your tooth of knowledge to see if you can determine how things are going."

Fionn did so and he said to the Man in the Light Grey Coat, "They are two mountains and two glens and two summer sitting-places away from us now, but Caoilte is no closer to the deer than when you saw it up there."

"Yes, indeed," said he, the Man in the Light Grey Coat, and they spent another long while sitting. Then he said to Fionn a third time, "Put your finger under your tooth of knowledge, Fionn, to see if you can determine how Caoilte and the deer have fared."

Fionn did so. "Well," said Fionn, "they are three mountains and three glens and three summer sitting-places away now and Caoilte is no closer to the deer than when you saw it up there."

"Well, if that is how it is," said the Man in the Light Grey Coat, "I'll have to go myself." And he set out.

But he felt that the cloak that he was wearing was too long: it was hurting his heels. So he returned saying that he could not go on that way; the cloak was so long that it chafed his heels. They located the Fenians' tailors and the tailors cut a piece from the cloak. The cloak was returned to him, he put it on, and off he went.

He may have travelled for a long time or a short time, but the weather turned wet and cold, and the Man in the Light Grey Coat turned back saying that the weather had become very cold and that the cloak was too short; he was feeling the cold on his ankles and he could remain outside no longer like that. The Fenians' tailors were located a second time and a little piece was put back on the bottom of the cloak to make it longer than it had been. The Man in the Light Grey Coat put on the cloak and off he went.[3]

However long a time he pursued the deer, he was drawing finally close to it, gaining little by little. But the deer made for a river, and if it reached the bank of the river and if it leapt across to the other side, no one in the world or the entire universe could catch it. But when the Man in the Light Grey Coat saw the danger – that the deer might escape him – he forged ahead even more swiftly than before and, just as the deer was measuring its leap across the stream or river, the Man in the Light Grey Coat caught it and brought it down. The deer was killed and carried back.

When they reached home Fionn's wife became exceedingly attracted to the Man in the Light Grey Coat – so much so that she wanted to do away with Fionn. She said to Fionn,

> "I am putting you under spells and crosses," said she,
> "And under nine constraints of the walking wandering
>   fairy mothers
>   That every lamb weaker and more misguided than yourself,
>   May take from you your head and your ear
>   And your livelihood,
>   If you do not bring me the head of the Feamain-Feòir."[4]

(And I am certain that would not be easily obtained, whatever sort of creature it was.)

So they had to begin building a ship; and however long it took them to build it, you can be sure that they spent a good while at it. And when the ship was ready and a crew was found to go on board, they sailed.

They sailed a long time until at last they reached the region where the creature lived whose head was to be taken. When they arrived at a harbour, they pulled the ship up seven times its own length on the green earth where the impertinent lads of the big town would not be mocking them[5] and they went ahead. And whatever things befell them or came their way, and whatever they had to do, in the end they finally reached the place where the Feamain-Feòir lived and his head was taken off. Then they took it to the ship and the ship was put out to sea and they returned home.

But she (Fionn's wife) was by no means satisfied with things as they stood. She feared that her scheme would fail utterly and to make things more difficult there had to be other tasks, so she said to Fionn,

> "I am putting you under spells and crosses
> And under nine constraints of the walking, wandering fairy-mothers.
> That every lamb weaker and more misguided than yourself,
> May take from you your ear and your head
> And your livelihood,
> If you do not bring me the head of the Bogan Balachaidh."[6]

There was no choice but to set out again and travel to whatever quarter that monster dwelt in. They set sail, and however long it took them to make the journey they reached the place. And whatever they had to do there – a battle or a fight or some conflict – they succeeded in slaying the creature and cutting off its head and bringing it back.

But she (Fionn's wife) was not satisfied with things yet, and she said to Fionn,

> "I am," said she, "putting you under spells and crosses
> And under nine constraints of the walking, wandering fairy-mothers.
> That every lamb which is weaker and more misguided than yourself,
> May take from you your head and your ear
> And your livelihood
> Unless you bring me the clawed cup[7]
> From the Great Smith."

There was nothing else to do; they had to set out and certainly there was a fearful distance to cover on that journey. They sailed on and reached land there, and when they landed as was their custom they pulled up the ship seven times its own length on the green grass where the impertinent lads of the big town would not be mocking them. And when the Man in the Light Grey Coat arrived up at the Great Smith's place he went in to talk to him. They spent a long time conversing – he had to go about it in a canny way – but eventually their conversation turned to the clawed cup. The Great Smith showed him the clawed cup, and as he turned it in his hands, regarding it and saying how lovely it was, he dropped the cup on the floor and it broke. Oh, the Man in the Light Grey Coat almost wept over what had happened, and the Great Smith said to him, "Never mind," said he, "about that. In fact, I am pleased that this has befallen it, for now I know that there was a flaw in the cup. And now we must locate all the smiths and make the cup over again and be certain then that it is good enough to stand up to any blow or fall or anything at all that happens to it."

"Oh," said he (the other one), "if that's how it is, the incident is not altogether so painful for me."

And all the smiths went to work and the clawed cup was made anew. And it was tested this time to make certain and the cup was as strong and as good as could be. And the Man in the Light Grey Coat, to be sure, saw his chance as he was turning the cup. And when he got the chance, he took a leap outside and off he went with the cup.

The smith and the others all got up to pursue him but the smith called out, "Oh," said he, "we'll let him go. It is not worth our while pursuing that man any longer, for I know now who he is. That is the Son of the King of the Golden Pillars and neither in this world nor in the universe," said he, "is there one who can keep up with him. It is just as well for us to let him go."[8]

So they arrived at the ship below and put the ship to sea and off they went. When they returned home they had the clawed cup ready, and the Man in the Light Grey Coat gave the clawed cup to Fionn and Fionn showed it to her.

"And now," said he (Fionn), "I am putting you under spells:

I am putting you under spells and crosses
And under nine constraints of the walking, wandering
fairy-mothers.
That every lamb weaker and more misguided than yourself,
May take from you your head and your ear
And your livelihood,
Unless you have one foot on the little house
And one foot on the big house
And your face toward every kind of weather that comes
from the sky,
When I return."[9]

And whatever journey Fionn and his companions made to the hunting-mountain – or wherever they went – when they returned, she had fallen dead with rage. And that is what I remember of the tale of the Man in the Light Grey Coat.

2   *O Cròileagan of the Horses*

This is part of the tale of O Cròileagan: it seems that they found a servant lad somewhere. He was near death when they found him, wherever they discovered him, and the King of Ireland asked if he was alive and one of the king's company said that the breath of life – a murmur – was still in him.

"In that case," said the king, "O Cròileagan is what we will name him. Raise him up and bring him with you."

Anyway, when the lad grew up he used to take care of the horses and it seems that he was very good around them. And people used to make fun of him: they called him O Cròileagan of the Horses, the King of Ireland's foster-son.

Now, there were many goings-on in the tale, but they all came down in the end to something concerning Céin: about Céin's leg. It seems that his leg was shattered and a man came – a leech of some kind came – to heal him. He could perform cures while he chanted a rhyme. And he would say,

"Stretch out your leg, Céin,
  So that I may put on it poultices of relief and deliverance
  and great healing
  Which will reach the bone and pass the flesh ...
  Who was born in a town in Upper France[1]
  And was broken in Bergen in Norway
  And listened to a mass in Dublin in Ireland, all in one day."

"I will not stretch out my leg," said Céin.
"For poultices of relief or deliverance or great healing
  Which will reach the bone and pass the flesh
  Unless you tell three true stories without a lie."

When he began then to tell the story – the first tale – he
came to a part of it in which they arrived at a certain place and
it seemed that a certain lady had been abducted by the warriors
there. So they hammered on the door and called out for battle
or combat[2] or for Anna an Diochlais, the daughter of the King
of Ireland, to be sent out to them.[3] And what they got was
battle and combat. And there were five hundred agile heroes
and five hundred complete heroes and five hundred brave
heroes with Cù Chulainn leading them. And when the battle
was over they set out and reached another place and called out
as they struck the door for battle and combat or for Anna an
Diochlais, the Daughter of the King of Leinster, to be sent out
to them. And what they got was battle and combat. And there
were five hundred complete heroes and five hundred agile
heroes and five hundred brave heroes and Iall of Greece[4]
leading them. And before he told the first story, he would say,

"But stretch out your leg, Céin,
  So that I may put on poultices of relief and deliverance
  and great healing ...
  Who was born in a city in Upper France
  And was broken in Bergen in Norway
  And listened to a mass in Dublin in Ireland, all in one day."

"I will not stretch out my leg," said Céin,
"For poultices of relief or deliverance or great healing

Which will reach the bone and pass the flesh
Until you tell three true stories without a lie."

When he began to recite the third story, he said that they went to this place and they struck the door and called out for battle and combat or Anna an Diochlais, the Daughter of the King of Leinster, to be sent out to them. And what they got was battle and combat. Five hundred agile heroes and five hundred full heroes and five hundred brave heroes were sent out and Fear Liath Mac Deamahainn[5] leading them.

And at the end of every tale, his companion would say, "My thanks to you, O God the King of the Hundreds and of the Powers. I am stronger today than I was yesterday and I was stronger yesterday than I was the day before."

And thus it went on until the leg was healed and it was found out for certain how everything had been. And that is what I remember of the tale as it was told by Archie Kennedy.

3   Ìseadal Son of the King of the Hunts, Fionn's Foster-Son

This story concerns Ìseadal Son of the King of the Hunts, who it seems was a foster-son of Fionn. And when they were at the battle, when they came to give an account of what had passed, Fionn would ask when they knocked on the door who was there at the door.

"It is I, Fiachaire, your son, and Ìseadal Son of the King of the Hunts, your foster-son."

And they were admitted and Fionn would ask how they had fared that day and his son would tell him how the battle had gone. And no matter how Fiachaire tried, Ìseadal Son of the King of the Hunts kept pace with him and Fionn would say, "Oh, Fiachaire, Fiachaire, you are too hard on Ìseadal Son of the King of the Hunts; he is only young. See that you do not press him so much."

And they would set out to another battle and the battle was going on this way for some time and then they would go to another battle. They would go out to battle and every time they came home, Fionn would ask how they had fared. Fiachaire, Fionn's son, would tell how things had gone and no matter how hard he tried the other one would keep pace with him and Fionn would say to Fiachaire, "Fiachaire, you are too hard on Ìseadal Son of the King of the Hunts; he is only young."

But at last they came to a battle when Ìseadal was killed. And they were engaging in battle – always offering battle – and Fiachaire was advancing and at last Ìseadal Son of the King of the Hunts was killed and beheaded, and Fiachaire had no choice but to put the head among the others where Ìseadal was struck dead.

The battle continued and it seems that the Fenians were winning, and there were withes to be strung with heads. And at the beginning and the end of the number of heads on the withes the head of Baoth Maol a' Chruachain was to be placed.[1] One of them asked the other how many heads there were and the other said that they were all there except for one.

"Well then," said he, "we must do battle and either your head or mine must go on the withe."

"Oh," he answered, "but that's not how it is at all," said he. "The nine withes are full now and at the beginning and the end of each full one is the head of Baoth Maol a' Chruachain."

"Well then," said he, "if that is so, we may stop: the battle is over."

4   *How Oscar Got His Name*

I heard a story from Archie Kennedy about Soup-Ladle, one of the Fenians. Because of all the soup he drank, they called him Soup-Ladle. And they were gathered somewhere: it seems that they had become lost, or that they were out on a journey and some hostile enemies happened upon them, and when they missed Soup-Ladle they began walking around and one of them called out then that they had found him.

"And is he alive?" said Fionn. "Oh, there is still some force

(*an t-osgar*) in him," said the other one.[1] "Well then," said
Fionn, "Oscar is what we call him. Let us carry him home."

And that is how Oscar got his name.

5   *Oscar and Mac a' Luin*

I heard an account from the late Archie Kennedy concerning the
tales of the Fenians, and the story he had about the journey of
Fionn and Oscar; however many others went with them I don't
remember at this time. But anyway, they went on a journey.

And, according to Kennedy's version, they went to see the
Pope. And it seems that the journey went well for them, and
when they were taking their leave, Fionn left the great sword
Mac a' Luin with the Pope as a gift. And they exchanged
farewells and went on their way. But unknown to the others,
Oscar stole back the sword and took it with him, concealing it
under his cloak.

And on the way home he said to Fionn, "Put your finger
under your tooth of knowledge to see what you will see and
hear."[1] And Fionn said,

> "A battle being fought and need of men
>   And the wind blowing over the host.
>   How hard it is without Mac a' Luin!"

"And what would you do with Mac a' Luin?" "I would,"
said he, "do away with the enemy. I would destroy them."[2]

I suppose that it was the Norsemen who were doing battle
with the Fenians at the time. At any rate, after a while Oscar
said to him again, "Put your finger under your tooth of
knowledge." This he did and it was the same story.

> "A battle being fought and need of men
>   The wind blowing over the host.
>   How hard it is without Mac a' Luin!"

And he asked what he would do with Mac a' Luin, and he

got the usual answer: that he would do away with or destroy the enemy.

The third time that he said this, it was the same story, except that Fionn appeared very sorry to receive this news a third time. And anyway, he felt something going up his back under his cloak.

"What," said he, "is on my back there?"

"Try and you'll see," said Oscar, and when he tried, Mac a' Luin was there.

"Didn't you do well by us," said Fionn. "You have behaved very wisely indeed. If you had given me Mac a' Luin while you were standing in front of me it would have given me such pleasure that I would have lost the ability to control myself and would have cut off your head."

And such was the story that Kennedy had on Mac a' Luin, and it seems that when they returned they were able to wreak great destruction on the Norsemen with Mac a' Luin.

6   *Fionn and the Strange Adversaries*

A story I heard from Archie Kennedy many years ago concerns Fionn mac Cumhail. And it seems that they were in a battle or in some hard conflict and, when things were turning against their opponent, he got assistance. The opponent used the Strange Adversaries, and when they came to attack Fionn he could not see them. At last Fionn realized how things stood and said, "Lift from me those who are invisible to me."

And the opponent paid no heed. But after some time he took the Strange Adversaries off Fionn, and then they went into battle for real – hand-to-hand I am sure – and Fionn managed to prevail.

There is a large part of the tale that I no longer have; Archie himself had forgotten most of it.

7   *How Conan Got His Name*

It was from Archie Kennedy that I heard the following story

about Conan, the most contemptible of the Fenians. It seems that Conan was crossing some strange, rugged country one day and he arrived at a hut. He looked in and there was a great hulk of a giant or some terrible creature sitting inside, so Conan said, "I never saw an open door that I did not enter through."

And in he went. There was a place for him to sit along the table, and he said, "I never saw a seat in a place that I did not sit on."

So he sat at that place. He looked and there was food on the table and he said, "I never saw food on the table that I did not partake of it."

He went to the table and began to eat the food, and at that moment the monster – the giant – was looking at him and his jaw was very close to Conan as he regarded him. I am sure he was considering how he would kill him, but when Conan was through with the food he said, "I never saw a chance to deliver a blow that I did not do it."

So he pushed the monster over and broke his jaw and did away with him. When he returned to the Fenians and told them what had happened, they all said that only the most contemptible of the Fenians would do such a thing. They were afraid to admit that he was valiant lest he begin on them. And that is how Conan got the reputation for being the most contemptible of the Fenians.

And I believe that it was Conan that said, "'If it's bad for me, it's no better for you,' as Conan said to the devil."[1]

And that was the saying: "'If it's bad for me, it's no better for you,' as Conan said to the devil." There you have the story of Conan, the most contemptible of the Fenians.

8   *Diarmaid and the Slim Woman in the Green Coat*

Whoever the Slim Woman in the Green Coat was it seems, according to some accounts, that Diarmaid O Duinn was eager to be in her company, that he was very much enamoured of her. I remember the late Archie Kennedy telling a tale that belonged to the Fenian Cycle. It seems that the Fenians were in hard straits and apparently under spells. They were sticking to the place where they were sitting and a cup of water was obtained which contained something to counter the spells and Fionn was sprinkling the water on them until the contents of the cup ran out and one of the Fenians was there who had not been detached from the floor at all. And he was calling out for them to lift him up and there was no way that he could be detached from the floor. And so he said, "O Diarmaid, O Diarmaid! If the Slim Woman in the Green Coat were in these straits you would do your best to help her."[1]

And according to the story he angered Diarmaid so that Diarmaid grabbed him and dragged him along and left the skin of his back and his thighs on the floor. And that is how I heard the story from Archie Kennedy about the Slim Woman in the Green Coat.

And people who listened often to his tales used to say if it were only the Slim Woman in the Green Coat ... (who needed your help) as if it were Diarmaid that said this. And that is what I remember concerning the Slim Woman in the Green Coat.

9   *The Death of Diarmaid*

Archie Kennedy had a tale concerning Diarmaid and Fionn. He had a large share of Fenian tales, but in this particular tale it seemed that there was something on the forehead of Diarmaid and any woman who saw it on his forehead could not help but fall in love with him. And it seems that Fionn's wife saw it and she fell deeply in love with Diarmaid. She felt a great longing for him, and that caused Fionn to harbour malice toward Diarmaid, because his – Fionn's – wife had departed with Diarmaid. And it seems that Fionn took the matter to heart and that he intended to put Diarmaid to death, but he did not want to have a hand in the death of Diarmaid or to be directly involved; he did not want to appear to be to blame in any way. Finally he sent Diarmaid to kill a poison boar somewhere. I'm sure that he tried many ways before to kill him, but it was not easy: Diarmaid was so stalwart. But he was sent to kill a poison boar; they expected when he went to hunt down the poison boar that it would finish him, and Fionn would not be blamed. But Diarmaid killed the poison boar and Fionn was not satisfied. Diarmaid was still alive and Fionn still harboured a good deal of malice towards him.

Fionn nursed his intense hatred towards Diarmaid and even though Diarmaid was so heroic as to kill the poison boar, Fionn was not happy that he had not met his death. So he saw fit that Diarmaid should measure the boar, and the boar was to be measured along its length. The measuring was to be done by foot-lengths, heel-to-toe, from one end to the other. Diarmaid began measuring the boar at its head, and he measured it down to the other end, that is, from the snout or nose of the pig down to the tail. Once he had done that, he was asked to measure back again toward the nose; measuring that way he was going against the direction of the bristles. Now, there was what was called a "Door of Death" on the sole of Diarmaid's foot and if any venomous point should penetrate it, he would die. As he was going up the pig Diarmaid stepped on a poison bristle which penetrated the "Door of Death" or the mole on the sole of his foot and he fell.

As he was approaching death he asked for water, and I believe that if he had got water, perhaps he might live and perhaps not. It was his last request, so Fionn went down to the water – there was a river or rivulet or a pond or a place where there was water – and he scooped some up. He put his two palms together and scooped up water and was going up to Diarmaid with it when he thought of the malice that was between them and how Diarmaid had stolen his wife – how his own wife had gone off with him – and he opened his hands. But he thought then that he had done wrong; he regretted that he had not performed the last request that Diarmaid had made, although there was the malice between them, and he returned to the water for some more. But he could no longer carry water in his hands.

And Kennedy used to say, "This is why no one can scoop

up water with his hands and carry it any distance." And
that is what I remember of the tale of the death of Diarmaid
O Duinn.

10   *The Amhas Òrmanach*

I got a short tale from Kennedy concerning a person who as far
as I remember was named the Amhas Òrmanach. And he was
so courageous and gallant; he had no fear of anything anywhere. So he set out to travel the world to see if something
would happen to him that would frighten him, and it seems
that he travelled throughout the world – whatever part he
could – and he encountered nothing that frightened him. And
he was returning home and nothing was happening to him.
But when he was close to home on his own land he grew
thirsty and bent down beside a little stream and was going to
drink from the stream. And as he bent over and was just about
to put his lips to the water a little fish swam by and stirred the
water. He jerked his head up and thought then how silly he
was to go travelling through the whole world to see if he could
see anything or if anything would happen upon him that would
frighten him when that tiny little fish in the stream beside his
own house had frightened him so much that he had panicked.

11   *Jack and the Master*

Once upon a time there was a poor widow who had three sons,
and they were all very poor in this world. The two oldest sons
were extremely smart and intelligent but the youngest, Jack,
was considered by everyone just a fool. So the oldest of the
lads said that he was going to go out to seek his fortune, saying
that when he had made a sizeable fortune he would return
home to the house and that they would be well off then.

So he set out, and whether the time that he travelled was
long or short, he arrived at the holding of a big farmer, a large,
grey-haired old man, who had an extensive piece of farmland

and cattle and was very well-to-do. And it seems that he was the sort of man who was hard on people. But they came to an agreement and settled on the salary he would pay. And the conditions were, should the lad ever express regret for having come to work for the farmer before a year was up, he would receive no pay at all – he would be let go penniless – and a strip an inch wide would be taken from the skin of his back, from the top of his shoulder down to his waist. So the lad stayed for a short length of time with the farmer. But it seems that matters were so difficult that finally one day, when the work had got on top of him so much that he did not think first, he said that he regretted coming there at all. And that was it. He had no choice but to start off on his way without thanks or payment, and a thong of skin – a strip an inch across – was cut from his back from the top of his shoulder down to his waist. So he arrived home in that condition, in great misery from how hard they had worked him and how scarce his food was and how he had been abused. And oh, his mother was extremely angry. And his brother was also quite angry about what had happened, saying that he himself would set out and approach that farmer to exact vengeance.

So he set out and, alas, things went no better for him than they had for the first brother. I am sure with things being so difficult there and people behaving so badly to him, that he felt regret and let it be known one day that he was sorry, so he fared exactly as his brother had. He returned home, and he too was miserable and sore. And, oh, his mother was truly unhappy about what had happened.

Then Jack, the youngest brother, the fool, said that he was going to set out. Oh, his mother advised him that he had better not go at all, that he would probably fare worse than the others. But he said that he would go anyway, and he set out and he reached the home of this grey-haired old man, the big farmer. He told the farmer his mission and the farmer replied that he had better return home, that his brothers had fared badly and that perhaps he would fare even worse. Oh, he said that he would remain there anyway, that he would give it a try.

So they agreed on the conditions, and the wage that he was to get was twenty English pounds per year. That was good enough; it would please him well enough, but the farmer told him that there were other conditions, too: "If you ever express regret over coming here before the time is up, you will receive no wage at all. And a strip of skin will be taken from your back, from the top of your shoulder to the top of your hip."

"I am satisfied with those conditions," Jack replied.

"There are other conditions, too," said the grey-haired old man. "If you refuse to do anything that I ask which you are able to do, you will be docked one month's pay."

"I am well satisfied with that," answered Jack. "But now," he continued, "there is a condition that I require."

"Very well," said the gentleman-farmer.

"That is," said Jack, "if I remain with you for a year my wage will be doubled."

"I am satisfied with that," said the gentleman.

"And I have another condition for you."

"Very well," said the farmer.

"That is," said he, "should you ask anything at all of me, and prevent me – hinder me – then from doing it, I will expect a month's wages."

"I am satisfied with that," said the master.

"And there is yet another condition," said he. "If you should scold me and complain about anything that I do, I shall be entitled to a month's wages."

"I am satisfied with that," answered the farmer.

So the youngest brother stayed to work. But on the first day he only got a very small amount of food, and he was tormented with work until he was fairly exhausted right down to his shoes. But on the following day when he was going out to work – it was nowhere near dinnertime yet – he went into the room where the cooking was done and there was a big goose on the roasting-spit. He snatched the goose off the spit and brought over a big knife and gave the goose a good whack, taking off one side of its breast along with a wing and a leg. Just then the master came in.

"And what," said the master, "are you doing there?"

"Oh," said he, the lad, "isn't it fitting enough that servants should be fed? And where this goose," said he, "is going now, no more need go, at least until suppertime."

And that did not please the old man at all so the lad asked him, "Do you have any regrets?"

"Oh, no," replied the old man. So Jack had his food and I'm sure that he took things easy for the rest of the day.

But the farmer said to him on the next day, "You must," said he, "go out to harvest the peats."

"All right," replied the lad. And when he went to get his breakfast, it seems he only got a very small serving of food.

"Well," said he, "I think that I would be just as well off getting my dinner and that would suffice for walking back and forth from the bog where the peat sods are."

"You will have that," said the maidservant, and she came in with a bonnach[1] and big lump of butter and a bottle of milk. She expected that he would take that over to where he was going to harvest the peats, but he did not move from where he was sitting. Instead, he ate every bit of the bonnach and of the butter and drank the milk.

"Well," said he, "I think that I could arise and begin work earlier in the morning," said he, "if I were to sleep in the shelter of the peat stack on the dry grass. So wouldn't it be just as well for me," said he, "to take my supper along?"

"Very well," said the maidservant. "I will bring you your supper."

And she thought that he would at least set out with that but instead he remained seated and ate his supper. When he had finished it, he arose and went to look for his master.

"What," said he, "is the custom for the servants to do in this country when they have had their supper?"

"Oh, indeed what," said the master, "but to go to sleep?"

"Thank you very much," said the lad.

So he went over to the stable – the byre – and he went up into the loft and took off part of his clothes and lay down to sleep. One of the servants told his master that he was over in the loft of the barn – or above the stable – going to sleep, and his master went over to look.

"What," said he, "are you doing there?"

"Oh," said he, "am I not going to sleep? The maidservant," he continued, "gave me my supper and didn't you yourself say that people of this region go to sleep when they have had their supper? Are you pleased with the way I have done things?"

"No," replied his master.

"Then give me," said Jack, "one English pound thirteen shillings and fourpence."

"You will have that," said his master "when you have had your nap."

"Do you regret my coming here?"

And, oh, the master was going to say yes. "Oh, I am still well-satisfied," he said instead. And so he did himself in that way.

Anyway, when Jack had finished his sleep he came and got his due.

And his master said to him, "You are," said he, "to go out tomorrow to plow on the ridge beside the lower cattle-fold. You will hold the plow."

So in the morning he went down and toward midday the farmer arrived to see what kind of plowman Jack was; and there he was with the plow running on the top of the ground, and the young lad who was with him leading the horses.

"And what," said the master, "are you doing here?"

"Well," replied Jack, "I am doing what you asked me to. Didn't you ask me to hold the plow? I am trying to hold the plow as best I can and that fool of a boy," he said, "is driving the horses and hurrying them so I can only do as I am doing."

"Oh," said the master. "Didn't I ask you to break the earth and turn the soil?"

"Oh why," said Jack, "didn't you tell me that correctly in the beginning? Would you like me to cease doing this?"

"Yes," said the master.

"Well, then," said Jack, "give me one English pound thirteen shillings and fourpence. Are you," said he, "happy with the work that I am doing?"

"Oh, yes," replied the master.

And he started over then and plowed at his leisure.

The next day his master said to him, "There are," said he, "three heifers that have strayed and I wish you to find them."

"And where shall I find them?" said Jack.

"Oh," said the master, "look where it would be fitting or natural for them to be, and where it would not be fitting or natural for them to be."

So Jack set out looking for the heifers. And his master arrived at the byre after a large part of the day had passed and there was Jack busily working at pulling the thatch from the top of the byre and looking inside; he would peer inside through the hole he had made pulling the thatch from the byre. He would try in one place and pull out another clump and look inside there.

"And what," said the master, "are you doing there?"

"Am I not looking for the heifers that were lost?"

"And did you expect that you would find them ... what would put them up here?"

"How should I know what would put them there? You asked me to look where it would be proper and natural for them to be and that is where I looked," said he. "I looked in the byre and I looked in the cattle-fold and I looked out on the meadow beside the cattle-fold, and they weren't there at all. And now," said he, "I am looking to see if they might be here in a less likely place."

And this did not please the farmer at all.

"Do you regret this?" asked Jack.

"Oh, no," replied the master. "You had better thatch the byre as if it were your own mother's little hut."

"Very well," said Jack. And he began to re-thatch the byre. And after a period of time the byre was thatched better than it had been before. And he got the lad who was attending him to supply him with fresh straw for the top of the byre. Then his master said to him, "Get going now and fetch those heifers as if they were your own."

So he set out and before the sun went down he had the three heifers in the fold.

His master said to him on the following day, "There is," said he, "a bog up in the meadow, and the sheep are about to get stuck in it as they pass through. But you get going," said he, "and build a road that meets the requirements of sheep's feet."

So the lad set out. And after a good part of the day, the farmer arrived up there and there was Jack busily sharpening a big knife.

"Is that your way of preparing the road as I asked you to?"

"Oh," replied Jack, "this is just the beginning. And anything well begun is already half done."

"And what," said his master, "have you done there?"

"Am I not sharpening the knife so that I can cut the feet off the sheep?"

"Why," said the master, "are you going to cut the feet off the sheep?"

"And did you not ask me to make a road which would meet the requirements of sheep's feet?"

"Oh, that is not what I asked you at all. What I was asking you was to make a road that would be good enough for sheep's feet."

"And why," said Jack, "didn't you say so at first? Are you ordering me to stop?"

"Yes, I am," said the master.

"That will cost you one English pound thirteen shillings and fourpence. And do you regret that you made me come here?"

"Oh, no, no," replied his master. He was quiet for a time. "No, no," he said again.

So that passed. And then Jack's master said to him, "I have received an invitation to a wedding and I'm going to take you with me so that I will not be led astray by strong drink; I will have to be home before midnight and you are to return with me. And when you see that I have had enough to drink and you want to put a stop to my drinking you can throw me a 'sheep's eye' (a sideways glance)."

So they set out to the wedding and the master began to grow quite merry after drinking a good deal. And as he was going to raise the pints of wine that were before him – going to raise the flagons of wine to his mouth – he felt a soft blow on the side of his jaw. Whatever had caused it fell, and when he looked what was it but a sheep's eye! He threw it aside and wondered what impudent rascal was inside or who in the world would throw that at him. After a while he was going to reach over for the pitcher of wine, and when he was extending his hand towards the flagon he received a soft blow on the other side of his jaw and whatever had done it fell on the table. And he looked and what was it but a sheep's eye! And he continued drinking – he was becoming very annoyed at what was happening but he continued anyway – but when he was opening his mouth, about to put away a good mouthful of wine, the third thing came and went right into his mouth. He spit it out of his mouth, and what was it but a sheep's eye! So he called out to the host, asking who was throwing that at him and he began to grumble.

"Take it easy," said Jack. "The host is not to blame at all for this. Did you not ask me to do this so that you would not drink too much?"

"And where," said the master, "did you get the sheep's eyes?"

"Where indeed did I get them," said Jack, "but in the heads of the sheep? In the heads of your own sheep," he went on. "For I was not about to go around taking the eyes out of the neighbours' sheep for fear that I would be arrested," said he, "and held fast, as they say, like a stone in lime."

"Oh," said he, the master, crying out, "I am sorry and I regret that you ever met me at all!"

"Now I have a witness against you," said Jack, "that you have stated that you regret this. So get for me my double pay immediately," said he, "that is, forty English pounds. And come into that room yonder with me," said he, "and lie down on the floor."

The master went into the room – reluctantly – and Jack began sharpening the big knife to take the skin off his back. The others there called out repeatedly for him to stop.

"Oh," said Jack, "nobody said anything to him about stopping when he took the skin off the backs of my two brothers and returned them penniless to their poor mother."

And when they heard what had happened, they agreed

that that was fitting enough. And when Jack had the knife sharpened to a good, keen edge he made three lines on the floor beside the master.

"I will grant you a condition," said he. "I will leave the skin on your back if you give me two hundred guineas."

"I will not," replied the master, "though you would flay the skin off me from the top of my head to my heels."

"Very well," said Jack. "I will flay a strip of your skin off you."

And he began, but when he had taken a little piece of the skin from his back, the master cried, "Stop! Stop! Stay your hand and I will give you the two hundred guineas."

"Now," said Jack to the people who were around him, "do not think badly of me at all. I did not have the heart to take the eye out of a rat, let alone eyes from sheep. Instead, I got half a dozen sheep's eyes from the butcher and I only used three of them."

And when they heard this, they took the two of them back into the room and they all got a little flagon of wine and drank Jack's health. Then they gave him a glass of wine and he drank one toast to every one of them and they set out for the big farmer's house. And the farmer had to go to a room that was high up in the loft and bring down the golden guineas and give the lad the two hundred English pounds in wages.

The lad set out for home. And he was very well set with his own wages going home and his back was whole and undamaged. And he had two hundred guineas to give to his mother and his brothers, who though they were cripples would be well off for a long time to come. And ever since then, they did not call him "Jack the Fool" but "Jack the Old Man's Hide." And there you have the story as I heard it.

12   *Great Brìd of the Horses*

I have part of a story or tale that I heard from the late Murdock Kennedy, who died a number of years ago. So much time has passed since I heard this tale; I only heard it once so I did not learn it completely. I just learned part of it.

The tale concerns a king in Ireland who had three sons: one was called Ullabhan, one was called Marbhan, and I don't remember the name of the third one at all. Anyway, one of the lads was put in charge of the kingdom after his father's death, and there was a band travelling around at that time and they were causing the kingdom great expense, for they had to be kept as guests whenever they arrived. They were musicians of some sort or belonged to some such profession and they were called the Cleith Sheanachair.

Since they were so costly, the young king decided to give up the kingdom and not to concern himself with those matters any longer. So notice was given and they sold everything belonging to the kingdom. Oh, the people of the kingdom bought various things here and there, and the kingdom was broken up.

But after a time the young king came to regret having left the kingdom and let everything go. He saw that it was a bad thing for the people to be without a king and for things to take the course that they had. So he sent notice that he would like to return to take charge of the kingdom and to restore things to their former state. Well, people were very happy with this, and everyone who had bought things from him, whatever purchase price they had paid for them, returned them to him for half of the original price, and the matter was settled as well as could be.

For a while things went well enough but it seemed that Great Bríd of the Horses – for she was the lord over the Cleith Sheanachair at the time – found out that the kingdom had been restored, and so they returned to visit. Now the young king was not at all willing to have them in the kingdom and he gave them his order to leave. They were not to stay in the kingdom at all or to be guests as they had been accustomed to be before. Great Bríd of the Horses said that they would not leave until they were given their three wishes. The king replied that they would get those and he set out expressly to determine what these were and to find out if certain conditions might be laid on him. She said that she required her fill of blackberries in January, and that she wanted her fill of the flesh of a boar that was never born, and that she wished to ride on the white horse with red ears until she was tired. The king replied that he would try to fulfil her wishes for her, but that there were certain conditions before these things could be delivered. Then he went to an adviser and told him how matters stood.

"Well," said the adviser, "as you were leaving you became angry when things turned against you – you and your father fell out with each other and you left – and you cast off your cloak and threw it on top of a knoll. Go to the knoll there and raise the cloak and you will find blackberries in January."

"Yes, indeed," he replied, "but where will I find the flesh of the boar that was never born?"

"Oh," said the adviser, "your father had a sow and she could not bear her litter, so they found a man who was good around stock and that man saw that the only suitable way to get the litter from the sow was to open up her side. And that was how they got the litter. They lifted out the piglets from the sow through the opening that they made in her side and one of those piglets is alive yet, and that piglet was never born; it was taken out through the side of the sow. You can find that boar and kill it and give her her fill of its flesh."

"Yes, indeed," said he. "But where am I to find the white horse with the red ears?"

"Oh, that is easy enough for you to find," said he. "When you kill the boar, keep the blood and you can rub its blood on the horse's ear until the ear turns red and no rain ever fell in Ireland that can dissolve or clean off that blood. And now you may go."

So the young king reached the place where the Cleith Sheanachair were and he said to her that these conditions – these demands – could be fulfilled for her entirely, but that she would have to grant him a demand in return; and if she could not fulfil this they would not receive a single share more of anything. His demand was for his seven satisfactions of the *Crònan Snagach*; it seems that the *Crònan Snagach* consisted of striking the joint of the thumb on their teeth to make a sort of droning. They tried it and whether they had to abandon the attempt or whatever happened, according to how I heard the tale from Murdock Kennedy, the Cleith Sheanachair went back, making for some other kingdom and they never again returned to bother the young king in Ireland. And there you have what I have learned of the tale of Great Brìd of the Horses and the king of Ireland and the Cleith Sheanachair, as they were known.

13   *The Death of Cù Chulainn*

I only have a piece here and there of this tale as it was. I heard it from Murdock Kennedy a long time ago. I am certain that had I paid more attention to the tale I would have learned it entirely. But I know that there were warriors named there, such as Cù Chulainn and great ones like that, and there was one they called Raven. And it seems that in a certain battle someone was killed and Raven cried out that it was Cù Chulainn who had slain him. But at that moment somebody came by and cried out that it was Raven who had slain him. But in the course of all the battles Cù Chulainn himself was killed. And the man who knew that Cù Chulainn had been killed was too afraid to tell the other one what had happened – whether it was Fionn or whoever it was. I think that it was Fionn who was there at the time. But he noticed that the man appeared to have something on his mind, so he asked him, "Is Cù Chulainn dead?"

"It was yourself," answered the other, "who was the first to say 'Cù Chulainn dead.' And you needed to do that," said he, "for had you said that before, I would have had to kill you."

Now, there was more in the tale about the Stone of Great Fergus – until the Stone of Great Fergus moved – where some evil man went to the stone and he began to ask the other one to move, or to arise, and Great Fergus would say, "Avoid me, O Cursed Son."

And he continued at this until at last he had to move the Stone, the Stone of Great Fergus. Whatever the conditions were, or whatever information was to be gained, that is how they found him. I don't remember any more of the tale.

14   *The King and the Foal*

A man offended a king, whatever the reason was. This particular man's wife died and he and his daughter were keeping house. It seems that she was extremely smart and she was good in every respect. But the king sent for the man – whatever the pretext – and the man went. And the king said to him in parting that he had to be back there the next day to tell him what was the most plentiful thing in the world and if he could not tell him that he would be put to death. The poor man came home and the daughter noticed that he looked extremely sorrowful. She asked him what his trouble was – he looked so cheerless.

"What good will it do me to tell you?" said he.

"Well," replied the daughter, "perhaps none, except whom else would you tell it to if you didn't tell me?"

So he told her how things stood.

"And why," said she, "did you not tell him the answer when you were over at his place?"

"And what could I tell him?"

"Couldn't you tell him," said she, "that there was nothing in the world as plentiful as sides?"

"And do you yourself think," said he, "that sides are the most plentiful things?"

"Oh, don't you know, dear father," said she, "that indeed they are? It does not matter at all how plentiful anything is in the world; there are at least two sides to it and there are many things which have more than two sides. There might be, for example, an inside and an outside and a top side and a bottom side and on some things a far side and a near side. You can name sides as being more plentiful than anything else."

So the following day he went back and he was so happy.

"Well," said the king, "you have come."

"Yes, Your Majesty," replied the man.

"Do you have an answer to the question?"

"Oh, yes indeed," he replied.

"Well, then, what is the most plentiful thing in the world?"

"There is nothing in the world as plentiful as sides."

"Oh, yes there is," said the king. "I do indeed believe there is."

"Oh, there is not, by your leave," said the man, "anything as plentiful as those."

"And what proof do you have that they are the most plentiful?"

"My proof is," replied the man, "that there are at least two sides to everything. However plentiful anything is it must have two sides and there are some things which have three sides and others with four sides."

"I am satisfied," said the king, "from that answer that you are correct. But you are to be here tomorrow," he continued, "and you will tell me what is the wealthiest thing in the world."

The old man went home and he looked just as sad and sorrowful as he had the day before.

"What is troubling you today?" said the daughter. "You look so heavy-hearted."

"Oh, what use is it to tell anybody or anyone at all what my trouble is? Are they not going to put me to death tomorrow unless I tell the king what is the wealthiest thing in the world?"

"So why didn't you tell him?"

"What could I tell him?"

"Couldn't you say to him that there was nothing so wealthy as the sea?"

"So wealthy as the sea! Do you really think so?"

"Oh, I am certain," said she. "Name anything on earth and the sea is much larger than that and it contains more of every-thing. And by virtue of that," said she, "is it not the wealthiest thing in the world?"

So he returned to the king's palace.

"You have come," said the king.

"Yes, Your Majesty," said he. "I have returned."

"And do you have the solution to the question?"

"Oh, I have," said he.

"Well, then," said the king, "what is the wealthiest thing in the world?"

"Oh, nothing on earth," replied the man, "is wealthier than the sea."

"Oh, yes there is," said the king. "Am I myself not wealthier than the sea?"

"Oh, no indeed, by your leave, you are not that wealthy. Remember," he continued, "that the sea is larger than the rest of the world; it is larger than the land and it contains more of everything and for that reason it is wealthiest."

"I must confess that I am satisfied with that," said the king. "But you are to be back here tomorrow and if you cannot tell me what is the swiftest thing in the world you shall lose your head."

The old man returned home and he was very down-hearted when he arrived.

"Well," said the daughter. "What is your trouble now, dear father? You look extremely cheerless."

"Oh, what difference does it make what is troubling me?" said he. "I will lose my head tomorrow unless I tell the king what is the swiftest thing in the world."

"And why didn't you tell him?"

"What could I tell him?" he replied.

"Could you not have told him that there is nothing in the world so swift as thought?"

"And do you yourself think," asked the old man, "that thought is that swift? Do you really think it is?"

"Oh, don't I know it is?" she replied. "Couldn't you your-self think of being in any part of the world at all, far away on the other side of the world? And is there a bird or a horse or any other creature who could go over to the other side of the world as swiftly as your thoughts would travel?"

"That is true," said the old man.

The next day he went over to the king's palace. "Well," said the king, "you have come."

"Yes, Your Majesty," said the old man. "I have returned once more."

"Well, then," said the king. "Do you have a solution to the question?"

"Oh, indeed I have," said the old man.

"Well, then," said the king, "what is the swiftest thing on earth?"

"Oh," said he, "it is thought."

"Oh, no indeed," said the king. "I believe I have a horse as swift as that."

"Indeed no," said the old man. "There is nothing in the world as swift as thought."

"And by what means," said the king, "do you intend to prove that? What proof do you have that thought is so swift?"

"Oh, by your leave," he replied, "your thought can be on the other side of the kingdom or the other side of the world and you can be there so swiftly that there is not a horse or a bird nor any other beast who could take you there near as swiftly."

"Ah," said the king, "I am satisfied with that answer. Now I am going to ask you another question," said he, "but this one is easy enough. Who is with you, or are you living alone, or how are you managing?"

"My daughter is keeping house for me," replied the man, "since she lives with me."

"Indeed," said the king. "I am going to ask your daughter's hand in marriage."

"Your Majesty, you may go to get her," said he, "but that is up to her. I will not ask her to marry you nor will I prevent her."

"That is all right by me," said the king. "I accept that."

So the king arrived and he asked her hand in marriage and she was quite willing to marry him. But when the marriage was ready and everything was finished, the king said, "There will, however, be a condition."

"Oh very well," said she. "Let me hear the conditions."

"There is a condition to be laid down," said he, "that if anything ever comes between us you must depart and leave the castle."

"That is all right," said she, "but I must impose conditions too or I will not be in the least willing to agree to any conditions whatsoever."

"Well," replied the king, "that is fitting enough."

"I wish for conditions to be laid down," said she, "that if anything comes between us that I leave the castle, but that you permit me to take three loads out of the castle as I am leaving for home."

"It is fitting enough," replied the king, "that these conditions be imposed."

So the conditions were laid down legally enough and they were made binding; they had to be fulfilled if such things should come to pass.

But anyway things were going ahead happily enough and they had a family – a boy was born. And at that time it was the custom to put a child in a cradle and rock him back and forth, so the child was in the cradle; he was perhaps about a year old. But there was a farmer in the region living next to the king who had a mare, and the mare had a foal and she went out on the mountain. The king had horses out on the mountain along with a gelding, and, however it occurred, the foal followed one of the horses home to the king's stable. The king claimed that the foal was his own, that it belonged to him and that he had the right to it since it was with the horse, and the man could not get his foal back. The king was going along with appearances and for this reason the man could not recover the foal, for it seemed that it belonged to the king – that it was his property – having come home with the horse. So the farmer came over to the house one day and the king had gone out hunting – he used to go out hunting with his servants – and complained about this.

"Now," said she, "come by early in the morning when you think that the king has just arisen, and bring along a bucket of salt and begin sowing it in the field. And the king will come out to see what you are doing and you will say to him that you are shaking salt. And be sure to talk as if you see this as most usual and fitting. And when he asks you whether you believe that the salt you are sprinkling on the field will grow, say to him that it is just as likely that salt would grow in the ground as it is for a gelding to have a foal. And now," said she, "I will say no more."

So the farmer came over early in the morning and he was sprinkling salt on the field – he had a bucket of salt and he was sprinkling it. The king went over to him.

"What are you doing there?"

"Am I not," replied the farmer, "sprinkling salt?"

"And do you really think that the salt that you sprinkle on the ground will grow?"

"I am not certain that it will," replied the farmer, "but I think it is just as likely for salt to grow in the ground as it is for a gelding to have a foal."

"That is certainly true," said the king.

The king was not happy to part with the foal. It seems that he knew that it was an exceptional foal – the stock was good and it was hard for him to part with it – and he went inside.

"This was your doing," said he, "giving advice to the farmer."

"Indeed it was," replied his wife.

"Well then," said the king, "I am sure that you remember the conditions."

"Oh yes," said she, "I remember them very well. All of them."

"Then you can get ready and go out of the castle and leave it and go off in whichever direction you please," said the king.

"Oh, that is all very well," said she. "But remember that I was to have three loads to take out of the castle when I left. That was the agreement. And if I hold to this agreement then you must hold to your own."

"Oh, yes indeed," said he. "That is fitting too. The agreements were set."

If the king were to go against the agreement that he had made, she could refuse to go from the castle. But he said that that was all right, that she could take the three loads with her. So she filled a chest of gold and silver and jewels and all sorts of valuables and carried that out and put it outside the castle and then she returned inside. The cradle was in the room and the young lad was in it and I am sure that he was sleeping at the time. She lifted up the cradle, and that was the second load that she was allowed to take out of the castle. And I am sure that the king was looking at the chest of gold outside and looking at the cradle and looking at the baby boy inside – at the heir to the kingdom that was in it. And surely he was holding his temples thinking how silly he had been when he made that condition. So all she did then was to walk inside and glance around and take hold of him and lead him out the door.

She had brought the three loads out of the castle and the castle could be anybody's then. So he said, "You can go back into the castle now and I will go in myself and carry in the loads that you brought out along with everything else from the castle."

And that is what happened to the old man's clever daughter and the king who was trying to get the foal from the farmer. This is the tale I got from Kate Kennedy.

15   *The Castle That Boban Saor Built*

Now, I have a tale concerning how a certain woman's cleverness came to the fore, and the tale came from Catherine or Kate, as we used to say, Kennedy – and it was from her that I got the story that I am going to tell now – when Boban Saor and his son were sent for to travel to some region where a castle was to be built. I believe that they were to go to France or some region of Greece.

So they arrived there, but before they left home at all the son's wife said to him, "Now," said she, "I am giving you some advice. You will take a fool for a sweetheart, whatever town you will be working in or staying. And you will find out," said she, "things from this foolish sweetheart that will be very useful to you."

And so it happened. He was courting some woman who was certain that she was going to marry him, so she held back no information. And what woman was that but one of the woman servants to the nobleman – to the king – who was there, and she knew about everything. And when the castle was nearly built and completed the lad found out from her that they did not intend to pay them at all, and that they might not be allowed to return safely to their own country. He was telling his father that night, when it came time for them to go to sleep, how thing were going, and the old man decided that he would find a way out for them.

And he told the nobleman one day that the castle was ready now, except for one detail that was left to do, and that that could not be done until he fetched a tool that he kept at home. Oh, the nobleman said, he would send a servant right away to fetch it.

"Oh, that won't do," said Boban Saor. "I must go over or my son and myself should go to fetch the tool. The wife would not entrust the tool to just anybody."

"Well," said the nobleman, "I will send my own son over to fetch it."

"Well, then," said Boban Saor, "in that case he must learn from me what to say when he arrives there, or he will not get the tool."

And that was what was done. The nobleman's son learned what to say to Boban Saor's wife when he arrived. When he reached the place he said that he had come over, that the husband had sent him to fetch a tool that they required.

"Indeed," said she, "and what did he tell you to say?"

"He told me to say, 'Turn alike and turn for turn, and the little tool will not come over here until the big tool goes over there.'"

"Oh, very well," said she. "Come down to this room."

And when they had gone down and through a door or two leading to some rooms, and had reached the room, she told him to enter, and when he did she locked the door; she locked the door on the nobleman's son and there he was. As time passed and he did not return the nobleman said to Boban Saor that it was strange that his own son had not returned with the tool.

"Oh," said Boban Saor, "your son won't return at all. He is being held prisoner over there by my wife. And he will remain there until the lad and I go home and we won't leave here at all until we get our wages for building the castle."

And Boban Saor and the lad received their wages and they got home safely. And that is the story I got on the cleverness of the lad's wife when she let him know or put him under an obligation to take a fool as a sweetheart. That is the story that I got from Catherine (Kate) Kennedy.

16   *Working with the Adze (Boban Saor)*

In the story about working with the adze, Boban Saor's son always wished to find out about working with an adze and the old man would never tell him everything about it. But the son's wife determined to trick him and get the information, and so one day, as they were working somewhere outside hewing lumber or at some kind of work, the young wife went to them with their dinner. And what did she have but boiled eggs which had been shelled – the shells had been taken off – and when they sat down to eat their food, the old man asked who had shelled the eggs.

"Oh," said she, "your own son shelled them with the adze."

And this caught the old man so swiftly that without thinking he answered, "Didn't he hold it close to his thigh!"

And the lad overheard him, and that was how he found out how adze work was done.

17   *Did You Ever See the Like of Me*

Here is a story that I heard from Alexander Kennedy. It is a great many years since I heard it told, more than fifty.

It seems that there was a certain man who engaged in tricks and strange ways, and he went to see a stingy old woman. And he had made a bet that he would get inside and that he would get food. When he came to the door she asked who he was or who was there and he said that his name was William Sit Down.

"William Sit Down," said she and he entered, saying, "That is the proper thing to do now that I have been invited by the woman of the house."

So he was in the house and he said to the ill-tempered old woman that she would have to prepare food for him. She put a little splash of water in a pot as she was about to prepare porridge and went off to fetch the meal. And while she was away getting the meal he poured another little splash of water into the pot. She returned with the meal and put it into the pot and to confuse her he said that it was too thin, that she would have to put more meal in it. And off she went to get more meal. While she was away he put another little splash of water into the pot, and when she returned he said that the porridge was still too thin and sent her away again for meal; so that it amounted to quite a nice amount of porridge. When they had eaten that, he got a chance and snatched up articles that belonged to the old lady – cheese or whatever was there – and she asked him again what his name was. He replied that when he was away he had various names and the name he had when he was travelling was Did You Ever See the Like of Me.

And when the old woman finally missed the articles that were taken she went out to look and there was no trace of him: he had taken off and fled. So she went down the road and called out to everyone that she met, "Did You Ever See The Like of Me?"

And I am sure that the people thought that the old lady had gone out of her mind calling out, "Did you ever see the like of me?" And I expect that they caught her and put her away in a safe place before she could do any harm. And that is all I remember of the story about Did You Ever See The Like of Me.

The MacLeans

According to the history that I got from them, these MacLeans came from Barra. But they maintain that originally they belonged to the MacLeans of Duart. It seems that they may have been brought over to Barra. Perhaps they were in North Uist. I don't know anything about that, but perhaps they were in North Uist and went from there to Barra.

It seems that over in Scotland there was Lachlann Gobha (Lachlann the Blacksmith) and Iain mac Lachlainn Ghobha (John son of Lachlann the Blacksmith); and Calum Òg, son of Iain mac Lachlainn Ghobha came over to Cape Breton. Now I don't know when he came over, whether it was after his children emigrated or whether he came over with them.

But that is of no great importance. Calum Òg was over here in Cape Breton. And since he was styled Calum Òg (Young Malcolm) I would guess that he would probably be one of the youngest in the family; certainly the name indicates there were two Calums in the family. But it was over here that he died. He was buried down in the graveyard in Big Pond or in Middle Pond, as they say.

And Niall mac Iain 'ac Lachlainn (Neil son of John son of Lachlann) arrived; he was a brother of Calum Òg. Now I cannot say for sure that Niall mac Iain 'ac Lachlainn actually came over – I never heard that he was over here in Cape Breton – but the children of Niall Mór mac Iain 'ic Lachlainn were here. And when I have finished giving the history of the progeny of Calum Òg I will say something then, whatever I know, about that of Niall Mór (Big Neil). I believe now that I should begin from Calum Òg down.

John son of Calum Òg and Neil son of Calum Òg and Alexander son of Calum Òg were living over in Middle Cape.

He also had a number of daughters such as Mary Calum Òg and Sarah Calum Òg, Catherine Calum Òg, and Annie Calum Òg, and so on. I won't go into too great detail concerning them because I did not get stories or anything else from them; I only knew that they were there.

But Donald son of Malcolm J. (Calum Iain), when a young man, went away to work and took up work on the railway. And it seems that he worked in the roundhouse, the house in which they turned the big engine used to pull the railway cars around. When the engine came in it had to be turned so that it would go out again, as we would say, facing in the opposite direction. He worked there a long time, a great many years, until at last he worked his way up to where he let the cars out. This job consisted of inspecting cars before they were taken; he was, as they call it in English, a car inspector. And if anybody should be curious or wonder what this meant and what was involved, I was given to understand that he went with a small hammer in his hand and would strike the iron wheels on the cars. He could tell from the sound when he hit the iron wheel whether there was a crack in it. And if the wheel – the iron wheel – was cracked he was able to detect it and it had to be corrected. The car could not be let out with a cracked wheel. And that's what I understood to be involved in letting the cars out. He had that job, I believe, until he retired. And I believe that his sight was growing bad – extremely bad – but that made no difference since his hearing was good.

And I used to go and visit the man until very shortly before he died. And we were always together telling tales and such like. He had some books of Gaelic songs and he would say to me whenever we met, "Be sure to come and visit me soon. I am still keeping the books so that you'll have some time to read them."

As for Michael (Mìcheal Iain Chaluim) – I have mentioned him often – I got a good number of items from him and indeed it was he who gave me the account that Calum Òg was buried in this country. Although I hardly got any stories from Calum Iain, I learned a good number of them from his son, from Donald whom I have mentioned, and from John. And there was an Alexander (Alasdair Nìll Chaluim) from whom I also heard stories. And, to be sure, there were the wives of these people, such as the wife of Michael (Mìcheal Iain Chaluim); I got expressions and such from her, and the same with the wife of Alasdair Nìll Chaluim: I got a few expressions from her too. And James Smith: he was raised at Michael's place and I got expressions and proverbs from him and heard stories told by him in addition to those I learned from various newspapers.

And I think now I have covered the history of those MacLeans – Calum Òg's branch – but I should add here that they were considered to be exceptional fishermen. It seems that they were fishermen in Barra although there was also blacksmithing among the older people all the way back to Lachlann Gobha (Lachlann the Blacksmith); it seems that they came into the fishing from that time on. John (Iain Chaluim) and Neil (Niall Chaluim Òig) were considered to be especially good fishermen over our way. John's son Michael spent some of his life on the fishing banks; he was at sea. And Malcolm, Neil's son, was considered to be a real fisherman; when they were out on the fishing banks he was the best man of all. One summer when they were engaged in fishing he beat all of the rest there with the size of his catch of fish. And he raised his family to the south in Irish Vale before he moved into the town and the children went to work for the railway and such places. He raised a big family; although he owned a place it was on the mountainside and there wasn't much room there for farming. But in those days he did so well fishing cod and herring that he was able to raise and feed his family. There is one short story that I think would be suitable to tell here. He himself used to tell it to people.

The only money he had at the time was enough to purchase a herring net. So he bought the herring net. And when the ice got thick enough on the Bras D'Or lake to put out the net, he set it out. And, as he used to tell people, it seemed that a large number of herring were going past at the time and they used to catch a lot of herring at once. He said that the first morning he went out and hauled up the herring net there were quite a few herring by the time he had finished. I believe he was

putting them in a bag out on the ice and he probably had a
little sleigh to pull them to shore. And what happened but
a man arrived who used to buy up things throughout the
countryside. There may have been people fishing somewhere
who needed bait or else he was going to market where people
would buy herring to eat. So this man arrived with a horse and
sleigh and stopped where he was on the ice where his herring
net was cast and asked if he had herring and he replied that he
had. So the herring were counted and the man took the herring
and paid him. And there were enough herring in the net in the
one haul to pay the price of the net so he had as much money
then as he had before he bought the net.

Now I should pass on an account of the family of Big Neil
(Niall Mór mac Iain 'ic Lachlainn Ghobha). He had three sons
who settled over at Middle Cape. But I cannot say whether Big
Neil himself settled there because I never heard anything
concerning him. People didn't say, "Here is where Big Neil
lived," or, "There is where Big Neil lived," but they did name
his sons Angus and Lachlann and Malcolm.

Angus was married to a Campbell woman. They had no
family at all; it seems that they were up in years when they
married. Lachlann was not married at all. And while I am
speaking of Lachlann they considered Lachlann Nìll Mhóir to
be a singer as good as was over there in Middle Cape in his day;
he could sing songs as nicely and as well as any there.

But Malcolm (Calum Nìll Mhóir) was married and his wife
was one of the MacNeils. She was a granddaughter of Ruairidh
Breac, Màiri Alasdair 'ic Ruairidh. And a son of theirs called
Donald was the only one that I came to know. That's the man
that I mentioned before in a story here and there that I put
on tape where I mentioned a Donald MacLean (Dòmhnall
Chaluim Nìll Mhóir). Donald was a farmer although he did
buy a little out in the country and went to markets to sell. He
used to work for people; perhaps he would go on errands for
them and so on. And he spent the last part of his life farming
until he gave it up. His health became so bad. And that was
Dòmhnall Chaluim Nìll Mhóir.

I have not mentioned the women who were married to this

branch of the MacLeans, and I think it would be an oversight
to leave them unmentioned in my account. There was a Mary
MacNeil who was married to Michael (Mìchael Iain Chaluim
Òig). She was one of the MacNeils who were living over in
Castle Bay in Cape Breton and she used to be called Nighean
Dhòmhnaill Òig (Young Donald's Daughter). Because of the
garden or orchard of valuable apples that her father had
over there where he lived in Castle Bay in Cape Breton they
nicknamed him "Donald the Apples." And I believe that he
was styled Dòmhnall mac Ruairidh if one went back that far
but it will suffice to say that it was Màiri Dhòmhnaill Òig
(Mary Young Donald) – or Mary Donald the Apples – who
was married to Michael.

And Elizabeth Kennedy was married to Alasdair Nìll
Chaluim from whom I got the stories. Elizabeth Kennedy was
a daughter of James Kennedy whom I mentioned before.

A MacKinnon woman was married to Malcolm J. (Calum
Iain Chaluim), the father of John and Donald from whom I got
the stories. She was a daughter of Donald Neil – I think that
the man was called Dòmhnall Nìll 'ac Dhòmhnaill Bhàin –
and she was a fine woman, easy-going, kind and courteous,
and a true Christian in her patience. I was very fond of her too.

Elizabeth, the widow of John MacDonald, was married to
Donald (Dòmhnall Chaluim Nìll Mhóir). She was the mother
of Dòmhnall Nìll Eòin Mhóir.

And I believe that this will suffice for a history of the
MacLeans. Indeed, giving a history of these men is no burden
to me because I am very proud to have been in their company
and to have received so much from them.

18   Duanach the Widow's Son

I have a short tale here and I was only very young – about
fourteen years old – when I heard it from Donald MacLean
son of Calum Iain Chaluim Òig 'ic Iain 'ic Lachlainn Ghobha.

The tale concerns a man whom they called Duanach the
Widow's Son. And, according to the tale, a giant was living

down in a deep glen. He was doing a lot of damage around, throughout the land too although he was living in the glen. And if anybody went to kill him, they failed. I cannot say why.

Duanach the Widow's Son set out; he was only a slight, little man but he was full of craftiness. So he set out on a journey to slay the giant. And it seems that he climbed to the top of the mountain. He put two boards on his feet, or he had some sort of little sled or, as they usually say, a sleigh which he had made, and so he rode on that down the glen until he arrived at the place below the giant's dwelling. And when he arrived there out came the giant.

"Where are you going and what brought you here, my pretty young fellow?" asked the giant. I am certain that the giant was going to threaten his life as this was a usual enough thing for giants to do. But before he got an answer the little man said that he had come to put him to the test and fight him.

"And what kind of fight could you put up," said he, "little and puny as you are?"

"Perhaps," said he, "I am strong enough after all to beat you in many ways."

So the giant said to him, "Well then, go over to the well and bring down water so that we can cook a soup or some food to eat."

And the little man asked him if he had a vessel for the water and he replied that he did. And when the little man grasped the handle of the vessel I am certain it was so heavy that he was barely able to lift it. So he wouldn't budge. He wouldn't budge then, for if he did go to the well with the bucket he would not be able to move it when it was full of water. The giant was growing impatient that he was not getting the water so the widow's son said that as far as he was concerned the vessel was not big enough to fetch water from a well. If he only had a way to bring the entire well home as it was, that would be worth the effort. But the giant told him just to bring the bucketful and that he did not want the well to be taken out just then. Oh, the little man would not listen to that. He said that he would not bother going to a well with such a small vessel and he angered the giant so that the giant went himself and brought back a bucketful.

Anyway they had to get sticks of firewood to make a fire to cook food and they went up the mountain. But the young lad would pay no heed to the giant: since he could not bring everything in the forest home at once, he did not consider it worth his while to bring home a load. This made the giant angry and since the lad was so difficult to please he said, "I will bring home a stack of wood myself."

And the lad would not take a single stick. The lad pretended to be angry because he could not get permission to take the whole forest home with him. I am sure that the giant was afraid that if the whole great forest were brought home it would rot before it was used.

After going back and forth they decided to make their supper. Time was passing, to be sure, and they were growing hungry. So a great, big pot was put on the fire and filled with water and, I am sure, bits of meat or some kind of game; they were going to make a soup. Duanach went out to a place where odds and ends were kept. There was a sort of little hut out there where things were kept for hunting and game and everything else, and along with the other things there were some sheep skins. Duanach got the sheep skins and he slapped them together as quickly as he could. He made a big sack out of them to cover his own torso under his clothes and while the soup was still cooking he came inside. He was ready to have some soup and they were going to eat some of it together. But the lad said that there was not enough there for the two of them.

"That's little enough for myself," said he. "I think that there isn't even enough for me."

Oh, there was plenty for the two of them, the giant said. Duanach said that he would not take any more unless he got all there was and that he was afraid there was not enough because he was so extremely hungry.

"Well then," said the giant, "dig into this and I will make some more for myself."

But the lad would not take a drop of what was in the pot if

the giant touched it; there was not enough. So he drank what was in the great soup pot all by himself, and of course he was pouring it down into the bag fashioned out of sheep skin which was under his clothes and the giant did not see what was going on. And when that was done and he had drunk all the soup and eaten all of the meat in the pot the giant fetched more food and he was very hungry. So he filled up the pot to the brim and when it was ready he began drinking the soup. And before he went about three-quarters through the soup he began to grow very full and Duanach started to make fun of him, of how slowly he was drinking the soup. And the giant said he had had enough, and Duanach started laughing at him again.

"Why," said he, "should you have had enough? Remember how big you are compared to me. And I thought that there wasn't enough in the pot for me."

And I am sure that just so he could be ahead of Duanach the giant put down all the soup that was there. He drank every drop that there was and it was no wonder that he was not feeling very well after that.

So after a while Duanach began to groan and complain and the giant asked him what was bothering him. He said that he was feeling a little too full; he was thinking that with the tremendous hunger he had felt before he had become too greedy, that he had eaten to excess. So he groaned for another little while and then said to the giant, "You had better," said he, "hand that big knife over to me. I feel too full; I want to get rid of part of the soup."

And oh, the giant did not think that this was proper at all but he handed him the big knife, and the lad ripped open his side and let the soup run out. But after a while the giant began to complain as he was stretched out on the floor going to sleep. He complained and complained. I am sure that he had awakened from sleep and begun complaining, which would hardly seem strange after drinking a whole big pot of soup. And Duanach asked him what was wrong and he replied that he was not feeling well; that he thought that he had eaten too much soup. Oh, the lad began to make fun of him as he helped himself to soup.

"Oh, you did not eat as much as I; I even ate a little more. And am I not small compared to yourself?"

But the giant continued his complaining and groaning and finally asked for the knife so that he could get rid of the soup. And the lad began making fun of him and asked him if he thought that would do any good, and he did. Well, it wouldn't he said, unless he gave himself a mighty slash with the knife to let the soup out: otherwise it would be no help at all.

"Didn't you see what I had to do, small as I am compared to you? And I nearly had to cut my belly right across from one side to the other."

But the giant was in such pain at the time that all he cared about was finding relief so Duanach handed him the knife saying, "As I explained, you have to make a big cut in yourself."

And the giant did that and the soup began to run out and I am sure that blood did too and as a result of that the giant died.

According to the story as I heard it from Donald MacLean, there was a reward offered for doing away with the giant because he had wrought such destruction throughout the country. And when it was found out that the giant had been put to death after so many men had tried to do it, I believe, and failed, and when the noblemen who had offered the reward found out who it was, Duanach was sent for and he received the large reward that was offered for slaying the giant. And he and his mother the widow were well off as long as that fortune lasted.

19   *The Man with the Long Tales*

There was once a king who had one daughter. And there was nothing on earth that the king was so fond of as long tales. So he made up his mind that he would not give his daughter in marriage to anyone except the man who could tell a story that he thought was long – I believe that nobody came to satisfy him – and so he required a tale that would last for a year and a day. And everything that the story-teller told had to be part of the same story.

Some people arrived – they hailed from every region – and began telling a tale. But the tale would last for a time and after that they had to give up and go on their way. Finally the king got so digusted that when somebody came to tell stories he warned him that, from that time on, anybody who came to tell a tale, if he told a tale that lasted a year and a day, would get the princess. But if he could not, it was better not to start at all for if he was unable to relate a tale lasting a year and a day the king would cut off his head; they were not going to keep anybody there for a long time telling a tale who did not have one that was long enough. Anyway a few came who thought they could tell such a tale. And there were some who had travelled – who had done quite a bit of travelling around the world – and they thought that with everything they could begin a story and tell it from end to end and it would last for a year and a day. But they could not. Every one of them failed and the few of them that did come were finally put to death.

So one day a man arrived who had heard of this – had heard what was happening – and who thought that he would be able to succeed. So he arrived and said to the king that he had heard about the conditions that the king had set, that he was offering a large reward and his daughter in marriage to the man who could tell a tale that would last for a year and a day. The king replied that indeed he was.

"But I am advising you early on. If you cannot tell a tale that will last for a year and a day on the same subject, there is a stake out in back of my garden and a number of heads have gone on the spikes out there."

The man just laughed saying not to worry about his tale. So he was to come in the morning and to begin telling a tale and to continue telling it until a certain hour in the evening. But he would have some time to have his dinner, and for his supper I think he would also be given more time. He was to spend the time from early morning until suppertime reciting the tale and, as I already mentioned, the tale was to be on one subject – about one matter – from beginning to end.

So he arrived early in the morning on the next day, the day he was to begin the tale. And he was to continue for a year from that day relating the tale. When he had settled himself he said that he was going to begin a tale, and that the beginning of the tale concerned his own father. He recounted how his father when he was a young man of marriageable age married and acquired a farm and began farming. And he was doing a little farming and he was progressing better as time went on. But somebody advised him, or he himself decided, that it would be most profitable to go into raising grain. So he raised grain and sold grain and stored it. He was sowing more and more seed until he had to rent land. After that he had to buy land at first and later on he rented land for all the grain he had. Finally there was one year when the grain harvest was so plentiful that he did not have room for it when it came time to thresh it. But the story-teller said that there was a hallow down near the place where they were living. About a mile away from the place where they were there was a big hollow and when a man would be up high on one side of the slope it was about a mile for him to go down into the hollow and climb up to the top on the other side. And for fear that a storm or something else would sweep away the grain once the threshing had been completed he began to store it in that hollow. And when the threshing was finished, the story-teller continued, it was fairly level across from hill to hill.

And, said he, "That in itself is of little consequence, for now I am to begin, and I have a little tale about every seed of grain that was there. And," said he, "before I get properly set to begin telling the story I am afraid that I will be running into such a great length of time that I will not be able to tell it in less than two or three years."

The king listened to him for a while. "I think," said the king, "that it is better for you to be satisfied with what you have told of the tale. I do not think that you will be able to complete the tale within the time that I set for you, so you had better take the reward and we will end the matter right there."

I am sure that the king recognized that the matter was based on a falsehood but the man was so expert that he was able to perform suitably. And I am sure that the king himself noticed that the man was smart enough to do this, so he got the reward and the princess.

20   *The Strong Woodsman's Son*

There was a man living with his wife in a hut at the edge of the forest whom they used to call the Strong Woodsman. Many wondered at his living at the forest edge where there were wild and dangerous beasts, but there were certainly some animals that were not so wild and dangerous and he made his living hunting. Nearly every evening when he came home he would bring an armful of old sticks – pieces that had broken off the trees during the winter and had parched and dried out. He carried these home to make a fire so that it would be easy for his wife to cook.

On a certain evening he was on his way home looking forward to returning to his wife and he began to fell a great, big oak tree. And a great misfortune befell him. The tree fell suddenly; he was caught under it and only just managed to crawl out from under, strong as he was. When he had fairly come to, he carried the tree back home, but when he reached the hut, both he and the tree fell to the ground. His wife heard the noise outside the hut and went out, and there was her spouse lying full length. So she helped him to his feet and into the house and he stretched out on the bed. She tried to give him all the hope and courage possible: nothing would be wrong with him. But he told her that she might as well keep quiet, that it was not worth her while speaking; he had received a blow from the tree and had been injured internally and had received his death-blow from that, and there was nothing more that could be done.

"But here," said he, extending his hand to her. "Here is a seed, an acorn from the oak tree. And after my death, you are to plant this acorn at the top of the manure pile over there beside the byre. Around the time that leaves come on the seed you will bear a son but he won't be like other children. You must nurture and raise him until he is strong enough to pull the oak tree – the oak sapling – that is growing on the manure pile out by the roots."

Then he turned his face to the wall, drew his last breath, and died.

When the burial and everything else were over, she was in a state of black sorrow and mourning, but she thought then about the conditions he had asked her to fulfil, so she went and buried the acorn from the tree on the edge of the manure pile and returned home.

After a length of time two brown leaves from the acorn emerged from the ground and at the same time a son was born to her.

When the son reached seven years of age she took him over to the manure pile to see if he was able to pull the oaken sapling from the ground and, oh, he couldn't. So she took him back home and was obliged to bide her time, nurturing and raising him.

After another seven years he had grown quite strong. But if he had, the oak tree had grown too, and when she gave the order to him to go over and pluck the oak out by the roots if he could, he was not able to. So she had to spend another seven years nurturing and raising him.

At the end of those seven years – by then she had been nurturing and raising him for twenty-one years – she told him to go over and pull the tree out by the roots. He went over and managed to pull the tree out of the ground and he took it over to the house and brought it to her saying,

"Here. Make firewood from this, so that you can kindle a fire with it."

"Well," she replied, "the first thing that I am going to do with this is to make a fire that will cook food for you to take on your journey. You must go out to earn your living. You have been living here twenty years and you haven't done anything yet, and I am getting tired of supporting you."

"That is true enough," he replied. "I must be on my way." And so he set out travelling, and whether the distance he

walked was long or short, he came to a great farm which
looked to be as large a farm as anyone had ever seen. There
was a great, big field there full of stacks – stacks of grain –
without number, and he thought to himself that if they were
going to thresh all the grain that was there a man might get
work. And there was a big barn on the land of a size he had
never seen before. So he went over to the house and when he
knocked on the door a maidservant came to the door. And
when she saw the big, terrible man at the door she was rather
afraid. She took a step back and took her time asking him
what he wanted. Oh, he said that he would like to talk to her
master, and it seems that he addressed her very civilly. She
returned inside and went to where her master was asleep in a
large chair in the sitting room, as was his habit after having
his food. So she wakened him and said that there was a large
man at the door – a man at least as large as she had ever seen –
and that from his size she would say that he was a giant. The
farmer arose and went to the door and, when he opened the
door and looked and saw the big, huge man there, he also took
sort of a step back.

"And what will you be wanting?" asked the farmer.

"Well," replied the lad, "I'm looking for work."

"Well, perhaps," said he, the farmer, "we could manage to be
some help to you in this. Do you thresh?"

"Yes," he replied, "I do without question." And he twisted
his arm as if he were working with a flail which, I'm sure,
frightened the farmer.

"Indeed," he continued, "if your hire me I expect that you
will have no cause to regret taking me on."

"I hope not," said he, the farmer. "I would say from your
size that you will be able enough."

So they came to an agreement about wages, whatever they
were going to arrange – he was going to have a trial period or
something like that. Then he asked the farmer, "When will I
begin threshing?"

And that surprised the farmer very much to see the hurry
the big lad was in to begin threshing. It was not usual for those
who came to him for hire to be in a hurry at all. So the farmer

said to him, "It is our custom to begin when the starlight
fades in the morning and to work until the starlight appears
again at the end of the day."

"Oh," said the lad, "that is very good."

So Big Ranald – his name was Big Ranald – went to the barn
to see what the people there were doing, since it was only
early in the afternoon. And he let forth a peal of laughter,
saying that the flails that they had there were just like
something children would use. He went up the side of the
mountain to the forest and felled two trees to make a flail
for himself when they began in the morning. And, oh, he
frightened the boys when they saw him coming; they said
that the sticks he was carrying were big enough to serve as a
mast for a boat.

So in the morning, long before the day dawned, he began
threshing and when he had finished threshing what was in the
big barn he started going out to the field and catching up a
stack under each arm, taking them in with him, and setting
about threshing them. By the time breakfast was ready, he had
finished what was in the barn. And long before noon the field
outside was full of straw and the barn was filled with grain.
He was surprised that no one was coming to see how he was
getting along or anything, and so finally he went over, taking
his time, and the farmer met him.

"And what now," said he, "am I to do?"

"Oh," said he, the farmer, "threshing." And the farmer was
very surprised at the number of piles of straw he saw out on
the field. So he said, "The barn is full."

"Oh," the lad replied, "what is in the barn is also threshed."
And that surprised and frightened the farmer very much.

"But," said the lad, "if I am to continue working like this I
must be given more food than before."

"Yes, indeed," said the farmer.

"I shall require a large cauldron full of meal as gruel for the
first day. And then I will require a good cauldron full of meal
baked into pancakes, and an ox two years of age on the next
day."

The farmer took a terrible fright and went up to the other servants and told them how things stood.

"I would give a month's wages more to anyone who could tell me how I am going to get rid of this big, fierce man," he said.

They put their heads together and thought, but none of them could see a way. But then one of them had the idea that, if the farmer went to see Big Angus of the Rocks, he could advise him for he was the oldest man in the entire country, and the wisest. The farmer made up his mind to go, and when he reached Big Angus of the Rocks he told him about the threshing and the food that the big lad required.

"Well," said Big Angus, "I don't know what I can do for you. Don't you know that there was once a prophecy made that a big man would come and that you would have to give up the farm? My grandfather used to tell that when I was very young." And Big Angus himself was quite old at the time.

"But," he continued, "we will attempt one thing anyway just to see how we fare. When you go home say to him that the water is becoming scarce and that you want a big well dug in the middle of the field. And when you get him down there at a good depth, there is nothing below but sand. I know that for a fact myself. You will get deep enough," said he. "Let every one of the servants be prepared then with a shovel ready in his hand and when you find his back turned to you begin throwing everything on top of him that he is bringing out of the well and perhaps you will smother him there. But be ready to flee if you do not succeed."

So when the farmer returned he said to the big lad, the Big Woodsman's son, that their springs had gone dry and that he would like to have a big well dug down in the field so that they would get plenty of water. So the lad began digging in the morning. I am certain that the earth was piling up very swiftly, but every one of the servants was ready and every one of them had a shovel. When they saw that he had bent down to lift up a shovelful of the stuff that was at the bottom of the well, they poured it all down on top of him. But he just threw it back up

as if nothing were falling on him but snowflakes, and so they
fled. When the well was finished he came up and went up to
the house. And they had all gone into hiding – had fled. There
was no one around to be found but the farmer himself, and he
was hiding under the table. The lad beat on the door, but no
one answered him, and at last he gave the door a blow and
broke it in. When he went inside, the farmer was getting up
from the place he had been and approaching him, and the big
lad looked very pleased with himself.

"How did you get along?" said the farmer.

"Very well," he replied. "The well is finished, but the ravens
were throwing stuff down on me as if they were trying to blind
me. They caused me a little bit of trouble but I got along
anyway. And what should I do now?"

"Oh," said the farmer, "you'll do no more today but rest.
You will prepare food for yourself."

The farmer set out as quickly as he could for Big Angus of
the Rocks and told him what had happened.

"Ah," said he, "it looks as if it's going to be difficult to do
away with him. But we won't give up the attempt. There is
still one way. You'll send him to plow tomorrow up at the
Crooked Ridge beside the Dark Loch. And if he remains there
until sunset there is a monster that emerges from the loch and
no man or beast ever went there that it did not swallow, so the
lad will not return alive."

When the farmer arrived home he told the big lad that he
was to go out the next day and plow the Crooked Ridge beside
the loch. He was no time at all getting two horses, so he threw
the plow over his shoulder and, leading the horses after him,
set out for the Crooked Ridge. He began plowing, and he
plowed there until it became quite late in the day. There was a
great oak tree right in the middle of the Crooked Ridge, and he
was plowing until it grew quite late. He heard a sound in the
loch and saw some sort of ugly beast or monster emerging
from the loch but he paid no heed; he continued plowing, and
when he was right in the middle of the Crooked Ridge, the
terrible monster came up and devoured one of the horses.

Well, he began scolding it, and asked it to return the horse, which was something it would not do.

"If you don't do as I asked," said he, "you will do the horse's work yourself." So he began harnessing the monster beside the horse. But when it was brought up beside the horse still hitched to the plow, the horse became so afraid that it took off for home. So then he caught the monster by the tail and knotted its tail around the tree, and the monster began turning and twisting and writhing until finally it pulled the tree out of the ground.

"Well," said he, "you've done very well." And he set on the monster with the tree until he only had a little stick of it left. Then he took the monster home with him.

But early on, the others had seen the horse coming and that pleased them greatly; they were sure that he had been devoured anyway. But at nightfall the lad came to the door, with the monster in tow, and went in. They asked him how he had fared.

"Oh," said he, "I got along very well."

"And did you see anything?"

"I didn't see anything," he replied, "that could frighten me. An ugly creature came out of the loch and devoured one of my horses, but I prevailed on it not to do the same thing again."

"And what did you do to it?" asked the farmer.

"Oh," he replied, "it's out there at the door. Come out and see it. But don't worry about that any more. What shall I do tomorrow?"

"Oh," said he, the farmer, "plowing."

"Oh, the plowing is finished," replied the lad. "No one who goes to that ridge to plow need worry any more."

"Oh," said he, the farmer, "do whatever you wish with that monster. What do you intend to do with it?"

"I'm not going to do anything with it," said he, "except to go and cut its head off and bury it over at the edge of the manure piles there behind the byre." So he went over and buried the monster.

The farmer set out to Big Angus of the Rocks and he told him what had passed.

"It looks as if we will not succeed at all," said Big Angus. "But we have one more chance. You will tell him this afternoon that the meal has grown very scarce and that he must go with a horse and sled and take bags of grain to the mill of Leckan.[1] And when he reaches the mill of Leckan it will be late. And if he is there after sunset there need be no worry that he will ever come out of there for the Big Brùthnach will put an end to him."

And so the farmer came home.

"Well," said he, "we are getting short of meal. We barely have enough for breakfast, so I think you had better take some bags of grain and go to the mill." And he told him where the mill was.

Oh, that was fine, and the lad put the bags of grain on the sled, hitched the horse to it and set out. He reached the place where the mill was, and the miller had just come home after he had finished everything, and the sun had set. He knocked on the door.

"Who is there?" said the miller.

"It is I," said the lad. He told him who it was – a servant of the farmer.

"Ah," said he, "what do you require?"

"To go to the mill to grind grain," replied the lad.

"Well," said he, the miller, "I will not go to the mill tonight for you or for anyone in the world. I would not go there for anyone in the world until sunrise."

"Oh, that does not suit me," said the lad. "We are short of meal at home and I must be back early in the morning with meal."

"Oh, I won't go there in spite of that," said the miller.

"Well," said the lad, "give me the key and I'll go to the mill myself and I'll do the work."

The miller gave him the keys and he set out. He opened the door to the mill, gathered some odds and ends together, and made a great fire under the oven and began to harden the grain. And when the grain had been hardened – had been parched – he started the mill turning and began pouring grain into the hopper, and the grain went through the hopper and between the millstones. When he had ground enough to make himself some good oatcakes – he was extremely hungry – he stopped the mill and made a number of them and put them up on top of the oven – it was still hot – so that they would cook there. And when they were cooked, or almost cooked, a big claw came down and one of the oatcakes disappeared.

"Leave that oatcake there," said he. "Put it back where you got it."

It took no heed. The claw came again and took another and that continued until all six of the oatcakes were taken.

"Put back the oatcakes," said he, "or you will be the worse for it."

But it paid no heed, so he and the Brùthnach – whatever kind of creature the Brùthnach was – started at each other and they levelled the oven, and in their battle they gutted the mill, and at the last of it the big Son of the Strong Woodsman put down the Brùthnach and he was conquered.

"And now," said he, "you are going to leave, and you will never return here again."

"I will," said the Brùthnach.

"But wait," said the lad, "you won't go yet." And he took hold of him by the neck. "You will not go at all," said the lad, "until you put the oven back correctly as you found it and set everything back up as it was before."

And when that had been done, the Brùthnach said, "Let me go now."

"Not yet," said the lad. "You will not leave here until you put back the six oatcakes that you took from me that I was going to have for my supper."

So he reached his big paw up to the edge of the chimney, and he brought down the six oatcakes, and he put them down on top of the oven. And the big lad threw him out the door of the mill and said to him, "Get going. And do not ever return," said he. "Do not ever return to the mill."

And when he had eaten the oatcakes, he began to grind the grain, and he finished the rest of the milling. And he put the meal in the bags, tied them on the sled, harnessed the horse, and set out on the way home, heading towards the miller's house. The day was just dawning. He knocked at the door. The miller heard that noise going on, and I'm sure that he regretted that he gave the keys to the lad at all, thinking that he had most likely been killed. And the miller was startled when he heard the noise, thinking that it was probably the Brùthnach who was still at the door, and he called out who was there.

"It is I," said the lad. "And here are your keys."

But the miller was afraid to get up at all. And when he realized that the miller was not going to get up, he said, "I'm in a hurry, for meal is needed at the house." And he threw the keys in under the door. "Here are your keys." And off he went.

Now Big Angus of the Rocks had cautioned them that if the monster in the mill had not killed the big lad to be sure that the servants, every woman and child, and all others there on the hill be ready to flee should they see him returning. They had a lookout stationed on the hill watching for him and the lookout came running down to the farmer's place saying that the big lad was coming with the horse, sled, and the bags of meal. They all fled and when he arrived at the house there was no one to be seen or found at the farmer's place.

"Well," said he, "they didn't need to flee on account of me. I wouldn't have caused them to flee at all, if only they had given me enough food. But I haven't lost anything; I have a good farm and livestock and everything that I should require. And since they have all left, it will all be mine."

He thought then that it would be fitting for him to bring his mother along, so he went home and arrived at the small hut where his mother lived and told her everything that had happened.

"And now," said he, "you are going to go with me."

"No," she replied, "I am not. I am getting too old to walk that whole distance."

"Oh," said the lad, "don't let the distance worry you at all." And he lifted his mother and put her on his shoulder. "You have looked after me long enough, feeding and nursing me, and now it is little enough to ask for me to take you along and look after you."

And the big lad returned home to the large farmstead and

brought his mother inside. And he worked there at farming
while his mother sat inside taking things as easy as she pleased.
And that is the story I heard of the Strong Woodsman's Son.

21   *The Woman Who Was Awarded a Pair of Shoes by the Devil*

There was once a married couple who through many years of
marriage had always been harmonious and happy. However
hard the devil tried to make them quarrel, he failed miserably
in his attempts on them and this angered him greatly. So one
day the devil met a certain woman who it seems was quite an
evil woman – a very bad woman – and he made a bargain
with her that if she would start that couple quarrelling he
would give her a pair of shoes. She agreed to try.

She tried for a long, long time, attempting every stratagem,
but without success. Some days she would talk to the woman
of the house, spending some time in conversation with her,
and then she would spend another little while talking to the
husband where he was working on carpentry or blacksmithing
or whatever his work was – I believe he worked mostly at
carpentry. She would spend some time conversing with him
but neither of them paid her any heed.

But one day she spoke to the woman of the house, saying,
"It's hardly worth my while telling you, but you would well
believe me if you were to see and experience what I am going
to tell you."

Oh, the woman said to her that she was not heeding her at
all.

"Never mind," said the evil woman. "When your spouse
comes home tomorrow evening and goes to stretch out on the
lounge there and falls asleep there is a hair down at the base of
his neck. Go get a razor and cut the hair and then you will
know how things really stand."

Well, as it happened, she set the wife to thinking until at
last she thought that there might be something to it after
all. So the evil woman went to the husband, telling him

everything – everything about his wife – and he would not pay any attention to her; he did not believe her at all.

"Never mind," said she. "When you go home this evening you will stretch out on the lounge and you will pretend that you are sleeping; you will begin to snore." (She had just finished talking to the wife the day before). "And perhaps you will believe me when you see your wife coming toward you with a razor to cut your throat."

With all the confusion that she had caused him the man was becoming good and tired of her anyway; I'm sure she had spoken to him so often that he decided to do as she said. Certainly it would only prove that she was wrong. So he did as she asked and when he was in a deep slumber and snoring in his sleep the wife thought of what the other woman had said to her; now she could find out. The other woman was only talking anyway; nothing would come of it. But when she came over with the razor poised above his throat he believed it then so he leapt up to his feet and they began quarrelling and I'm sure that it was indeed fierce. Probably they nearly came to blows, quarrelling as violently as people ever have.

On the next day when the evil woman went to get her reward the devil was so frightened by how evil she was that he put the pair of shoes at the end of a long, thin stick and stretched them out to her while he remained on the other side of the fence. He was too afraid to approach her.

And that is how I got the tale from Michael MacLean concerning the devil and the evil woman who was awarded the shoes.

22   *The Three Knots*

This tale I heard for the first time from Hector MacNeil who lived over in Middle Cape. We used to call him Hector Angus the Postman. He only told a part of this tale. He did not recount as much of it as I heard later from Michael MacLean (Mìcheal Iain Chaluim Òig 'ic Iain 'ic Lachlainn Ghobha).

And according to MacLean's recitation it was his own

relatives who figured in the tale; they were the people who were travelling in the boat. And they visited a place, an island or some place on their journey to market. And there was an old man and an old lady in the little house there so they went up to ease their fatigue. Perhaps it had grown so calm that there was no good sailing at the time.

In any case the old people asked them whether they had tea or tobacco and one of the crew said that they had a little on board. He went down and got the little bit of tea that they had and brought it up. He gave the tea to the old people – to the old couple – and they shared the tobacco generously with them. The old man asked one of them – the one that he thought to be the oldest – whether any of his family had been in the battlefields and the man answered yes, that he had lost two sons on the field.

"Isn't it a shame," said the old man, "that you did not come to me before they went to battle."

"Yes indeed," replied the other.

"Oh, if you had come," the old man continued, "they would have been magically protected from the lead."

So after they had rested themselves and spent some time in conversation one of them said he thought they had better try to go on their way now to see how they would do. The old woman told him to stop for a moment. She went over to a corner or somewhere, or a small room and returned with a thread; it was a piece of wool thread, I'm sure, and there were three knots in it.

And she said to him, "Here. Take this with you since you are the one who is in charge of the boat today. You will take this with you and when you are well out take one knot out of the thread and you will get a breeze. Keep on, and when you are well underway and you think that she can take more of a breeze take another knot out of this string and you will get a good, strong, favourable wind. But be absolutely sure that you do not take the third knot out of the thread. For if you do things will not go so well."

So they left and when they put their boat in order and got it out they undid a knot from the thread. No sooner had they released the knot than a small, light, favourable, and fitting breeze sprang up and they sailed forward. But the man in charge of the boat decided they should take on a little more breeze so they loosened the second knot, and when they did there came a strong, driving breeze and things were very favourable for them. They were sailing ahead as well as they could please.

When at last they were about to enter the harbour – they were so close to being inside the harbour that they thought themselves safe – he undid the third knot from the thread and cast the thread out to sea. But as he did the storm broke and they barely got into harbour without being drowned. But they managed to reach the harbour and when they were in at the market they brought along tea and tobacco in good quantity to take to the old couple to last them for some time. When they were finished and prepared to sail, they sailed back, getting quite a favourable breeze. They came in to the island – the place where the couple was living in the hut – and when they entered, they were cordially received; they delivered the tea and the tobacco to them and got great thanks for that.

The old woman turned to one of the men. "You did not do," said she, "as I asked you."

"Oh indeed I did," said he.

"Oh no you did not," said she "do at all as I asked you and, since you did not, I had a very hard time saving you from the storm."

And she came over and she showed him the thread. "Here," said she, "is the thread that you threw away. It served you well to be so close to shore; I experienced enough hardship saving you as it was. But we are pleased that you returned safely anyway."

They stayed with them for some time and then took their leave.

And there you have the tale that I got from MacLean, who said that it was his grandfather's or his great-grandfather's brother who was one of the men there; the story was that closely associated with him when he told it. And I believe that it was from them that the story came to where Hector MacNeil first got it. And there you have the story as told by MacLean.

23   *How The Fairy Suitor Was Tricked*

I got this tale from Michael MacLean one night when I was
visiting and he was telling us a story – there were quite a few
people in visiting that night, people there as well as myself at
the time – about a man who was courting a girl – at least she
thought that he was courting her – but the way things were
happening seemed quite strange to her.

And this is what happened. Her people went to a wise man
who gave advice – perhaps a tinker who used to advise them
or a tinker woman. So she indicated that the suitor would
require a ringlet of hair from the girl. And she instructed them
– put them under some obligation as they say – that should he
demand it she was to give him a lock of hair from the tail of a
cow. They had a big cowhide hanging there from which the
tail apparently had not been cut. When he asked her for the
locks of hair it seems she showed him that and it was given to
him.

She and her family were sitting inside one night or early in
the evening, and a noise was heard; the hide was moving and
out it went and off they went after it, and they never found a
trace of the hide. Whether it entered the Fairy Hill or
wherever it went it was never found.

And people used to add that, if the daughter had given him a
lock of her hair, he would certainly have taken her away in
the same way he was able to take the cowhide.

And the hide disappeared, to be sure, without returning.

Perhaps it was from this story, once it had circulated, that
the expression originated that was used for someone who was
talking pointlessly or talking about something he intended to
do that was never done: they used to say that he was nothing
but a hair going with the wind.

24   *The Night It Rained Porridge*

I have a short story here that I heard from the wife of Michael
MacLean (Mìcheal Iain Chaluim).

It concerns a widow with one son who was a sort of half-wit. But the son was big and strong and it seems that she was clever. So she sent him off with a cow to market to see if he could get something for the cow; I am sure that they were getting short of food to feed the cow or some other reason, or perhaps she was an extra one.

So off he went with the cow, and when he was at the market a man approached him. "What do you want for the cow?" he asked.

"Oh," he replied, "I want something for her."

The other man said to him, "Open your hand then." And he spat in his hand.

"Here is something," he said, and the half-wit handed him the end of the rope with the other hand. "Here is the cow," said he, and he started out on his way back home with his fist closed, so happy that he had gotten something for the cow.

But when he was crossing a small river he slipped on one of the stepping stones as he was making his way across the river from stone to stone; he opened his hand and the spit went away. So he started groping around in the stream to see if he could find it, and who came along but a pack merchant or a peddler, as they would say in English.

"What are you doing there in the river?" said the peddler.

"I am looking for something that I have lost. I lost my something."

The other man also slipped as he was crossing. "Here is something," said he.

"You found my something," said the lad.

"I did not find something," replied the peddler.

"Yes you did," said the lad and they went at each other and he killed the merchant, or the peddler as he was called.

He buried him in a hollow and took his packs home with him. His mother asked him what had happened and he told her. He said that he had lost his something and that the other man had found it and that they had fought. So she told him to go stretch out, that he was tired after coming from town and that he was so fatigued that he should sleep a while and take off his shoes; his feet would get more rest by being bare. She herself got a pot and put water in the pot and meal and made a thin porridge and shook that out around the house. He used to go out of the house anyway before he went to sleep to see what kind of weather it was or for whatever reason, so when he arose after sleeping for a while she awoke and told him it was time to get up and to go and sleep properly.

He walked outside barefoot and when he came back in, "It is raining porridge," he said.

"Is it?" said she.

"It is," said he. "There is porridge on the ground. It is raining."

"Oh well," said she, "go and sleep. Don't worry about that any more."

But she found out from him where he had buried the man he had killed and when he had gone to sleep she went to the hollow and the man was buried there. So they had a small ram in a field and often people used to call one of those animals "Peddler." This one used to travel around all over the place if it got loose. She killed that animal there and she buried the other body somewhere else far away, to be sure.

Sometime after that, whether the time was long or short, two policeman came to the house asking if any trace had been seen of a certain man, the merchant that was going around, the peddler.

"Oh," said the half-wit, "I killed that peddler."

"Did you indeed?" said one of the policemen.

"Yes I did," replied the half-wit.

"And when did you kill this man?" said he.

"Oh," said he. "Wait a moment. It was the evening of the day;" said he, "the night it was raining porridge."

And he only seemed to be a crazy fool anyway.

"Where did you put him?" said the other man.

So he told him where he had put him and off they went. They were saying to each other, "Did you hear the crazy man there talking about the night it rained porridge?"

And they were walking down anyway and they passed the place.

"Oh well," said one of them, "we will go to see what is

buried in the place that he was telling us about. He hasn't a grain of sense."

When they went down and dug down into the ground, they found a ram buried there.

"Didn't I tell you," said one of them, "that he was not all there; that he was without his sense? Look there," said he. "That's the peddler he was talking about."

And they kept on their way. And the packs and everything in them went to the widow and to her son. And that is the story I got about the night that it rained porridge.

25   *Stirling Castle*

I heard a short tale about Stirling Castle, about when Stirling Castle was built. It seems that the devil was given charge of the project – he was the one doing the work. It would have cost them so much, I am sure, to build a castle, but the devil would do it under certain conditions. I believe the condition was that he could take the laird away as his prize if the laird did not know his name by the time the castle was completed. So he – the laird that is – went to a wise man, an intelligent man (I am sure often as not he was called the Old Blind One), and the old man told him to be around the work as often as he could to see if he could hear at all the name of the man who was in charge. And it happened that he heard somebody say "Thomas Jock," and he remembered that name. And perhaps another time he heard one of the workers who were labouring on the castle say "Thomas Jock." But in any case when the castle was finished the devil said – for it seems that it was really he – that he was now going to demand his wage, to ask for his pay.

"Well," said the laird or landlord, "we agreed on the condition that if I knew the name I needn't bother paying."

"Yes indeed," said the devil.

And, as I said before in the story, when the devil said that that was true – that there had been such a condition – the laird or landlord turned and said, "You are Thomas Jock."

And the devil went away crying out, "Stiring Castle completed and poor Thomas Jock destitute!"

And away he went and I am sure that he travelled surrounded by flame or in some such way. And that was all there was to it.

And there you have the story that I heard from MacLean on the building of Stirling Castle.

26   *The Miser and the Tailor*

Someone was once asking me about tales of misers, men who were cautious and would not spend money or anything, who were so extremely careful. And I did hear a story about one person who it seems was an extremely cautious, miserly man. And he was saving up his money; there was not a piece of silver that he had or of gold that was not being saved.

And finally a tailor came to his house one day and said to him, "I see," said the tailor, "that you are in need of a good suit."

"Oh, I am sure," said the miser, "that I do need one if only I had the means to buy it."

Well, the tailor told him that it would not be difficult at all for him to pay for it. And it seems that the miser, when he was showing his treasure to people, used to require that they pay to see it; they had to give him at least a coin for this whether it was a shilling or sixpence or whatever. But the tailor told him that it would not be difficult to pay for at all.

"I will take your measurements and make the suit for you if you give me your assurance that you will show me your treasure and your savings. But," said he, "I won't ask to see that until I return with the suit."

The miser said that he would do so if the tailor was willing to go ahead with that. He was willing enough himself, and so the tailor took his measurements and believe me he was very careful. He returned home with everything written down correctly and you can be sure that he chose the very best cloth that there was to make a suit for the miser.

And a good suit was made, believe me – the suit was made
very well indeed – and when it was ready he took it to the
house and he said, "I have returned with the suit."

"Very good. Well," said the miser, "since you have come I
am sure that I too must stand by my agreement just as you
have done."

"That will be fine," said the tailor.

So the miser went to look at the suit and it looked very
elegant indeed. So he said to him, "Let's go then," said he.
"Come along with me so that I can pay you for the suit."

And down he went. He began opening doors. He opened a
lock on a door and opened the door and went through one
room and opened the door to another room. When he undone
the lock he opened the door and there was the money on the
floor. The tailor looked at it. He gave it one look and he turned
around to leave.

"May I look at it once more?" he asked.

"Oh, I don't know," said the miser. "Oh I am sure," he said,
"that I can permit you to do that."

The tailor turned around and he looked at the money again,
and they went back up. The miser locked the doors and when
they reached the other room the tailor told him that he had
better put on the suit so that he could see it on him and see
how well it fit him, and if it did not fit him as it should, that
could be fixed. The miser put on the suit and the suit was so
well made that it fitted him perfectly. The miser spoke to him
then: "Well," he said, "it is bad for me, tailor, to keep this suit
without any means of paying you for it. You have made the
suit so well and it fits me so snugly and it is well made in
every way."

"Oh," said the tailor, "never mind about that. I have already
been well paid for it."

"No," replied the miser, "you have not. I don't understand
at all how you were paid."

"Oh indeed," replied the tailor, "I was paid very well for it. I
saw your treasure and then I turned around and I looked at it
again."

"And what use was that to you?"

"Oh, didn't it do me just as much good as it is doing you now? And now," he continued, "what will happen if you yourself are only as I was? I took a last look at it and I left, and that is what is going to happen to you eventually: you too will look at the treasure for the last time and will leave it there."

"That is true," said the miser. "That is true. But that is not the way it will be at all. Since you have opened my eyes and brought me the vision to see how things are, you will go back with me to that room for I must now pay you well for the suit. Whatever you want for it, you must take. And I must spend the greater part of the treasure that is there before I leave so that I will get some use from it."

And there you have the story of how the tailor helped the miser out of his difficulty.

27   *The Two Misers*

While we are on the subject of miserly men, there was a man John MacLean (a grandson of Iain Chaluim Òig 'ic Iain 'ic Lachlainn) who told me a story about two misers.

It seems that one of them lived in Cape Breton Island and another lived on the mainland of Nova Scotia. And however it was that the one heard stories about the other, he made up his mind to go to see him. When he arrived at the place where the other miser was living on the mainland he went up to the house. He had found out where the man lived and when he arrived at the house the other man was not inside; he was up in the field planting potatoes, or cultivating them. He would not stop at all to talk to the visitor but kept right on working and asked him who he was. The man replied that he himself was considered to be a terrible miser down at the east end of the country – down somewhere in Cape Breton Island – and that he had heard about a careful, miserly man that was over here and had come to see him. The other one just kept right on with his work without stopping at all.

But when evening arrived they went down to the house.

When they went inside there were two places there – whether it was two pieces of wood for them to sit on or boxes or whatever they sat on – and when the man from the mainland sat down on the box he took his pants down off his backside. The other one asked him why he was doing that.

"Oh," he replied, "why should I be wearing out the seat of my pants sitting around and not getting a stroke of work done?"

So that was miserly enough, and the visitor thought that this was certainly the stingiest man he had ever seen or heard of. He lost his patience and could not wait until he got home to tell the story to his brother, and so he asked if there were any way that he could write. He said that he had a brother and he wanted to send word to his brother about how he had met this remarkable man.

"I would like to tell him that I met you. I am too tired," said he, "to be going off in a hurry and I am afraid that it would take me too long to reach home so that he could get the message."

"There is nothing here," replied the other, "for you to write on unless you find a piece of old gray paper that came home on something from the store, if that will do for you."

"Oh I am sure that I will have to make do with it."

So a little stub of something was found – whether it was a cinder or a piece of pencil or something – with which he could write and he wrote down a little message on paper. And at the time that he was writing it was dark and the miser had a small candle which he was holding over toward him. When he had written down the message on paper, saying that he had met a miser and a few other words with it, the other man asked him, "Are you finished writing?"

"Yes, thank you," said he.

And he blew out the candle. "We don't need light at all since we are only sitting and talking."

And there you have the comical story that I heard about the misers, which I am sure was doubtless made up.

The MacIsaacs

Since I have been giving a little bit of history of the fine people from whom I learned part of the tradition and the joy and the humour that was going, I should recall the MacIsaacs down that way, the children of Big Archie MacIsaac. Alexander and John and Donald and Angus were the four brothers that I became acquainted with.

Angus was full of a kind of cheerfulness. He used to tell stories and he could make them up as well. He made them up in great numbers and with great ease. And he could invent long ones too; some of his tales were extremely long. He knew himself that they were not true and when he was finished telling one of these big stories, after he had let out a little laugh, he would say, "And that's no lie."

He worked in various places out in Canada, though perhaps he was not so far out west as he pretended to make his story. But he was good in the blacksmith shop; he could do extremely nice work there. He was an extremely gifted man. They would tell me that all he had to do was look at a horse's feet and he could make shoes that would fit snugly.

Angus was a humorous man as well and enjoyed going out visiting to houses and wakes. He was such a sociable man that he could entertain people in a way that was altogether amazing; an evening in his company would please everyone.

As for John, he was just as cheerful and easy to be with as the others, but the poor man was deprived in a way; his hearing was defective. It was difficult to learn from him because he would speak very softly, at the same time believing that he was speaking loudly. You had to be very attentive. It would not do for you to turn your face from him when he was reciting a story for fear that you would miss words. And that was very difficult because when he was reciting stories he could go any way at all, or so it seemed, that the course of events took in the story. If a smile came on the face of character in a story he would almost laugh himself; and when a man in the story frowned John would do the same. And if the character asked someone who had addressed him to remain quiet, John would get the scowl on his face and would pretend to threaten the other man: "Shut your mouth. What will I do with you?"

And you would think that he was that man and that the story was happening right in front of him. Sometimes that would make you laugh, and that was certainly no trouble for him. In fact he enjoyed making you laugh, and for that reason it was hard to learn a tale from him; you had to be so attentive before you got every word. But it was nice to be with him, and when he would go to a place where there was a wake he would start out telling a short story. When he finished the short story, another one would come up a little bit longer than the first. They were like the shoe lasts – each one coming a little larger and larger until finally a big, long tale would come out. There was one big, long one that I did not manage to learn because he knew it so naturally and fluently and proceeded so smoothly with it that it was a little too fast for me; I would try to learn it but there were some words that were not loud enough for me to hear. It was a special story: *The Tale of the Son of the Old Woman with the Three Sheep.*

In any case he was an extremely cheerful and sociable man. We all praised him and everybody had something to say about John; they would laugh whenever they talked about John's stories.

His brother Donald was himself a cheerful, fine man, fond of company and conversation. I was not very well acquainted with him, but I knew about him through things that he used to say. But I did see him – I was in his presence – and he could make a very neat job of telling a story. He had no trouble taking it one way or the other, but it was so well done and so complete the way he told it. Perhaps Donald was not the kind of man who would set the world on fire with his hurry but nonetheless he raised a family – a good one – and they turned out to be people of some consequence.

Alexander was a fine man, a quiet, personable man, and a nice man to talk to. Without a doubt he was extremely good at repartee: he had an answer ready for everything. But he was personable and never impolite in any way; he would never give you an answer except one he felt was fair. He composed songs easily, some good ones. If he wished he could make songs that were not entirely complimentary but he never did so without good reason, and he could make humorous songs too. And very probably he was the way the bards used to be; there had to be a lot of the imagination of the bards in songs for them to be good, and there was some of that in some of the songs that he composed for humour and amusement. He also made songs that were quite clever; he composed a song to the soldiers who went to the World War and he made a good job of it. He composed a song as well about the time a friend of his had a sawn pine tree kept in the byre which was stolen. In addition I should also mention that he was the seventh son; eight sons were born to Big Archie MacIsaac along with one daughter. According to people's tradition, he used to cure the king's evil (scrofula) too.

28   Jack Fury

There was once a man and it seems that he was extremely cunning and independent in whatever he did. And he went to work for two people who were extremely stingy. I'm sure they did not care if they ever paid a man as long as they got enough work out of him.

Anyway he went to work for them, and the work that he went to do that day was to go to a field some distance away and plow it with the oxen. He was a strong man and quick-tempered, and as he was going around with their oxen a bird alighted and started to sing in a tree. He thought that somebody was making fun of him and he decided it was the bird. So he picked up a large stone to throw at the bird and what did he do but strike one of the oxen, and he killed the ox; the ox fell over dead. There was no help for it and he continued plowing, but he skinned the ox and in the evening he took the oxhide with him to town.

He arrived at a certain place there, and where was that but the shoemaker's. And he was thinking perhaps that the shoemaker would need leather and that he might buy the oxhide and get it tanned. But when he arrived, it seems that a gentleman was with the shoemaker's wife while the shoemaker was away. So he said to the gentleman, "Well," said he, "you have been caught in a compromising situation and it will not go so easily for you as you might expect when I see your host and tell him."

The gentleman replied, "Please, don't say anything. I will give you five English pounds to keep quiet."

"Oh," he replied, "five English pounds! What is five English pounds to me? Don't you know that I am not going to conceal this matter for a trifling sum of money?"

"In that case," said the gentleman, "I will give you ten English pounds."

"I'll have nothing to do with it," said he. "I am not going to let this matter concerning my good friend pass for such a trifling sum of money."

"I'll give you twenty pounds," said the gentleman, "just for keeping quiet."

"Well, then," he replied, "I would not mind being quiet, since you are so concerned about my remaining so." So he got twenty English pounds for the oxhide.

Later that evening when he reached home they asked him how he got along, and he said that he did not get along very well at all, although he began well enough. He got along very well at first while he was plowing, but some creature was making fun of him and he threw a pebble at it in order to drive it away or kill it or something.

"And," said he, "I struck one of the oxen and I killed it."

Well, believe me they were angry then. He continued, "I skinned the ox and I took the hide with me and went to town and shouted to see if there was anyone who would buy an oxhide, and they bought the oxhide from me."

"And what did you get?"

"I got twenty pounds for it."

"And do you think if we took the hide of the other ox in, that they would buy it?"

"Oh, I don't know," said he, "but I think that if I had a number of oxhides with me, I could have sold them."

So they killed the other ox and went to town, calling out, "Who will buy an oxhide?" And people started after them with their dogs; they drove them all the way home. They were angry when they arrived back, but I am sure that they did not show many signs of it. But he was canny so he listened to how things were going and heard them planning to do away with him that night as he slept in his bed.

Anyway he entered, and there was an old lady in with them, or two of them. And he went over to one of them – and he was almost crying – and said to her, "I have bad news for you. They are talking about doing away with you tonight. But," he said, "if you come over and sleep in the bed where I am sleeping now, you will be safe enough."

And the old woman came over and slept in his bed, and he went and slept in another bed somewhere. That night they came and did in the old woman.

Jack arose in the morning and they looked at him. "And what," said they, "brought you here?"

"And why," said he, "shouldn't I be here?"

"And where did you sleep last night?"

"I slept in the bed over there," said he. "The old lady came to me complaining that she was not getting enough sleep, and I said to her that she would be better off sleeping in my bed; my bed was quite good and I would go over to the old lady's bed. And I slept well enough in her bed. And I found nothing wrong with it."

Oh, that made them angry, but they did not let on at all. They said to him, "Now you must go and bury the old lady."

"Oh," replied he, "I will not go with her today. You must give me time. I will go with her tomorrow morning."

And so it came to pass. He set out in the morning and he took the old woman with him and a basket on his arm. He travelled with the basket and the old lady in tow and he reached his destination just as the day broke. Early in the morning he reached the place of a gentleman – a king or some kind of gentleman – and he left the old woman standing up at the well with the basket on her arm. There was some sort of fence surrounding the well and she was leaning against it. He went up, knocked on the door, and complained to the gentleman. He said that he and his mother were travelling around and that they were so poor in the world; they were travelling around with a basket of eggs to see if they could get some food to eat. The king said, "Tell her to come down."

"She won't come down," he replied. "She has given out. She is so tired that she can't come down. She has given up walking, and I'm tired myself."

"Well, then," said he, the king, "I will send down a servant to talk to her and ask her to come down, so that you will get food until I buy the eggs from you."

And the lad said to the servant as he was leaving, "Now," said he, "my mother is very deaf and you may have to give her a slight push to make sure that she hears and realizes you are speaking to her."

So down went the gentlemen's manservant and when he reached there he spoke to her and shouted to her, but she did not answer, so he gave her a slight push and she fell into the well. Jack started weeping and lamenting.

"You have killed my mother," said he. "And how am I going to stand being so destitute in this world without my mother?"

"Oh, take it easy, take it easy," said the gentleman.

"It is easy enough for you, my fine fellow, to say that. But as for me, I have lost my mother."

"Listen," said the gentleman, "take it easy there."

"Oh," he replied, "I will do nothing of the sort. I am going to take this matter to the law. Your servant pushed my mother into the well without just cause and she was drowned. And I am going to take that to the law."

"Oh, take it easy," said he, the gentleman. "Take it easy. I will give you a settlement."

"Money means nothing to me," said he. "What good will your money do me compared to my mother?"

"Now," said he. "I will give you ten English pounds to keep quiet about the matter."

"Ten English pounds for my mother!" said he. "Is that not a paltry settlement to give me for my mother?"

"Well, then," said he, "I will give you twenty English pounds."

"Well," said he, "perhaps, since you are a gentleman, and doing as well as you are, perhaps you are not entirely to blame, and I may accept that and we will leave this matter as it is as long as you look after my mother and everything, and see that she gets a decent burial and is taken care of."

That was done, so he went back and the others asked him if he had buried the old lady.

"I did not bury the old lady," he answered. "Why should I? I went and sold her."

"And how," said one of them, "did you sell the old lady?"

"I went to town," said he, "and I called out to see if there was anyone who would buy an old lady. And they all gathered around and they began. One would say 'I will give you so much for her,' and another would say, 'I will give you more than that for her,' and finally I got twenty pounds for her."

"And do you think," asked one of them, "that we would get that for the other old lady?"

"I don't know what you could sell," he replied, "but I believe that if I had had three old women, with the rush everyone was in to buy an old woman I could have sold all of them."

So they did away with the other old woman that night and took her to town to sell her. But dogs were set on them and they had to flee or the police would have been sent out after them, so they had to make for the woods.

They reached home and when they did the only thing to do was to do away with Jack Fury immediately. They grabbed Jack and they put him into a large sack, bound a string good and tight around the sack, and set out; they carried him away to drown him. But it seems that the day was quite warm and on their journey they threw the sack to the side of the road in a certain place and continued on a short distance to where there was a tavern for a drink of beer before they went with

Jack to cast him into the river. And Jack heard a sound down the road. He decided that it was a cattle-drover coming. He heard the noise of the cattle walking and so he began to complain and complain, saying, "I will not marry the king's daughter; I certainly will not. I will not marry the king's daughter in spite of them. Even if I were put to death I would not marry the king's daughter."

A drover came up to him. "What," said he, "are you saying?"

"I am saying," replied Jack, "that I will not marry the king's daughter. Why should I marry the king's daughter when I am in love with another maid? And now they are threatening to do away with me unless I marry the king's daughter."

"Well," said the other, "I would marry the king's daughter."

"In that case," he replied, "untie the string from the mouth of the sack and let me out. You can marry her. I don't want her at all."

So the poor drover was put into the sack and the string was bound around it and Jack went off with the cattle.

When the others came out of the tavern the man in the sack was saying, "Oh yes, I'll marry the king's daughter."

"Do you hear," said one of them, "what that soft-headed fool is saying?"

They continued on with him and the man kept saying, "I will marry the king's daughter. I will marry the king's daughter." And he was thinking – they were carrying him along – that they were going to drown him or do away with him unless he married the king's daughter because of what the other man had told him. In any case, they reached a certain place, threw the drover into the river, and down he went with the current.

But after a time when they had returned home, there came Jack with a drove of cattle. He stopped up at the gate and hollered and hollered to them until one of them finally said, "There's Jack back again. Go to meet him."

"I will not go to meet him at all," said another of them. "I was afraid enough of him at the end of it when he was alive, and I will certainly not go near him now that he's dead."

The first one said, "Well, someone has to go to meet him, so we'll go down together."

They went out and he called to them, "Hurry up! Hurry up and open the gate and let in the cattle."

"And where," said one of them, "did you get the cattle?"

"Didn't I find them," he replied, "where you threw me? Down in the river. When I reached the bottom of the river, I never saw cattle so fine. There they were."

"Were they plentiful?"

"Plentiful!" said he. "If there were as many as four people with me, we could not have possibly caught all that were there. All I took was the worst of the drove. I did not have the time nor the help to take the rest."

"And do you think," said one of them, "that if we were there, we would find cattle, too?"

"I don't know what you would find, but I know that had I had help, I could have got many more cattle."

"Well," said one of them, "you can take us to the place."

"I won't take you anywhere," said Jack. "Go there yourself."

"Oh," said one of them, "you have to take us there to see if we can get some more of those cattle."

"If you are so determined to go there," said he, "then I'll go with you. But you must go to the exact place where I went. It is not worth your while going anywhere else except for the place where I myself went."

And it seems that that was a steep place with big rocks and the like and a strong current. Jack said to them, "Take along you own sack. I'm not going to follow you with sacks at all."

When they arrived there one of them was put in the sack and tied and Jack said to the other one, "You can throw him into the river."

And as the man went under he made a gurgle of some sort.

"What did he say?" said the other one.

"He said," Jack replied, "that he sees a large drove of cattle and they are just getting ready to flee from him."

"Quick," said the other. "Tie me in the sack."

"What sort of talk is that?" said Jack. "Won't you get in and be patient about it?"

"Oh, hurry, hurry," said the other. "I am in a hurry to go and help my friend."

So the other man was put into the sack and Jack tied the string around it and rolled him down – he plopped into the stream – and Jack returned home. And he had the big drove of cattle along with what money he had gotten for the ox's hide and for the old woman; all of these things he had for himself.

And there you have the story that I heard about Jack Fury as told by John MacIsaac.

29   *The Man Who Received the Three Counsels*

Here is a story I heard from John MacIsaac and another man, Angus MacMullin. It is some time since I heard it from Angus and a long time indeed since I heard it from MacIsaac.

It concerns a man who left his home to seek employment: they were running short of everything so he told his wife that he was going to go away for a while to work. So he set out and hired on with a man some distance away and it was very good; he liked it. The wages I am sure were only small but he was so faithful and conscientious anyway that he did the work that needed doing as well as it could be done. Finally he was about to return home and his employer asked him about advice, saying, "I could give you advice. I could give you advice if you would take it."

He said that he would and, as the reciter told me, "It is going to cost you," said the man, "five pounds" – or however much it was. Anyway it was a third of what he had earned there, and he paused for some time to think it over. Finally he said he felt that it was just as well for him to take it. And the advice that he was given was not to take the short road at any time but to choose the long, clean road, for that was safest for him on his journey; he had a long way to go.

So he paid so many pounds for the advice and I'm sure that he had to follow it. Then the man said to him, "I will give you another piece of advice."

"Yes," he replied.

"If you take it it will cost you five pounds" – or six pounds or a half or a third of his wages. Oh, he remembered that

perhaps it would be better for him to take it since the distance
was so long and the advice might be suitable. So the man said
to him, "The advice that I am giving you is not to spend a
night in a house where there is an old man with a young
wife."

So part of his wages was gone but the man said to him then,
"I have another piece of advice that I could give you if you
will take it. But if you do take it it will cost you the rest of
your wages."

He said that he would take the advice, and the other man
advised him not to do anything in the evening or at night
without serious reflection that he would regret having done
on the morning of the next day.

So he prepared to leave and there was a little in wages –
perhaps a week's or so – coming to him. That was given to
him along with a loaf of bread and the man told him to make
sure to take it home and that his wife be there when he opened
the bundle and to give it to her.

So off he went. He was travelling along the road and a rider
came up to him and they began conversing. They reached a
short cut and the rider said that he was going to take this road,
that it was shorter.

"I won't take that road myself at all," said the man. "I
prefer to follow the long, clean road."

He remembered the advice that was given him and continued
on. But the rider had not gone far when he encountered thieves,
highwaymen, who took his money from him, and since he
escaped from them with his life there was nothing that he
could say.

But the other man continued on his journey. He reached a
house late in the evening and went up to it. Inside was an old
man and a young woman. I believe he got food from them and
they spent some time conversing and then he got up to leave;
he wasn't going to spend the night there anyway. And he went
and hid himself; there was a haystack there or hay inside a
barn and he went in. Then some people came to the house. At
least one man and perhaps two approached the house that
night. And it happened that one of them had his back against

the place where he was concealed in the hay. The man leaned his back against him, so he reached out through the hay and caught the tail of his coat. He had a small pair of scissors in his pocket and he cut a piece out of the coat and put that into his pocket and the other man went away.

He set off then at daybreak – he had slept there all night but when dawn came off he went. And he had just gone down to town when he noticed a tremendous commotion there so he asked somebody what was wrong and the person replied that there were two sailors who had been caught; a man had been murdered up in these parts the night before and these sailors had been caught and they were taking them to court. Oh, he said he thought he would go to hear them, and they said without a doubt he could go: if he wished to go that was all right.

He went to the court-house and entered and there was a man condemning the poor sailors. And when they were in danger of being convicted he stood up and asked whether they would permit him to say a little concerning this case. They replied that he could say something if he would give testimony. He said that he would do so. He stated that it was neither of the sailors – these poor lads – who had committed the crime the night before. They asked what proof he had and he replied that to his knowledge they were not present at the scene. However he said there was someone who was there last night and that he could recognize him by a certain means. Yes, by what means was that? He replied that the man had come down, that he had leaned his back against the place where he himself was hiding in the middle of the hay and when he was close to him he reached over and caught hold of the bottom of the man's coat and cut a piece from it with the scissors.

"I have it here. And anyone," said he, "whose bottom coat hem fits this piece is the man who was there last night."

The guilty man was about to run out but was stopped. They looked and there was a piece missing from the back of his coat. They tried it and the piece cut from the man's coat was the one that fit it. It was a young gentleman from the region who had committed the crime; he was going to get away completely and the poor sailors were going to be condemned on his account. So I am sure that the sailors were very grateful and that they expressed their deep gratitude.

So he continued on his journey and when he reached home it was nighttime. By this time he had been a long while away working and a great change had come over things. When he went into the house it was dark and he saw a man stretched out on the bed. He thought that it was somebody who was staying there while he was away and he went to get a knife or an axe or a sword or something to kill him. But he thought of the advice that his employer had given him on which he had spent five or six English pounds, and that he should take it. And the advice was not to do anything at night until he thought it over or he might sorely regret his deed in the morning. And he made up his mind that he would justly determine what was going on. He went up to the bed to see who was in it and who was it but his own son; he had grown so big by then. He had grown though the father had not noticed at all, and the wife asked him what wages he had gotten and he replied that he had been paid wages but that he had spent them on the pieces of advice that were given to him and that this advice given to him had been very useful too.

"And oh," said he, "here is something that he said to me."

And he reached over the loaf of bread to her.

"Here," said he, "is a loaf of bread that he sent with me and he told me not to open it until you yourself opened it."

So she went over to the table and a knife was put to the loaf of bread and it was opened and his wages poured out of the loaf. Every penny that he had earned while he was away on his journey had been put into the loaf of bread. And because he was so faithful that he had heeded the pieces of advice from the man who had given him the wise counsels, he reached home safe and well.

And that is the tale of the man who received the three counsels.

30   *The Forgetful Minister*

There was once a minister who was extremely forgetful.
He couldn't remember what day it was – he could barely
remember from day to day. And he was looking for a manservant to take on. A certain young man came to him who
was I am sure pretty much up on tricks: he didn't care what he
did. Anyway, he was quite clever. So when he was going to
hire on with the forgetful minister he asked what wages he
was paying and the minister said twenty English pounds when
horns grew on a horse. Oh, that was good enough. The forgetful
minister had a duck that laid an egg every day and that was
how he knew what day of the week it was, and the duck
would lay an egg early in the morning and the minister would
keep track of the eggs.

One morning the minister was fixing his shoe – he was
sewing his shoe together. He had just begun sewing the shoe
and had made two or three stitches with the thread in the
shoe when the manservant came inside in a great rush and
said to him that the duck had just laid the seventh egg and
that today was Sunday. So the minister went out in a great
hurry and the servant said to him that he had better hasten,
that they would be waiting for him to appear at the sermon.
So he left in a great rush and just pulled on the shoe. He set
out in great haste and ran until he entered the church. And
when he was going down towards the pulpit to give his sermon
there was a little old woman proceeding slowly to a bench.
What did he do but when he moved a little to the side he trod
on his own shoelace, and he was in such a rush that it tripped
him. Down he went head first and struck the old woman and
down she went. She struck her head on the bench in front of
her and she was laid low.

Once that had happened, the lad told the minister that he
should leave, that it was not advisable for him to stay around
there at all, and that he had better not remain seeing how things
had turned out because people might think that he was intoxi-
cated or that something was wrong with him. The matter was
so vexing for the minister that he decided he would leave.

They were in a hurry to leave and the servant said that he had better set out without losing any time on food or doing anything, but just take off immediately. And the servant filled his own pockets with bread and they set out. They walked and walked on their way to visit at a house. Eventually they reached the house, but as they were on their way the lad now and again would put a bit of food into his mouth and chew it, and the minister asked him what he was chewing. Oh, he said he was chewing little stones he was picking up off the road and that they were very good; when he got them down they never seemed to run out at all. The minister said to him, "Give me some."

"I will not," replied the lad. "Get some for yourself."

So the minister picked up two or three of the pebbles, put them into his mouth and tried to chew them but they nearly broke his teeth; he had to spit them out again. After a while he saw the young lad chewing again and he asked him, "What are you chewing there?"

"Ah," the lad replied, "I am chewing horse manure."

"Will that serve as food?"

"Oh yes indeed," replied the lad. "It will. It certainly will serve as food and it is so rich. Try a little bit of it."

"I will not," said he, "try any of it at all."

"But when I told you about the pebbles you complained."

But he decided to try it so he put a little bit in his mouth and he expelled it from his mouth again, spitting it out.

"You nearly poisoned me," he said.

"I never did anything of the sort," replied the lad. "You did it yourself. And you were saying as well that I broke your teeth. I didn't do anything to you; you were the one that picked up the pebbles."

So they continued their journey and when they reached the house the people were not home. So they had no choice but to go inside and begin to prepare something to eat. And the lad said, "You make," said he, "something for us to eat. Don't bother to ask me to do anything like that."

So they found meal or flour or something and he began to put something into a container and wet it in order to begin

making some sort of little cake. And just then who did they
see coming but the people who lived in the house! The lad did
not let on at all until the people were right there at the door.
The minister just thrust his hands into his armpits for fear
that they would see the dough on them and the lad went and I
am sure he set the vessel which held the dough to one side.
The rest of the dough which he did not take up on his hands
the minister gathered together and put into his armpits, so he
could not shake hands with them.

"Oh," said the lad, "he is not used to shaking people's hands
at all, but pay no attention to him. Just leave him alone."

Well, he was satisfied enough then that the lad had
apologized for him. Anyway they were conversing and their
supper was prepared and meat and soup and food put on the
table and couldn't the lad made noise! The minister could not
eat anything: his hands were in his armpits covered with dough
and he could not eat a bite. And as John used to say, the lad
would raise a spoonful of the soup and would make a noise
ffffff sucking the soup off the spoon. And oh, that was making
it so difficult for the minister; he would look at him and start
swearing and look at him again. Then the lad took up a piece
of meat on the fork: he would stab the fork into a piece of
meat and would lift it up so high that the minister would see
it. Then he would put the piece of meat into his mouth and
begin chewing it and the minister just shook his head. And at
last he wished that the lad and the meat and everything else
there, as John himself would say, were out on the rubbish
heap.

When dinner was over it came time to retire. So they went
to sleep, and the minister kept saying to the servant, "I'm
hungry. I am about to starve."

And the servant would say, "Shut your mouth. What will I
do with you?"

But the minister kept saying, "I'm very hungry."

"So, what will I do with you?"

And the minister kept on, "Did you leave behind the rest of
the food? Don't you know whether you did?"

And the lad would answer, "Yes, it's over there. It's over

there in the cupboard so go and get it. And if you get soup and things bring them over to me. Bring me part of it."

"But how will I find your bed?" asked the minister.

"Oh you will," replied the lad. "You'll take the end of this string with you: and I'll tie the other end of it to the lock on the door to the room. And you just follow this string right back."

So off he went and when he went inside to where the meat and everything else was he set to helping himself as best he could to the meat and the soup and so on. Then he remembered that he had to take something to the lad so he followed the string back. But where was the string now? The lad had switched it over to the room where the old man and the old woman were sleeping. And there they were in deep slumber when the minister entered the room.

"Here," he said. "Here is the soup for you."

And the others only made a snoring sound in their sleep by way of reply. And the minister thought that the lad had gone to sleep and he grew angry and he poured a whole container of soup on them in bed.

He returned to where the meat and the things were in the cupboard and while he was away the lad switched the string over to the door of their own room where he himself was sleeping. And when the minister came in,

"Did you bring me," said the lad, "the soup or anything at all?"

"Yes," said the minister, "and you were asleep."

"Oh, indeed I was not asleep," said the lad. "I was waiting for you and you didn't come at all, and please note that I'm a little hungry now."

"Oh," said the minister, "there is nothing I can give you. What there was is gone. I brought in the last of the soup."

"Are you sure?"

"Oh yes," said the minister, "I am."

"Go," said the servant, "and look again to see if there is anything left."

So he went back and put his hand down into a pitcher that was there and there was a piece of meat at the bottom of it.

But he couldn't get the piece of meat out; it was in his fist and his fist got stuck in the neck of the pitcher and there was no way to take the meat out. The story wouldn't be right anyway if he could.

He came back to where the servant was – the string was back where it was supposed to be – and he said to him, "There's a piece of meat here in the pitcher but I can't get it out."

"Oh," said the lad, "don't talk to me that way at all. What kind of silly things are you saying?"

"I can't," said the minister. "I can't get this piece of meat out of the pitcher."

And while this was going on the old man woke up and started scolding the old lady asking what was going on now. Said he, "You changed the bed and now this bed is full. You must have thrown up in bed."

"I did not," said she. "I was asleep."

"Even if you were," he replied, "you must have. Go out and take that off. Get something to wash it off your clothes. It's not proper to be in bed like this."

But just then the lad was speaking to the minister.

"Go out," said he, "and you will see a big stone at the end of the house or somewhere near by. Strike the pitcher against the stone and it will crack and you'll get your hand out that way."

It was pitch dark when he went out and there was a white heap out there – the old lady – rubbing the stuff off of her clothing. He knocked over the old woman and struck her and flattened her. Then he returned inside and he said that he had struck the stone and that it had said "Ouch!"

"Oh," said the lad, "you have done some harm."

The lad went out to look and there was the old woman laid low. They had to get out and get out right away; there was no time to be lost lest they be seen and what else could they do but flee?

The lad told the minister that it was not advisable for him to go in a vehicle or to wait for a vehicle – riding was best for him. He could leave without losing time harnessing up, he would not make so much noise on the road, and they would travel faster. It was still pitch black outside and the lad said, "I have the horse ready here."

So he went over. He crossed over to the stable to get the horse ready ahead of the forgetful minister. "I want my wages now," he said. "Hasn't the horse grown horns?"

"Has he?" said the forgetful minister.

"Oh yes," replied the lad. "And did you not promise to pay me twenty English pounds when the horse grew horns?"

"Oh, you will get that," said the minister, "now that you have reminded me."

And he took the bills out of his pocket and handed them to the lad.

"Put your hand over here," said the lad, "so you won't have to take my word for it."

He reached his hand over and what did they have out there but the bull! He put his hand out and the lad guided his hand over until he set it on one of the bull's horns.

"Oh," said the minister, "the horse has grown horns sure enough."

When he had been paid his twenty pounds the lad said to the minister, "Get up on the horse's back and I will go behind you."

The minister got up on the back of the bull and the lad gave the bull's tail a twist and the bull let loose a bellow and out he went and headed down. He went over a cliff or something and that was the end of the forgetful minister. And the lad got twenty English pounds and he was better off than many at the time.

And that is the tale that he had about the forgetful minister.

31 *Monday, Tuesday*

This story concerns two old men who were living in some part of the world; it seems that they were on each side of a glen. And it seems that one of the old men was very cheerful, funny, full of fun and games, singing songs and ditties, and always passing his time cheerfully and amiably. But it seems that was not at all the nature of the other old man; he was rather ill disposed. This old man was perhaps the way people would often describe someone who was not happy or good-natured or well-disposed: they would say that there was as little affection in his heart as there was in an owl. But the other old man was cheerful and would always be working on some mouth-music or a little ditty of a song whenever he was going or coming.

And according to the story he went out, climbed up the mountain, and came to a place where there was a door opening into a hillside, and he could hear the fairies inside playing a tune. And it seems that they were not having much success at the time and were just going back over "Monday Tuesday Monday Tuesday Monday Tuesday Monday Tuesday." The old man stopped – I am sure that he had some snatch of a tune or a rhyme from a song going anyway. But when he heard this he stopped to listen and he noticed that they seemed to be almost beginning to quarrel over this; they weren't getting very far with it at all. So he jumped inside the door and said "Wednesday!" Just when they had finished saying "Monday Tuesday" he said "Wednesday!" and right away they said "Wednesday" and "Monday Tuesday Wednesday," and they were so pleased that they had found another piece to add to the tune.

A little old man came over to him and said that he would get whatever reward he wanted for having done so well by them. Oh, he did not want a reward at all; there was nothing that he required – gold or silver or any kind of treasure – but he mentioned that he would not mind being rid of the hump that he had on his back. Immediately the hump was removed and put over on a table, the sort of table where they took their meals. And there he was standing straight as a young soldier. He went down to his home, as cheerful and happy as was usually his custom.

But the other old man in the neighbourhood – the cross one – came over. He saw him and became curious as to what had happened. The old man told him how he had fared and the other thought that he would try to get rid of his own hump. So he set out and he climbed up the mountain. But that old man had no cheer nor happiness nor keenness at all and no taste or understanding for song or music. He did not believe in it, like some other unfortunates, I believe, who were on the face of the earth. And when he arrived the fairies were working on the tune that the other old man had improved. So he added something and spoilt the tune for them. That angered them greatly, so they carried him inside, and instead of giving him a reward they fixed the hump on him that they had taken off the other man. And when he returned home he had a great big hump, or perhaps there were two humps on his back like a camel.

32   *Angus MacIsaac's Trip to the Moon*

At this time I would like to tell you a story or tale that was made up by Angus MacIsaac (Aonghus 'Illeasbuig Mhóir).

He was telling us that he went out hunting with an old musket and that there were geese sitting on the lake, down at the border of the lake along the edge. The shoreline ran in a great curve there, and they were lined up along the curve of the shore. And how could he manage to kill them when they were lined up that way? If they had been out on the loch in a straight line it would have been easy enough, but there they were, in a curve along the shore. So he bent the barrel of his musket, bent the ramrod, rammed home the shot and fired. The ramrod went through all the heads, and there they were on it, with the ramrod through their heads. All he had to do was to go down and catch them, and he began to take them away.

The geese were knocked out. They were delirious or in a faint, as they would say, unconscious at the time. But as he was carrying them away they regained consciousness and began flapping their wings. Up they lifted and I'm sure out of foolishness, as he claimed, he tried to hold them. But they lifted him off the ground – they were so strong – and kept on flying.

And up they flew. They were flying and flying, rising up, and he kept his grip on them. But once they had gained a certain altitude he couldn't let go lest he fall and be killed, so he kept on ascending, and when they were passing the moon he let go of the ramrod and let the geese go on. He leaped off the ramrod and planted his feet on the threshold of the moon. The Old Man in the Moon was standing at the door, but he did not recognize Angus and Angus did not recognize the Old Man in the Moon. How could they, not being acquainted? But the Old Man in the Moon was extremely kind to him. He invited him in and gave him food and Angus stayed a while conversing with him. They passed the time this way.

But Angus wanted to return to earth, and the Old Man in the Moon said to him that he had better stay for a while yet. "If you would just stay with me," said he, "and help butcher the pig."

The Old Man in the Moon had a good-sized pig over in the barn. So he stayed with the Old Man in the Moon; he stayed for two or three weeks with the Old Man in the Moon and helped him kill the big pig. And when they had killed the pig, he got two barrel-staves at the back of the barn that belonged to the Old Man in the Moon. He asked him for the two staves and, yes, he could take them. Then he asked him for some of the pig's lard. Yes, he would get that; there was certainly enough of that. The pig was fat and there was a lot of lard. So he prepared the staves and he rubbed a great deal of the lard on them and finally he had them ready so he waited. The first evening there was a rainbow he jumped off the moon and slid down the rainbow and down he went until his feet struck the ground behind Eaton's Store in Moncton.

And that is what happened to Angus MacIsaac the time he went out hunting and took a trip to the moon.

33   *The Big Pig*

I have a story that was made up by Angus MacIsaac (Aonghus 'Illeasbuig Mhóir). And as you hear it you will see that the man was astounding in his ability to make up stories and in his sense of humour.

He made the story up about an old woman who happened to meet him, and whatever kindness it was that he showed the old woman she was so pleased that she said she would have to give him some reward for what he had done. So she gave him a small box about the size of a snuff box with a few small holes in the cover. Inside was a little piglet. And she gave him a small quantity of golden dust or, as he himself said (in English), *gold dust*, and this was the food that was to be given to the piglet; little grains of this were to be fed to it.

So he went home with the little pig very pleased with it. He took the piglet out of the little box and shook a grain or two onto the floor and the piglet ate that and it began to grow. And he said that it grew so fast: it grew out backward and it grew out forward. At the very beginning he said that an old man could go at his leisure shaking the food on the ground. He could do this by throwing a little of the food on the ground and going ahead step by step. And when he put more on the ground the piglet grew so big that it would reach that too.

But, as time passed and the piglet was eating the gold dust, it grew so quickly that at last he had to get a young man to feed it. And old man could not keep up with it since it was growing so fast. The young man would stand at its mouth and pour the meal on the ground, going forward as fast as he could, and when he put the next bit of meal on the ground the pig's head was already there from growing so fast. At last even the young man was not able to do it. Even if he ran he could not keep up with the pig. So he had to get a man on horseback – and he had to have a good horse too – to go with the gold meal and sprinkle and throw it on the ground toward the growing pig.

Finally the pig got so big that it had grown to an awful size, and a show had come to town, a circus as they say in English. So he went to the people in charge and asked them if they were willing to exhibit the pig at the show. Oh, yes indeed; they were willing enough. And when the pig was brought there – I'm sure that it was brought on great big railroad cars –

the elephants climbed up on its back. They were walking around on the pig's back. And they told him – people who were a little distance away and who saw this – they said that wherever that beast had come from it had to be removed from the field entirely for there were lice or some kind of creatures on its back. He told them that they had no cause to worry, that it was just the elephants from the circus on the pig's back. It appears that the pig was big enough then.

By then the pig had grown so big that the time was coming to butcher it. And they had to get an engine from the railway company – a little locomotive – and they had to mount a big knife on the front of it in order to bleed the pig. To take the bristles off and to scrape it they had to build great fires around the lake until the water boiled. When they had it scraped and everything ready there was no way for them to weigh it; there was nowhere to put it to weigh it. The biggest sets of scales in the world could not weigh it. And it turned out that they had to estimate how many pounds a certain part of it would weigh. So they got surveyors who measured land with a compass and a measuring chain, and they measured it crosswise and lengthwise – how many hundred feet – and went to work with paper and pencils. They had all kinds of high-powered scholars hired to figure out the total poundage and to give it according to the measurements.

And, he said, with the time they lost on everything they had to do between measuring it and weighing it, the flavour turned so bad that a large part of the pig was lost before they found the time to salt it. And that is the tale of the Big Pig told by Angus MacIsaac.

The MacMullins

As far as I have been able to determine this family of
MacMullins came from North Uist. When Angus MacMullin
(Aonghus Alasdair 'ic Nìll 'ic Iain 'ac Mhurchaidh 'ac
Dhòmhnaill) was a youth he went to live with his mother's
people on the mainland of Nova Scotia where they had been
fishing for years. He fished out on the bay of Canso with his
maternal uncle and with others up there. Then he came back
down and settled in Johnstown or the Red Islands, as the place
was called at the time. He used to go fishing with Frenchmen;
it seems he was a good sailor, very skilled at repairing his nets
and making herring nets, and extremely courageous at sea. He
also did a small amount of farming but his place was ill suited
for it; it was nothing but steep slopes. He did well at fishing in
the Bras d'Or Lake also, catching cod and herring; he was skilled
at dressing herring, cleaning it, and salting it, and so on.

He himself could not read Gaelic, as was also true of the
Kennedys; they could not read Gaelic but they were so replete
with tales of every sort that I think even if they had been able
to read Gaelic they wouldn't have had anywhere left to fit in
the tales they read. But to return to Angus MacMullin, he
used to compose stories too. He used to invent short, pleasant
stories which he himself, along with everybody else who
listened to them, knew were not true. But he never claimed at
any time that they were the truth. He just made them up to
entertain people and to pass the time. He used to set them up
so well, whether he was telling you a long tale or a short tale.
He was able to order it extremely well and in a way that
would appeal to you – it was so enjoyable. That was the way
he had with tales. There was one night he was with people at a

wedding or some occasion sitting outside in a car alongside the house and he was naturally holding forth. There were some people around him in high spirits and one of them went over and asked, "Who's telling the lies here now?"

And Angus answered, "Somebody who knows how to."[1]

Similarly he was an excellent singer with a melodious voice. Most of his songs were in English, the reason being that when he was over on the Nova Scotia mainland there were Irishmen about the place where he was living; through his fishing he met some of them and learned a good number of Irish songs. He could really sing them; he sang them in such a tasteful way that all of you wanted was to pass the time listening to him. He was a welcome guest wherever he went since he was such a sociable man; if people saw him going by and had a good idea where he was going that night to pass the time you could be sure that they would drop in to hear him. It didn't matter whether he was telling true stories or not; the lies were only harmless ones. People used to pass the time happily with him this way.

Now I should give an account of Hector, Angus's son. He too was a very sociable man who could read Gaelic and sing songs and was good at learning them. He could pick up songs extremely quickly. When he came on a house-visit people would make him start singing songs, and perhaps he would sing three songs that you had never heard him sing until that occasion. That's how fast he was at picking them up.

We were always good friends and knew each other well. Many's the time we consulted each other about things; one would ask the other what his interpretation of such and such a word was or how we should translate it. And during the last few years when I would come into possession of books I would lend them to him so that he could spend some time reading them. He used to attend the meetings of the Gaelic Society and it was a great pleasure for us to have him. He would tell short, funny little stories at every meeting. He could make anyone laugh who had the sense or a taste for humorous anecdotes. I was sorry when I lost his support – when the time came for him to depart from this brief world.

34   *The King of Egypt's Daughter*

There was once a young man in a certain part of the world
and, since employment was scarce and work could not readily
be found, he decided one day that he would go down to the
pier to see if there were any sailing vessels in hopes that he
would be able to strike a bargain with a captain. And it
happened that there was a sailing vessel in at the time, so he
went to talk with the skipper of the vessel and was hired on.
He was to stay on the vessel for a certain number of years –
some years and a day – and a wage was settled, conditions
were agreed on, and when they were ready they sailed.

And however many years he sailed, when that number of
years and the day had passed, the sailor said that his tour was
now completed and that he wished to leave. Well, the skipper
was unhappy to see him leave because he had been so good on
board, but he would not oppose him. But he asked him how he
intended to leave now that they were out at sea.

"If you give me," said the sailor, "the longboat with a sail, a
compass, and a little food to put on board, I will be able to sail
right from here." So everything was fitted out and the sailor
was given his wages, and he took leave of the skipper and the
others on board and set sail.

Whether a storm arose or he went off course, whatever
happened, he sailed for a time until he reached an island; I'm
certain that he did not know at the time that he was on an
island. He landed and beached the boat, pulled it up, and went
walking around. He climbed up in the mountains, noticing
then that he was on an island, and he saw a hut on the other
side of the island and made his way down to it. When he
reached the hut he beat on the door and a young woman opened
the door and looked at him.

"Isn't it an unlucky thing for you," said she, "to arrive
here!"

"Yes, indeed," said he. "And what is the reason for that?"

"The reason," said she, "is that this is a sea-pirates' lair.
The ship on which we were sailing was caused to founder and
they took everything that was on her and took me along with

the rest. All the others on board were put to death, and they sent the ship down to the bottom. I'm the King of Egypt's daughter and I'm being held a prisoner here by the three pirates. Right now they are out at sea, but when they return you are not going to be at all safe."

"Well, be that as it may," said he, "I'll stay here until they return."

Whether the passing time was long or short, one of the pirates came down to the hut and saw the man sitting inside and asked him where he had come from. The sailor replied that he came off a wrecked ship which was torn apart in a storm, and that he had been fortunate enough to cling to a piece of wood that was floating on the surface. He had kept hold of it and was driven around the ocean until at last he came to rest on this piece of land.

When the second pirate came home, he questioned him, and the sailor gave him the same story that he had told the first pirate, and when the third pirate arrived he had the same story for him. So they agreed that since he had come to them in those straits he could stay. So one of them said that they were going out to sea to plunder and that he was to stay on land and to walk the shores to see what he would come upon there.

"And we have," said he, "a rule here on this island: the man among us who does best during the week becomes lord or king of the island until someone else does better than he. And whoever does, the title goes to him."

The pirates took off on the ocean, and he was going around on the shore and I'm sure with what he had hidden – the little bit of money that he had – when they returned home in the evening, he had gathered more along the shore than they had out on the ocean. And by virtue of this it was agreed that he would become king of the island for the week.

So they continued going to sea and he remained on land. But one day he began thinking that the time was right; he had begun to reckon the length of time they were out at sea, so he said to the young woman that it was time for them to be taking off. They got ready, though she wasn't at all eager to take this opportunity in case they might be captured, but at last she agreed to go. They were only a very short distance out to sea when they heard the stroke of an oar, and when they looked the pirates' boats were coming after them. Well, she began crying and lamenting, saying that they were now worse off than they had been before.

"Never mind," said he, "we are not lost yet."

And before the pirates caught up with them they entered a bank of fog and he put the boat onto another course; he changed course when he entered the fog patch, and they could no longer find him. But the young woman was even worse off once they entered it; now they were lost and she thought they would never get out. He told her not to worry at all about finding their way out and that he would continue on course with the boat.

Whatever length of time they sailed, they reached a seaport. He brought the boat into the wharf and went up to an inn to spend the night there. They intended to stay there until they could see whether they would find a chance to go to Egypt. Anyway they went to the inn and engaged rooms and, as they were on their way up to their rooms, they noticed a corpse hanging up there. The woman took to yelling and crying loudly.

"It was bad enough," said she, "to be with the pirates, but isn't it terrible to be with murderers now?"

"Never mind," he replied. "I will find out the meaning of this before we go a step further." He went down to the proprietor of the inn and asked him what was the meaning of the corpse hanging there.

"Well," said he, the proprietor of the inn, "it is always the custom in this town – it has been the rule for some time – that the body of anyone who leaves this world with debts is to be hung in the inn for so many days as a visible example to those passing back and forth so that they will be sure to settle their own debts before they leave this world."

"And," said the sailor, "would it be permitted or regarded as correct for another man to pay those debts off?"

"Oh, yes indeed," replied the innkeeper. "That would be all right."

"Well," said he, "we will take it upon ourselves to pay the debts that this man has incurred, whoever he may be."

"Very well," said the innkeeper. "I will send for the merchant to come here tomorrow morning and we will settle the matter."

They retired that night and on the morning of the next day the merchant was sent for and arrived at the inn. The sailor asked him what debts were owed by the man, the merchant told him, and the sailor agreed to pay them. "Very well," said the merchant, "I am well satisfied."

So the sailor settled the debts owed by the poor man and sent for a grave-digger and told him to clothe the body and to give him a gentleman's burial, and that he would pay the costs. That was done, and however long they stayed in the town, he would go down to the wharf daily to see if there were any sailing vessels coming around. One day a great sailing vessel came in and he went to speak to the skipper. He found out from the skipper that they were about to sail, and he obtained passage to Egypt on the vessel, mentioning that there was someone accompanying him. And that was all very well; they were to set out on their journey the next day.

He and the King of Egypt's daughter went down to the wharf, and when the skipper of the vessel saw the girl, he thought that he ought to recognize her. He went down to his own room where he had a picture of the King of Egypt's daughter, and sure enough it was she. But he did not let on at all.

They went on board and set sail. But the skipper gave an order to one of the sailors on the vessel to throw him overboard at the first opportunity. It was not advisable for that sailor to challenge the skipper, but he conveyed to the other man what was supposed to happen, saying that he would not do what had been asked.

But in the end, Jack the sailor went overboard, and down he went. He caught hold of a connecting rope that was underneath between the boom and the bow of the vessel, and there he remained. And the story went around that the sailor had fallen overboard, and when she heard the news, didn't the girl take to screaming and complaining, but the skipper told her not to be upset at all.

But the boat became becalmed. It was not moving – there was a dead calm – and Jack was seen swimming alongside the vessel. Right away the skipper gave the order to throw him a rope to try to bring him aboard. And sure enough he managed to grasp the rope and came aboard quite smartly. So that was settled. But one night when he and the skipper were up on the top deck keeping watch the skipper saw his chance. The ship was tacking back and forth and on one of her tacks across the skipper gave Jack a shove and out he went into the sea. He knew then that there was malice behind the skipper's actions so he did not attempt to return to the vessel; he struck out from it, calling out to the skipper, "I will be in Egypt before you."

And he kept on swimming. Whether the time was long or short, he kept on at his own pace until at last he gave up. He couldn't swim any further; he was just trying to stay above water as best he could. It looked as if he had just about given up completely, lying on the surface between two waves.

"Is my plight not a pitiful one!" said he. "All the big waves I have surmounted during my time at sea, and now it seems my lot to sink down between two of them right here."

Then he heard a blow or a noise as if from a boat, and when he looked, there was a black longboat beside him and a middle-aged man sitting at the oars. "It seems to me," said the man, "that you're in a fix."

"Oh," replied Jack, "I am in a fix. My time has come."

"Oh, I don't know," replied the older man, "that your time has come yet. If you were to make an agreement with me," said he, "I will take you safely to a harbour."

"It is difficult for me to make a deal with anyone in my present circumstances."

"Well, if you promise to do what I ask of you, I could see that you were at a harbour in time."

"Well," replied Jack, "how can I promise something that is neither there nor within my power?"

"Well," the man replied, "the promise I am asking is to give me your son on the day that he is three years of age."

"It is difficult for me," said Jack, "to give someone my son or my daughter at any age since my life is at an end and I have no wife, son, or daughter."

"Well," the older man said, "if you promise we will see about the rest."

So Jack got into the boat and stretched himself out on the deck, so exhausted that he fell asleep. And however long a time he slept or however long their journey took, at last they reached Egypt. They came into port and Jack was there a number of days before the skipper landed. He had found employment and was working at the shore around the wharf when the big vessel came into harbour. The King of Egypt came down with his servants and they went down to the wharf and the skipper of the boat came in with the king's daughter and she was received with great pleasure.

"I see," said the king, "that you have found my daughter."

"I have," replied the skipper.

"We will go up now," said the king, "to the castle, for there are agreements to be kept. I promised that whoever should find my daughter would have her in marriage."

"May I," said she, "say a few words?"

"Yes," replied her father. "You have my permission to speak at any time at all."

"This is not the man who found me. I was found by the man you see working over there."

"Oh, indeed. We would require some proof of that."

"There can be no such thing," said the skipper.

"Oh," said the king, "we must settle the matter somehow."

"Go over there," said she, "or call him over here, so that he may give you a little of his life story, and you will learn that things are different from what you believe at present."

The man was called over and was asked where he hailed from and the way the world had treated him, and he began telling his story, I believe, from the time he went on the sailing vessel until he was thrown off the vessel by the skipper. When the King of Egypt heard what had been done to him and all the rest, he ordered that the skipper be shackled and deprived of his freedom for the rest of his days, and that the sailor be taken to the castle, and that he be dressed in garments suitable for a person of his quality. A great wedding was arranged, and Jack and the King of Egypt's daughter were married.

But, with the passing of time, she grew heavy with child and gave birth to a baby boy and there was much more happiness and rejoicing. But time passed and passed swiftly, and soon the period of three years had run its course. And the day arrived at last when the young lad was three years of age. The older man came around; he knocked on the door, was invited in, and entered. When the older man had been sitting inside for a while, the sailor told his wife the conditions to which he had agreed in order to save his own life while he was at sea.

"Well," said she, "hard as it is, a promise must be fulfilled."

So the lad was brought to the older man. And he lifted him up and placed him on his knee and said, "You have been as good as your promise, which promise has been fulfilled tonight. It is in fact a long time since you paid me."

"I don't understand," said the sailor, "how I could ever have paid you."

"Oh," replied the older man, "you may remember when you were at the inn and took down the corpse that was hanging from a rope and gave it a respectable gentleman's burial and paid off the debts. Now the lad is going back to you as he should. And he has my blessing that every good fortune will meet him and the rest of you."

And there you have the story that I heard about the sailor and the King of Egypt's daughter.

35   *The Fair-haired Doctor*

This tale concerns a doctor whom they used to call the Fair-haired Doctor. It was related that he had more talent or learning than many other doctors and that he could see – so they believed – through people's bodies.

And there was a young woman singing a song at a frolic or a

milling or some gathering, and somebody told the doctor that this woman had a sweet, melodious voice. He replied that sweet indeed was the voice coming out over a frog. But what did that mean?

So the story finally came around, I am sure, to her parents and something had to be done about it; the doctor had to prove that this was so. So he told them that he could do this if they gave him the opportunity he required. According to what he said this involved water with salt added. The drink was made so strong with salt that it was barely potable. The girl had to take some of this and was not to take a drink or anything else for some time, perhaps for twelve hours after that.

The doctor himself arrived and I believe that he knew the proper time. There was a basin or a vessel of milk in front of the girl and she was to keep it there. Finally the frog came out of her mouth and went down to the milk, and the doctor snatched up the basin immediately. The frog jumped out of the milk trying to return to where it had been, but the doctor was too quick for it and it was prevented from getting back into the girl's mouth.

The doctor took the frog home with him. I believe that it had a vessel at the kitchen end of the house where it would swim in the water and so on, and it used to go around through the house. But one morning as they were having their breakfast a crumb of food – whether it was a piece of boiled egg or whatever – fell on the floor and the frog ate it and died.

The wife was sorry about what had happened, that the food had dropped off the table, but he himself was pleased to find out what caused the death of the frog.

And there you have the tale told by Angus MacMullin concerning the Fair-haired Doctor and the frog that was lodged in the young girl's body.

36   *The Bad Mother's Daughter*

As the tale had it, there was a farmer who was quite well off and he had three daughters. A man came courting one of the daughters and married the oldest one; another man came and married the next oldest. Finally a young man came along and it seems that he was warned that the other daughter was pretty hard to get along with; she was fairly independent. So an agreement was made and the marriage was performed, and when they were going home he had his dog with him – he had a good horse and the dog was with him – and he asked the dog to do something that he knew the dog could not do. And when the dog did not do it he shot it. They continued along the road until they came to a river and he asked the horse to leap across the river and the horse could not jump it. He tried and the horse would not go across it, so he told her to come down from the horse's back – they were riding double on the horse's back – and she was not going to come down at all.

"Well," said he, "if you are not coming down willingly you're coming down against your will."

So she dismounted from the horse's back and he said to her, "Take the saddle with you."

And she was not going to take the saddle with her at all. He told her that she had better take it while she had time so she took the saddle off the horse's back and he shot the horse. They kept on until they arrived at a bridge or a place where the river was narrow and she asked him what was wrong. She said that what she had seen seemed very strange to her.

"Indeed," said he, "and what seemed so strange to you?"

"It seemed strange," said she, "that you shot the dog when it was doing no harm."

"And didn't you hear me asking it to do something that it didn't do? It didn't do as I asked, and it was the same with the horse. I asked it to do something and it wouldn't do it for me. And since it would not do as I asked, it was of no use to me. And that is the way things always are for me."

So they went home and in the morning when the day dawned and they were awake he said, "Put on your pants," said he.

"No, I will not," said she.

"Very well," said he, "if you don't put them on today, remember not to ask for them again."

And things continued that way.

One day their father-in-law sent for them. They were over
visiting at his house and he called the three men down to the
room.

"Now," said he, "I am going to lay down some conditions
for you, but you have to give me your solemn oath that you
will not say a thing to your spouses. You are to be here one
year from tonight – the three of you along with your wives.
And the one of you whose wife is most obedient will get a
reward. But don't let your wives hear anything about this
during the whole year."

So the year passed and they came visiting, the three men
and their wives, the old man's three daughters. And he took
the men down to the room where they talked while the women
went to play cards over at the table – the three daughters
playing cards with their mother. The old man kept an eye on
things now and again, and when he saw that the oldest of the
daughters was arranging the cards to deal them around – she
was shuffling them at the time and getting them ready to deal –
he said to her husband, "Call your wife."

So her husband went to the door. "Come on down here,"
said he.

"As soon as I deal the cards," she answered. And she dealt
the cards out and went down and asked her husband what he
required.

"Oh," said the old man, "never mind now. It's over."

So the old man was keeping a good sharp eye on things, and
when he saw that the second daughter was getting the cards
ready to deal he signalled to her husband and he went to the
door.

"Come here for a moment," said he.

"I will," said she, "as soon as I deal the cards." And she
went down to them and asked what was going on.

"Oh," said the old man, "never mind right now. Let it pass."

The old man was keeping his eye on things and when he
saw that the youngest daughter was getting ready to deal the
cards he signalled to her husband and her husband came up to
the door and called to her, "Would you come down here a
moment?" said he.

She threw the cards down on the table and she jumped up to the room where they were sitting.

"What business did you have with us?" said she.

"Oh," said he, the old man, "I am the one who has business with you and here is a reward of twenty pounds. You are the most obedient of the three men's wives, and the most obedient of my three daughters."

And there you have Angus MacMullin's story concerning the gentleman's three daughters.

37   *The Lad, the Girl in the Cradle, and the Ring*

Angus MacMullin told a tale concerning a young boy who went to a house where there was a young baby girl in the cradle who was squalling and crying at the time. It seems she was only very small. And the boy said that he thought that if he were to have that kind of woman in marriage when he came of age he would drown himself. And an old woman who was present spoke, "Never mind my dear," said she. "This one may be your spouse yet."

After this, with the passage of time, as the girl grew up he used to see her fairly often, but he had no wish at all that the prophecy be fulfilled. One day as they were taking a walk down the road they came to a bridge over a river and he took a ring from his pocket. He showed the ring to the girl and said to her, "Take a good look at this ring so that you may recognize it again."

And he threw the ring into the river. "And don't let me see your face again until you have the ring for me."

So he set out and went somewhere to find work.

The girl went to earn her living with some people and wherever they were living they were close to a fisherman's place, whether it was a river or a lake or whatever. But anyway they caught a fish – it was a trout or a salmon it seems – and she was to clean the salmon, take the insides out, prepare it, and cook it for their dinner. When she split the fish down the front she felt something in its stomach. To be sure she cut its stomach to see what it was, and what was it but the ring, and she recognized it.

She kept the ring safe, and whether a long or a short time elapsed she saw the man coming up to the house where she was working as a maidservant. And when she saw him coming she took herself off to her room and went to bed apparently ill. But when the man came to the house the host said to him in the course of their conversation, "Well," said he, "a strange thing happened here when you were coming up to the house. Our maidservant became sick and took herself to bed, whatever it was that happened and affected her so quickly."

"Indeed," answered the man. "Would it be any trouble to you if I were to see her?"

"Oh, it would be no trouble at all for you to see her," replied the man of the house. "She's down here in a room."

When he went down there he looked at her and recognized her.

"I believe," said he, "that I asked you never to show your face or countenance until you had the ring for me that I threw into the river. And now you did not conceal your face."

"Well," said she, "go over there to the little drawer. Pull out that little chest and give to me the handkerchief that is inside, and then you will know how things stand."

He went over and gave her the handkerchief and when she had opened the knot in the corner of the handkerchief she extended the ring to him.

"Here," said she. "Isn't that the ring?"

"So it is," said he. "I see now that there is no way that we can be separated; what was meant to be has happened."

And the outcome according to the tale that MacMullin told was they were wed a short time after that. They were happy and contented for the rest of their days and led a long, happy life.

38   *The Widow's Son and the Robbers*

There was once a widow with three sons. Things were growing scarce, including game, but one of them had to go out hunting and so the oldest one set out to hunt. But the weather was so rough that he returned; he had to come back home. Then the second son went out but the weather was so adverse that he also returned home. But the youngest son said that he would go and he would try anyway. Oh, they kept telling him that he need not bother; since they had failed he shouldn't even take the trouble. But the youngest son set out.

He took a bow and a number of arrows with him – I am sure that he filled the quiver with arrows – and set out. He travelled and travelled, and even though the weather was bad he entered the great forest where there was some shelter for him though there was no game to be found. But he continued travelling and travelling and still he came across no game. Finally night descended and he was so far from home in the forest that he thought he had better stay where he was. Even if he tried to return he would only get lost and perhaps would be in danger. So for fear that wild animals would come upon him sleeping he climbed a large tree. He took the bow and the quiver of arrows and stayed up there among the thick branches.

After a while he heard talking – people talking – and three big robbers appeared with a quarter of meat which they were carrying between them; one of them was carrying it and another had a big pot. And very close to where he was, at the base of the next tree, they kindled a fire. They made a big fire and sat around in the warmth of the fire and the pot was hanging and boiling. The quarter of meat was cut up and put into the pot; they were going to have a big feast. One of the robbers asked the other to see if the meat was close to being cooked. And as he extended the fork and took a little piece of meat from the pot and was just about to put it up to his mouth, the lad in the tree shot an arrow and knocked the fork from his hand. The robber turned to the one next to him and scolded him, asking why or what made him do that kind of thing. The other answered that he had done nothing. But after a while the big robber asked this one to try the meat to see if it was cooked yet, and he replied that he would not, that the other one should try it. So the second one tried it. He put the fork into a small piece of meat and raised it and just as he was going to take it up to his mouth and taste it to see if it was cooked the lad sent down another arrow and knocked the fork from his hand. So that robber began to scold the other robber, asking what possessed him to do such a thing. And after a while the big robber told one of the others to try the meat again to see how it was coming along – whether it was nearly cooked. But the other did not want to try it at all.

"Well then," said the big robber, "I'll try it myself." So he put the fork into the piece of meat and raised it, and just as he was about to put it toward his mouth the widow's son sent down another arrow and knocked the piece of meat off the fork.

"I see now," said the big robber, "who was responsible for this foolishness." And he looked up.

"Aha," said he. "There he is up above. Come down," he said, "and do not be afraid."

"No, I will not," said the widow's son. "I'm safe enough where I am." And he remained up there with his quiver of arrows.

"Come down," said the big robber. "I see that you are extremely skilled with a bow. So come down to eat something with us and I think that you will suit us very well. We need you and I think that you will be very suitable to us."

So he came down out of the tree, taking his time, hungry after being in the forest all day. He descended and sat with them at the fire. Oh, they told him not to worry at all; nothing was going to happen to him. When he saw the big men coming he did not know who they were or what kind of men they were, but he hoped he might have some sort of fun at their expense.

"Now," said the big robber – he seemed to be the leader of the robbers – when they had eaten, "What we need you for," said he, "is your skill with the bow and arrow. We know that the nobleman has chests of gold and silver in the cellar and we have no way or means to get in there to steal them. He has a little black dog with a white spot on his chest."

He said that the white spot was just a shade larger than a shilling coin and that was the only way to kill the dog, that the spot on his chest had to be hit.

"And I think," said the big robber, "with your skill with the bow that you could do it. So you will travel with us."

The widow's son had no choice but to go with them. But he did not let on a thing and I am sure that he was watching out for himself too. But surely he had heard that a large reward had been offered by the nobleman to catch the robbers – to do away with them. They were doing a lot of damage throughout the kingdom.

So they set out from there and when they approached the nobleman's residence everyone had retired. But the dog ran a short way toward them and I believe that the lad went ahead a little while the others remained further back. And when the dog was coming towards them after hearing the noise they made, the lad released an arrow, and it hit the white spot on the dog's chest and the dog fell dead, and it happened that it did not awaken anyone in the castle. They crept up to the castle as stealthily as they could and when they arrived there was no way or means to get in under the castle: the place was girded about completely; there was no hatch nor doorway nor any other opening the could enter. There was nothing for it but to begin digging with their swords, and so they dug; they took turns digging, making a tunnel through which they could enter. When the hole was big enough so that the lad thought that he could manage to squeeze in he told them to stop and he would try to see if he could get in. He managed to get inside and no doubt the tunnel grew narrower the farther it was dug in.

When he got through he told them to send in a sword so that he could dig from the inside. And so it happened: a sword was given to him and he began digging from the inside and after a while he said to the smallest, "See now if you can get in."

So he tried. "Oh," said the lad, "the tunnel is still too narrow. You had better leave it until I dig out some more."

And then he said to them, "Now try it."

The other one tried again and the widow's son saw that he could get through so when he got in far enough the lad cut off his head. He dragged the robber into the cellar and put him to one side, and when he began digging again he told the next one to try. The tunnel was almost dug out enough so that the next one could manage it, and after he had spent a little time digging away with the sword he told him to try now. The next one came in and he managed to get inside far enough so that his head too was cut off. So the lad dragged his body in and put it to one side. Then he told the next one to stop a while until he was sure that the space was big enough for him to enter. And when the big robber's shoulders were through the lad cut his head off and left him there.

Anyway he stayed in the cellar for the night, and in the morning the first person awake noticed that there was no trace of the dog; none of the usual barking or anything. And someone looked out of the castle window and saw a pile of dirt on the ground. And where did that pile of dirt come from? What would leave that there? So out they went and looked and there was a man stuck in the hole in the cellar wall below and a big pile of earth out on the hill. They had to go and see what was wrong; it seemed that the man was not alive. And when they descended into the cellar, there was the widow's son sitting there, probably on one of the chests of gold or silver or in some such place. He was sitting there anyway or perhaps he was even asleep at the time. But when they went over to him he told them everything that had happened. He told them how he had killed the nobleman's dog even though he was sorry to have done so; how he had thought to him-self that if he managed to kill the dog and the robbers got to the cellar that he would then be able to kill them in the way he had and that was his reason. Oh, the nobleman forgave him right away for killing the dog even though it was a fine dog. And he had performed such a great deed; those three great brigands who had done so much damage throughout the countryside had been done away with and the country was safe and free of their plundering for good. And the nobleman gave the lad a big reward for doing so well, and found out from him everything that had passed. Then the lad's mother was sent for and his two brothers, since they were so poor in worldly possessions. They were sent for to come and work as servants for the nobleman. And the widow was to stay in the house – she was to have a room of her own – and the widow's son was given the nobleman's daughter in marriage. It was agreed that he would have half the estate as long as the nobleman was alive and that the whole property would be in his name when the nobleman departed from this world.

And that is what happened to the widow's son who was so skilled with the arrow and slew the dog and the robbers.

39   *The Golden Bird*

There was once a king or a nobleman – we'll say that he was a king – who had an orchard or a large garden which contained a large number of trees. And there was a certain tree there on which grew apples that were different from any other apples to be found. When one of the apples on the tree would ripen it would become a golden apple. The king or nobleman used to go out to look at the tree quite often, and one evening when he went out there was an apple on the tree which by the next day was going to be ready and ripen into a golden apple. But when the morrow came the apple had been plucked from the tree. There was another apple on the tree that seemed about to be ripe and was to be picked on the next day, but when that day came there was no sign of the apple. This aroused the king's anger, and he required that a vigil be kept over the orchard to see who was coming to steal the apples. One of the king's sons – the oldest – went out that night to keep watch over the garden, and at midnight he grew sleepy and fell into a deep sleep. When he awoke in the early morning the apple had been taken and his father was not at all pleased with that course of events.

Soon another apple was about to ripen and someone had to go out that night to keep a watch over the orchard. The king was displeased that the oldest son had not done a good job the night he had kept watch and he would not allow him to go out again. So the second oldest son said that he would keep watch. But he fared just as the first one had: at midnight he grew so sleepy that he fell into a deep sleep and when he awoke at daybreak the apple as usual had been taken from the tree.

Another apple was about to ripen on the tree and they feared that this one would be stolen along with the rest. The youngest of the sons said that he would keep watch and see what was happening, and I am sure that they were fairly reluctant to let him out. When the two oldest sons had failed, what would he accomplish? But they agreed finally to let him, since he could do no worse than the others.

So he went out to the orchard to keep watch and the night passed slowly. It reached midnight but he stayed awake and heard the flapping of wings. He looked and there was a great, magnificent bird flying towards the tree, and down it came and snatched away the apple. Before it was able to go any distance he loosed an arrow and struck the bird, but he did not bring it down and he did not kill it; he just knocked a feather out of its tail or wing. He observed where the feather landed and he picked it up and took it home with him.

At daybreak he arrived home with the feather. The king looked at it – he examined the feather and turned it every which way – and agreed that if he had the bird from which the feather came it would be as good for him as if he had all the wealth in the world; the feather that came from the Golden Bird meant that the rest of the bird must be like that.

So it was decided that the oldest son would set out to see if he could discover where the Golden Bird was. So he readied himself and set out, and on his journey he approached the edge of a forest that bordered the road where he was walking and a fox came out. And he raised the gun to fire at the fox and the fox addressed him: "Don't shoot me. Spare my life and I will give you some timely advice."

But he paid him no heed. And the fox said to him, "When you reach such and such a town you are to go to the little dark inn; you will not go close to the big inn where there are many lights."

"And what would you know, you ugly beast?" said the lad and he fired the shot, but the fox was moving at the time and he did not hit him. The fox disappeared into the forest and the lad continued travelling on his way. When he reached the town he did not remember the fox's advice, and even if he had he would not have heeded it. But he went to the inn – the one full of light and brightness – and he stayed there and I am sure that if he had a good deal of money when he set out he spent it. He did not move from that place; he forgot where he was going. He had been warned at the beginning that if he went there he would forget where he was going and would lose interest in his journey.

So when the king and his sons finally accepted the fact that the oldest son was not going to return, it fell to the second son to undertake the journey. And when he was on his way, who came out of the clump of woods but the fox. And the lad raised his gun to fire at him but the fox asked him to hold; he would give him some useful advice which he would do well to follow if he intended to succeed. The fox told him that when he reached the town and saw a dismal-looking inn with hardly a light to be seen at all to go inside, but not under any circumstances to go to the big, well-lit inn or he would lose interest in his quest.

"What would you know about that," said the lad, "you ugly beast? How would you know about that?"

And he raised the gun and fired the shot, but the fox had moved and he did not hit him. The fox disappeared into the forest and the lad set out. And when he reached the town the big inn was full of lights and looked so fine that he went into it. But he did not go near the little dark inn at all and he was not long there – I am sure that they were drinking and carousing – before he forgot where he was going and lost interest entirely. But he had wearied of the whole matter anyway.

Then the youngest of the lads said to his father that he would like his father's permission to set out.

"I am sorry enough as it is," said his father, "to be missing my two sons without your going off, young as you are. And however insignificant you may be, it's a shame for all of you to be lost to me."

"If you give me permission to set out," said the youngest

lad, "I will do so. And if the Golden Bird can be found I will find it."

So off he went and when he came to the place on the road and approached the clump of woods the fox came out of the forest.

"Don't fire at me at all," said the fox.

"Oh," said the king's son, "do not worry that I will fire at you. I would not be so ill disposed as to fire at a fine-looking animal like yourself."

"Well," said the fox, "I will give you some advice. I know where you are going. You are setting out to look for the Golden Bird."

"Yes indeed," answered the lad.

"Well," said the fox, "I will give you some advice. When you reach such and such a town go into the small dark inn where there is only very little light to be seen. But you are not to go at all close to the big inn that is full of lights. But you still have a long distance to go. The distance you must walk is so long that it will be a long time before you arrive there. But if you get on my back I will take you there in a shorter time than it would take you to go on your own."

So the lad climbed up on the fox's back and they set out and the fox went up and over hills and down hollows. He went so fast that the lad's hair whistled in the breeze. Late in the evening they came to the outskirts of the town. The fox stopped at the edge of the forest.

"I can go no further," said the fox, "lest the hunters see me. You keep on and remember my advice."

So the lad set off for the inn – he passed the big inn with its shining lights and made for the little dark inn – and he went in there and spent the night. Early in the morning he arose and went on his way and continued travelling to the place where the Golden Bird was. He had not gone far when the fox met him again.

"Oh," said the fox, "there is a great distance before you today. But first I am going to give you some advice. When you reach the place where the Golden Bird is to be found you should hire on with the king to take care of birds. And when you get your chance, and the house and everything is quiet, there is a golden cage and a wooden cage on the table next to the place where the Golden Bird is kept. You will put the Golden Bird in the wooden cage and take that one out under your arm. Unless you do this it will be the worse for you; you will not get the bird and perhaps you will not get out alive. So get on my back and I will take you that far in a shorter time."

So he got up on the fox's back and off they went. The fox travelled so swiftly over and down hollows and up hills and on the level ground that the lad's hair whistled in the breeze. They arrived close to the king's abode and the fox said, "I must remain here. If I go outside the forest the hunters will see me and my life will not be safe. Remember the advice that I gave you."

So the lad went to the king's palace and obtained employment and it was his job to take care of the birds. When he found the house quiet at midnight and everything and everyone had gone to sleep, he went into the room where the Golden Bird was. There was the Golden Bird with a wooden cage and a golden one on the table. He looked at the golden cage and it looked so splendid. And he thought that it would be ill fitting to put a bird as splendid and beautiful as this in a cage made out of sticks; he thought he should put it into the golden cage. And no sooner had he put the bird into the golden cage than the bird let forth a terrible cry and everybody in the castle woke up and down they came and he was caught before he got out of the room. They threw him into some sort of prison that night. His trial was scheduled for the morning and it looked as if he were going to get the worst possible treatment. But anyway he was brought to court, and since he had tried to steal the king's bird he was to be put to death. But the king said that he would grant him clemency on one condition.

"Since you are so bold and smart that you came to steal the Golden Bird, perhaps you would do something that I require. And if you accomplish that, I will give you the Golden Bird. I desire the swift steed belonging to a certain king. That steed is so swift that he can catch the swift March wind but the swift March wind cannot catch him. If you bring that horse to me by the bridle I will give you the Golden Bird."

So he set out and the fox met him. "Well," said the fox, "you did not take my advice."

"No I did not," replied the lad. "I believe that had I done so I would not be in this trouble."

"Well," said the fox, "I must show you clemency yet another time although you have done as you have done. And this time I will give you more advice. When you go to the king's castle and hire on there, your job will be taking care of the horses and you will see how everything is done. The swift steed is kept inside in the stable and there is an old, rusty bridle in there and there is also a golden bridle. You will put the old, rusty bridle on the horse. Do not put the golden one on him for if you do it will go none the better for you."

So they went off at great speed as before with the lad on the fox's back and the fox travelling over hollows and hills and level ground. He travelled so fast that the lad's hair whistled in the breeze. When they arrived close to the king's palace the fox stopped and said, "I must remain here without leaving the forest lest the hunters see me. Keep my advice in mind."

The lad kept on to the king's palace and sought work as a servant in charge of the horses. And he saw how everything was done there, and I am sure that the king had more than one stable-boy in his service. But at midnight, when he found things quiet and everybody asleep, he went inside. The horse was there and he put the saddle on it. But he thought as he was going to put the rusty bridle on it – such a fine, beautiful horse – that it would be a slight and an insult to put the rusty bridle on the horse, and so he put the golden bridle on instead. And when he did the horse let out a neigh which nearly shook the stable, and they all woke up. Before he could escape from the stable he was caught by the other stable-boys and the guards and put in prison that night and sentence was passed on him in the morning. He was sent to his trial in the morning and the king ordered him to be put to death.

But then the king thought perhaps that should be changed and said, "Although I am condemning you to death, perhaps I will extend you clemency. Since you were so smart and so bold as to have attempted to steal the steed, perhaps I might be able to use you. I desire the daughter of a certain king in marriage, and if you succeed in bringing this girl to me, the horse will be given to you as a reward."

So off he went. He went some distance and the fox met him. "You did not take my advice," said the fox.

"Indeed I did not," replied the lad. "Certainly if I had I would not be in this situation."

"Then I must forgive you once again, it seems," said the fox. "But we shall be on our way. And I am giving you advice in the beginning, so keep it in mind. When you go in you will be in the king's house and you are to avail yourself of whatever chance there is. And when midnight comes the king's daughter will enter a room to wash and comb her hair before she goes to sleep. And when she is passing you on her way to the door of the room go up and give her a kiss. And there is no way in the world for her to refuse you from then on. You will say to her that you wish her to go off and marry you and she will be perfectly willing to go. But, if she asks your permission to take leave of her father and her mother, tell her that there is no time to do that. For if she does it will go none the better for you."

So the lad went. He was in the king's palace and he had been hired on as some sort of servant. He kept an eye out and when he saw the king's daughter going to wash and comb her hair before she went to sleep, he caught hold of her and gave her a kiss just as she was coming out of the door to the room. And the king's daughter was not able to say a word about it, but if he asked her to marry him she would have to agree and that was all there was to it. He said that he wanted her to marry him. She replied that she would do so but added that she would have to take leave of her father and her mother before departing. Oh, that could not be – there was not time for that – but she began to beg and entreat him and at last she was almost weeping about leaving the castle without taking leave of her father and her mother. At last he agreed that was certainly the proper thing and when she went inside to see her father the people in the castle awoke. He was captured and thrown into prison and tried in court in the morning and a death-sentence was passed. But the king said to him, "I would give you the girl on one condition, if you are able to fulfil it. And if you cannot you will pay with your head."

"I would like to hear what task that is," replied the lad, "before I am to be killed at least."

"Well," said the king, "there is a mountain over there facing my house and it spoils the view from the castle. I could see out over a great portion of the kingdom from that castle window except for the mountain being there; it spoils the view of the whole country for me. And all who have tried to remove the mountain – to knock it down – have failed and have paid accordingly. And that is what is going to happen to you."

So the lad retired, and three days, I believe, was the time given to him to do this. So he began shovelling away at the mountain, and I am sure that as he was shovelling at the mountain the mountain was probably growing bigger. Things were going from bad to worse for him, but on the second night the fox approached him and said to him, "You did not do as I asked you!"

"Indeed not," replied the lad. "And if I had I would not be in this fix."

"That cannot be helped now," said the fox. But the fox began working and in the morning at daybreak the mountain was levelled and there he was shovelling. I am sure that every time he threw one large spadeful away that a good many others followed it. The mountain was levelled down so low that you could see over it from the window in the king's castle. And now the king handed over his daughter to him.

Soon they were under way on their journey.

"Now," said the fox, "the king who wants this maiden in marriage will give you the fine, valuable horse which was desired by the king who possesses the Golden Bird. But you will hand over to him the king's daughter and the king's daughter will be standing outside when he gives you the golden horse by the bridle. So when you get the golden horse by the bridle, hand over the king's daughter to him. And," said the fox, "be prepared and try out the horse to see how good it is and as you pass by, snatch up the girl and put her on the horse behind you and no man in the kingdom will be able to catch you. And I will be parting from you here since we are close to the king's palace."

And so it happened. He came with the king's daughter to the other king to deliver her and said to the king, "I have brought you the princess. And she will be handed over to you when I have the horse by the bridle."

"So it will be done," said the king, and the horse was brought out of the stable and the bridle was put on it and it was handed to him. He was going to try out the horse to see how good it was and it gave a sudden spurt of speed and he snatched up the princess and off they went and they could not be caught with the swiftest horse in the kingdom.

He went on his way then and the fox met him after he had gone some distance.

"Now," said the fox, as they were approaching the place where the Golden Bird was kept, "you will leave the king's daughter here at the road. She will stay around where I am. And you yourself will go down to the house with the horse and the king will give you the bird. You will place the bird in the cage and put it on the fencepost – the gatepost – and leave it there while you give him the horse by the bridle. Then say that with his permission you would like to try out the horse around the castle so that he can appreciate its swiftness. The king will be pleased by this and as you pass by you will snatch up the Golden Bird and there is nothing in the kingdom that will catch you."

And so it came to pass. The Golden Bird was brought out and the lad said, "If you please, I would like to make a circuit to try out the horse for you so that you can appreciate its swiftness."

"I would be most willing," said the king.

So the lad leapt into the saddle – the Golden Bird had been put in a cage on the gatepost – and off he went around the castle and as he came by he snatched up the bird, travelling at such a pace that there was not a creature in the kingdom that could catch him. And he kept on going until he reached the place where the girl was – she and the fox – and he lifted her up behind him on the horse's back.

"And now," said the fox, "I have three pieces of advice for

you. The first is do not spend two nights in the same house under any circumstances. And do not take anyone off the gallows – do not buy anyone from the gallows. And do not sit beside a well or a deep pit of any kind." And the fox took his leave of the lad.

The lad reached the town and they spent a night in a certain place, but they would not spend more than one night there and set out the next day. But the lad saw a fearful bustle in the town, a crowd gathering and everybody appearing to be in a hurry and excited when they arrived. So he asked what was happening there. Oh they said that they were going to hang someone today for a crime of some sort that was committed – or for an accusation made against the man for a theft. And the lad thought he would go and see how things were progressing and he saw the man that they were going to hang, and inquired whether the man could be bought off the gallows. Oh, yes indeed. If the fine were paid, the man could be rescued. So the lad paid the fine and his brother was freed and they set off for home.

But on the way home they grew tired and were obliged to rest a while.[1] And what did he do but sit beside a deep pit somewhere like an old well, and when they had been there for a short while one of them saw his chance and they gave him a push. Down he went into the pit and the others went on their way. The princess had to remain silent; it would do her no good to say anything anyway.

When they reached the king's palace the king asked what had happened to their brother and one of them replied that he had fallen over a cliff or into a pit or somewhere or other.

The king was sad that his son had not come home, but there was nothing he could do and the times were not very happy. The horse would not eat its food and the bird would not sing and the princess was very sorrowful – not a word could be gotten out of her.

But anyway we'll leave that as it is for now and return to the poor man who was thrown into the well. There was nothing in the pit but mud and slime, but at least there was no water there to drown him. And there he was with no way out; he could not get out. But presently the fox came.

"You did not take my advice," said he, "and now you are in a bad state."

"Yes indeed," answered the lad. "Now I am done for."

"Well," said the fox, "perhaps you are not altogether done for yet. It seems I must help you once again for you were kind to me."

The fox went down – he lowered his tail as far as it would go – and the lad grasped the fox's tail. By climbing up the side with his feet he managed to get out of the awful pit.

"And now," said the fox, "there are people searching the forest for you. Your brothers are fearful that you may not have been drowned and that one way or another you escaped. Some of their soldiers or guards are out searching for you, and you must be very careful."

So he continued on, taking his time and he met some sort of beggar who was travelling around trying to get rags of clothing, perhaps, or some small assistance from people he met and all he wore at the time was rags and tatters. He was poor indeed.

"What would you ask," said the lad, "for giving me your clothing?"

"Well," said the beggar, "old and poor as I am, if you are making fun of my clothing, it would be little enough for me to take this stick to your back."

"I'm not making fun of your clothing at all," replied the lad. "But I have a special need of it. I will give you my own clothing in exchange and will pay you well in addition."

So they exchanged clothing and the lad donned the beggar's clothing and gave his own to the other man. He gave him a fairly good payment for it and I am sure he warned him to keep out of sight for a while lest he be seen. And he set out, for he doubtless had a good distance to travel.

And at the king's palace they noticed that the horse began to eat. And the bird began to sing a little as a bird should. And the princess regained her cheer and began to look happy, saying that the man who had rescued her was still alive and must now be on his way.

After a time a pathetic-looking tramp approached the dwelling. He reached the house – they didn't suspect him of being anything but a poor beggar approaching the house – and he was allowed up to the house. When he reached the house she recognized him and told his father, and indeed the father recognized him once she had told him that it was his own son. He recognized him, particularly when he had a good look at him, though the lad was dressed in rags. And the other two brothers were driven away – perhaps they were sent to an island, or he intended to put them on an island. But I believe the lad gave the order to extend them a reprieve; he asked his father to leave them alive and in the kingdom, but they were to be servants and live as ordinary servants.

So he was dressed – a fine, elegant suit worthy of a prince was donned – and a great wedding-feast was arranged. He and the king's daughter were married and there was a big wedding; it lasted for some time.

But a day or two after the wedding he was walking down to the shore and the fox met him.

"Now," said the fox, "you must kill me."

"That is something I could not do," the lad replied.

"But you must," said the fox. "If you don't I am lost; it is better for you to do as I ask. When you kill me you will cut off my four paws and throw the carcass into a pit and the paws on top."

So he did that and set off for the castle and to be sure he was very sorrowful over what he had done; it was troubling him greatly. But he heard someone calling him and he stopped. He turned around and there was a fine-looking young man there, a handsome man.

"I am the fox," said the young man.

"Is it you?" said the lad.

"Indeed it is," he replied. "I am the fox and I am also the brother of the princess who is married to you. I was put under spells and turned into a fox. And that is why I wanted you to win my sister in marriage."

The young man was indeed a gentleman and was highly regarded in the kingdom along with the rest of them.

And that is the tale as I heard it.

Angus MacKenzie

Angus MacKenzie (Aonghus Sheumais Mhurchaidh Bhàin)
belonged to the MacKenzies who came to Christmas
Island Parish. He lived for some time over in Johnstown
at the place of a Donald MacNeil (Dòmhnall Sheumais 'ic
Eòin 'ic Dhòmnhnaill Dhuibh). His grandfather's sister – a
sister of Murchadh Bàn as far as I can determine – was
married to this Donald MacNeil (Dòmhnall Sheumais) and
that was the reason he lived with them for a time. He was
staying with them when I heard the story I have recorded
here.

Years later, when he had returned to Christmas Island,
married, and raised a family, I went to his house to see
him. He remembered visiting at our place and got the news
from me of the country over there and the people he had
known particularly well. And he began giving me small
accounts concerning things that had happened when he lived
there, and we continued to go to visit him from that time on;
whenever we got the chance we would go over to see him.
He was an extremely cheerful man and very witty. He always
had the right answers and he could turn things around so
easily.

He was married to a MacLean, one of the MacLeans descended
from Calum Òg. There was one of the MacLeans I did not
mention at all when I spoke of John, Neil, and Alexander.
They had a brother by the name of Archie (Gilleasbuig
Chaluim Òig) who settled over in Christmas Island Parish. It
was from these people that MacKenzie's wife was descended.
I believe that she would be a great-grandchild of Archie
(Gilleasbuig Chaluim).

40   *The Soldier Who Was Refused a Drink of Water*

There was a soldier travelling the road and he arrived at a house. And it seems the people were very stingy in that house. The soldier requested a drink of water – I am sure although that is all he asked for but that he hoped for more if he could get it – but when he asked for the drink of water the man of the house told him that there was a stream down the road where he could get his drink. The soldier thanked him and assured him that when he reached water he would recognize it.

So he left the house and did not go very much farther down when he arrived at another house. He went up to that house and asked if he could have a drink of water and they told him to come in; he would certainly get that and perhaps he was more in need of food than he was of a drink, although a drink was all he asked for. He thanked them and said that without any doubt he was fairly in need of food, and so he entered and got a drink of water and food was given to him. He was well received and invited to stay a while with them; he must be tired travelling and had better spend some time there and at least recover from his fatigue.

He stayed a few days in that house and I am certain the people over in the other house were very curious as to what was going on. And he asked the people he was staying with what sort of people were over in the other house; they said that they were very stingy, people without much charity at all. He told them that they had refused him a drink of water and that it had not pleased him at all – the man had been soldiering for a long time – to be refused a drink of water.

But so great was the curiosity of those people concerning the goings-on, as they constantly speculated about what was happening in the other household where the soldier was staying, that they finally tried to find out. And there was an old woman with them – whether she was his mother or hers or whoever she was, she was there – and they put her into a big chest and took it over to the house in which the soldier was staying. They said that they were going on a journey somewhere and wanted to leave the things that were in the chest – they were valuable – in the house lest something happened to them while they were away. Their neighbours were happy enough to do that for them and the chest was brought inside.

It seems that the soldier harboured some ill-will against them for what they had done, and he said that he was going to investigate the contents of the chest. Oh no, that would not do; the chest that the others had sent over was not to be opened. Oh, he said that he would open it, that it was no trouble for him to do; so he opened the chest and inside was a little old woman with cakes of cheese in there beside her. The soldier took a piece of the cheese and crammed it in the old lady's mouth and shoved it down her throat and the poor old lady choked to death.

On the morning of the following day the others returned offering the excuse that something had happened and that they were not going on the journey as they had expected. Some problem came up; the people they were going to see were away, or some silly reason. Almost any excuse would serve in that situation anyway. They took the chest home with them, and when they opened it, intending to find out so much, there was the old lady dead inside. It occurred to them that they had made a mistake in not putting water or milk in the chest for the old woman, that she had choked eating the cheese.

So then word was sent around that the old woman had died and a wake was prepared, but I am sure that the soldier did not go near the wake-house at all. But when the wake was finished the old woman was buried, and the soldier said that he was going to exhume her. And oh, no, that would never do. But he said that he was going to exhume her; he was not finished with those people yet.

So he dug up the old woman and set her upright – I believe down at the gatepost was where he set her first. Her family did not understand what had been done, but they sent for their neighbours to see what they would say about it.

When the neighbours went over they claimed no knowledge

about what had happened unless the soldier knew, the stranger who was with them. Oh, he said that he could not say anything for sure except that they had not spent enough on the wake, that they should have paid out more for the wake. So there was another night's vigil and more was spent on people around.

The old woman was buried once more, but the soldier was still not entirely satisfied with the matter and he said that he was going to exhume her. And oh, no, said his hosts, certainly they would not do it; would it not be better to leave her alone now? But he said that he would exhume her; he was not at all satisfied that they had gone to enough expense yet. So he exhumed the old woman and this time he set her up at the barn door. When they arose the next morning, there was the old woman at the barn door. So they went over to their neighbour's house once more. Oh, the soldier said, the cause was still the same as far as he could understand: not enough expense had been laid out for the wake. So there was a wake one more night as the man had said, and I am sure that the old woman was growing rather odoriferous for all the time they had kept her.

But she was buried and the soldier said on the next day that he was going to exhume her again that night. So he dug up the old lady and put her in at the stable door. Soon word came to the house where the soldier was to go over. He went over to see what was going on; they said that the old woman was inside the stable and that they intended to leave – to go away – but that none of them had the courage to bring the mare out. The soldier said that he would bring out the mare, and I am certain that he asked a good deal for this too. So he brought out the mare, the harness was put on her and she was hitched to the wagon, and off they went.

And when they had left he let out the filly and bound the old woman on the filly's back, and when the filly neighed the mare gave an answering neigh. So out went the filly when she heard her mother's call and away she went. Meanwhile the others were going down the road with the horse and wagon, and when they looked back the old woman was coming after them riding the filly. And they hurried the mare so much, not taking note of where they were going, that they finally went down a slope and fell into a pit. And I am sure as the expression has it, that they broke their necks and were killed in the pit. And I am sure also that the old woman was buried and did not arise again.

And that is how the soldier got the best of the people who were so stingy to him that they would not give him a drink of water.

Joe MacLean

Since I have given the history of the MacLeans at Middle Cape and Irish Cove, I should now give an account of the MacLeans who lived at Christmas Island, one who moved to Big Pond. Some of them moved all over Cape Breton Island, and among them was Joe MacLean (Eòs Pheadair Chaluim Ghobha). Calum Gobha (Malcolm the Smith) was the son of Alexander the Big Smith, and apparently Alexander the Big Smith went over to Cape Breton and his son Malcolm – he was called Calum Gobha – raised a family there. When I was over in the Gàidhealtachd in Scotland I met one of the MacLeans who was a great-grandson of Michael the son of Alexander the Big Smith. And Michael MacLean son of Joe (Eòs Pheadair Chaluim Ghobha) is a great-grandson of Calum Gobha.

In any case Joe MacLean was an extremely cheerful, happy man and an exceptionally good raconteur of short stories. I was always happy to be with him. He was married to a MacPhee woman from Big Pond, a daughter of Mìcheal Nìll Dhòmhnaill, descended on her mother's side from the Campbells and the MacDonalds.

41   *The Shirt of the Man without Worries*

This is a story about a rich man in a certain part of the world, who was ill for a number of years. He went to every doctor in the surrounding cities but could not get cured.

One day a young doctor came to a nearby town. Upon hearing about him the man prepared himself and went to see the doctor. After the doctor had made a thorough examination of his condition he said that there was one cure; if it could be found it would probably cure him. And the rich man said that if it could be found he would like to obtain it. So the doctor told him if he would put on the shirt of the man without worries, it might cure him – if it could be found.

So the rich man hired two servants who he felt would be very faithful to undertake a journey to obtain the shirt of the man without worries. They travelled and visited many parts of the world on their travels, but they met with no success at all. But, finally, one day as they were going along the road they saw a middle-aged man sitting outside beside a little shanty of a house who appeared to be very cheerful. So they went up to talk to him, and the man was extremely cheerful and friendly. They spent some time questioning him, and one of them asked him whether he had any worries. Oh, he said that there was nothing worrying him at all, and why should there be?

"And are you certain," said one of them, "that you have no worries?"

"Oh, I am very certain of that," replied the man. "Why should I worry? Don't you see the lake down there close to the road? It is full of fish; we get fish every time we go out on it in favourable weather. And don't you see the plain of farmland surrounding my place here? We take crops from here as good as we wish for. There is no seed that we plant that does not grow abundantly and fruitfully. So why should I worry when matters are so secure?"

"Yes indeed," said one of them. "We are very pleased that we came upon you. We are looking for something and remember that we don't expect to have it without paying for it. We will pay well for it regardless of the price."

"Oh," said the man laughing, "I don't have anything to sell you at any price at all."

"Well," replied one of them, "we wish to buy your shirt. We require it for our master and whatever the price is we are willing to pay it."

The man let out a great burst of laughter. "Well," he said, "it is difficult for me to sell you or anybody else a shirt when I don't wear one. I don't wear a shirt at all."

So they departed: they took leave of the man and were very

heavy hearted returning after all the travelling they had done over the world to find the man without worries and finding that he possessed no shirt. They returned home, and went to the rich gentleman, and told him what had happened. He was pleased that they had returned, and when he asked whether they had found the man without worries they said that they had.

"Well," said he, "did you bring me his shirt?"

"Oh," said one of them, "it would have been difficult for us to bring you his shirt. When we asked the man for his shirt he laughed and said that he did not possess one."

"So," said the rich man, "that man had no worries and he did not have a shirt at all."

"Yes indeed," said they.

"Well," said the rich man, "if that is so, I will have no further need of the shirt of the man without worries. And now I understand what use that was to be to me."

And the outcome for the rich man was that he let his worries go and began to distribute his wealth to other people until finally he had no worries at all.

And that is how the story ended from Joseph MacLean.

John MacNeil

John MacNeil was the son of Dòmhnall Dhòmhnaill 'ic
Iain 'ic Iain. His father also used to be styled Dòmhnall Mór
Nìll Mhóir because it seems that his father Dòmhnall mac
Iain 'ic Iain died very young. And as for John's mother Sarah
(Mór Nìll Mhóir) she was styled Mór Nìll Mhóir 'ic Iain 'ic
Lachlann Ghobha. So John MacNeil's mother was a daughter
of Neil MacLean (Niall Chaluim 'ic Iain 'ic Lachlainn Ghobha).
And I believe that there was an inherited capacity that was
passed down and that made them so good at telling stories; or
perhaps they were just good at it anyway.

John MacNeil was a good singer with a strong, clear voice.
He was also an extremely nice fiddler and a very competent
one. I heard him play at dances and I heard him play when we
were sitting in the house just passing the time. Often we would
enjoy ourselves listening to his funny sayings and listening to
him imitate people. He and I were so friendly that he would
call me "my brother Joe" and I would call him "my brother
John." That's how close our friendship was.

42   *The Young Lad Who Quit School*

This is a story I heard from John MacNeil more than fifty
years ago. It concerns a little boy who was going to school.
And one day at school it seems that some of the bigger, stronger
boys were mean to him and tore his clothes. When he came
home he said that he was not going to school any more but
was going to set out to seek his fortune.

So after travelling for a long or a short time he came to a
gentleman's house, and the gentleman welcomed him and

asked him who he was. He answered that he was a young lad
looking for a master. And the gentleman said, "Well, you're
the kind of servant I've been looking for to help me with
various things. Are you good at caring for horses?"

"Yes I am. I could care for horses well enough." So he hired
on with the gentleman.

But one day the gentleman said to him, "We should go out
and hunt for a while today. Are you good at hunting?"

"Oh," replied the lad, "I don't know how good I am but I
think that I could do a little hunting anyway."

They arrived at a place where the road forked in two[1] and
the gentleman said to him, "You keep on down that road and I
will continue on the other road. In the evening we will return
and meet here. Whichever one of us comes back first will just
have to wait until the other one arrives."

And so it was and they went off.

The gentleman returned in the evening, having found no
game at all on the road that he took. It seems that game was
very scarce. But he had been waiting at the head of the road –
where the road forked in two – since he returned and it was
getting late and there was no sign of the lad. But then he saw a
dark spot[2] some distance down the road approachng him. And
when the dark shadow came up to him, what was it but the
lad covered in game – dead animals and birds, I am certain,
that he had shot. The gentleman was indeed pleased with that
and he was proud of the servant who had hired on with him.

The lad continued taking care of the horses and he was very
good at feeding and currying and maintaining them. He was so
good around everything that finally the gentleman agreed to
send him to the bank to fetch some money. So the lad set out
toward the bank and withdrew the money from the bank, and
when he was on his way home a robber met him – a highway
robber – and demanded that he give him everything in his
purse. The lad was not at all willing to do so but the robber
put a hand on his pistol and said, "Unless you hand over your
purse I'll take your life and the purse too."

The lad threw the robber his purse and continued on home.
He related what had happened and the gentleman was pleased

that he had reached home alive and had not been killed on his way back.

So a day or two later the lad said, "I am going to take with me the worst horse from the stable."

"Where are you going?" said the gentleman.

"I am going to the bank."

The gentleman said to him, "You had better not go anymore. Perhaps you will not be safe travelling to the bank. The robbers may kill you."

"Oh I will try anyway," said the lad, "just to see how I fare." He set out with the worst horse in the stable and the robber met him on his way.

"Where are you going to today, my fine fellow?" said the robber.

"Oh," replied the lad, "I don't want to tell that to anyone."

"Well," replied the robber, "it wouldn't do you much harm to tell me."

"All right," said the lad, "perhaps it wouldn't. I am going to rob the gentleman's bank."

"Indeed," said the robber. "And when you are on your way back will you be returning by this road?"

"Oh, I'm sure," said the lad, "that this road is just as good for me to take as any."

He set off toward the bank and he got a small sack at the bank and I am sure that he went out and got small pieces of glass and clay shards and the like and filled the bag with these to make it appear full of money. He was returning in his own good time when the robber met him.

"Well," said the robber, "you've returned."

"Oh, yes I have," replied the lad.

"And did you manage to rob the gentleman's bank?"

"Oh, I was able to get a good deal out of it."

"Well then," said the robber, "hand over your purse."

"Oh," said the lad, "I had not intended to do that at all."

"Well, you had better," said the robber, "if you want your life to be safe."

The side of the robber's horse was to him and he had an excellent horse at the time. So the land threw the sack which supposedly contained the money into a hollow filled with thistles and brambles and stickers.

"There you are, go get it."

The robber dismounted from the saddle and down into the hollow he went into the brambles and spiky branches and everything else. And the lad leapt onto the back of the robber's horse and took off home and left the old horse where it was – a horses which was not much use.

He returned home to the gentleman's house with the horse and the gentleman said, "Where did you find the horse?"

"Oh," replied the lad, "I got the horse from the robber. This is the horse that belonged to him. I threw the bag of money down into the brambles and he went down after it so I leapt into the saddle and I took this horse and left him the old one. I made sure he couldn't catch me anyway."

"Well then," said the gentleman, "I believe we will keep this horse until he comes for it. But it's unlikely that he will come at all."

But when they were taking the saddle off the horse it puzzled him that the saddle was fairly heavy. So they examined the saddle and the money that had been stolen – the robbers had met the lads who were taking money from the bank for the gentleman and had been waylaying them for a long time and robbing them – and the money was stashed in the saddle. So the gentleman got back all the money that had been stolen from him over a long time. And he couldn't let the lad go any more but he kept him with him and he was a servant to the gentleman from then on. In any case I never heard that he went to work anywhere else from that day.

And there you have the story that I got from John MacNeil.

Mrs Michael MacNeil

She was a Campbell woman (Anna nighean Dhòmhnaill Iain Dhiarmaid) married to Michael MacNeil (Mìcheal Ruairidh 'ic Iain 'ic Eachainn Bhàin).

Michael MacNeil's wife was an extraordinary woman. She was a midwife who used to travel throughout the country in those days, and it seems that she was prosperous and happy in her profession. She had a good singing voice and a large repertoire of good songs. As for mouth-music, she was a very accomplished singer; it didn't matter whether she was just reciting the words or singing them to a tune. She was exceptionally good at it.

43   The Little Old Man with the Grains

Here is a story that I heard when I was just a small boy. I was only about ten years old when I used to hear a woman telling us a story concerning what they used to call "The Little Old Man with the Grains." And I saw the tale years later in a book, and it was an ear of corn that the man got, seed. But in the tale told by the old woman that we learned, it was seeds of grain.

He was going to town or on some errand and left the grains at a house. He asked the people there to watch the grains until he returned, whenever that was or after however long a time. And when he returned they told him when he asked for his grains that the hen had come in and had eaten them.

"Well then," said he, "I'll take the hen."

"Oh no, no," said they. But he scooped up the hen and went on his way.

Soon he reached another house and left the hen there and asked them to take care of it until he should return to fetch it after a time. Soon he came back to fetch the hen, and when he asked for it they told him that the cow had walked on the hen's leg. She had broken her leg and the hen had to be done away with.

"Oh well then," said he, "I'll take the cow."

"Oh no, no," said they. But he took the cow and off he went.

He arrived somewhere else and left the cow there and told them to take care of the cow until he should return for her. However long he was away, when he arrived back and asked where the cow was, they told him that the daughter had taken it down to the stream to have a drink and the cow had slipped and fallen on the ice and broken a leg and they had to do away with her.

"Oh well then," said he, "I'll take the daughter."

"Oh no, no," said they. But he snatched up the daughter, and put her in a sack and set out with her. And he was travelling down the road, and the ending in the book was that as he was going down the road he got tired of carrying the sack – the daughter was fairly heavy – so he let the sack down onto the ground and went into a public house or somewhere to have a drink or catch his breath or whatever. And when he was inside someone came around and the sack was opened up and the daughter was taken out. And the weight of the daughter in stones was put into the sack. And whoever it was took the daughter with him.

But he came out and he took the sack and he was getting so weary of carrying it that when he reached the shore of the lake he threw the sack that he thought contained the daughter out into the lake.

And there you have the tale of the little old man with the grains.

44   *The Fox, the Wolf, and the Butter*

The first time I heard the following story was from the wife of Michael MacNeil (Mìcheal Ruairidh 'ic Iain 'ic Eachainn

Bhàin). And the next time I heard it was from Hector
MacMullin, son of Angus MacMullin, who also used to tell
me stories. Even though there was a slight difference between
them in the way the story went, both were quite similar. So I
am going to recite the story as I remember hearing it from
Mrs Michael MacNeil. I was only very young when I heard it.
I think I was no more than twelve years old or so.

The story was about a fox – whatever Gaelic word you prefer
to use – and a wolf, as they are often call it.[1]

It seems one day as they were walking along the shore they
found a container of butter – perhaps the kind of container
that could be called a tub – and they hid the tub until they
could find the time to take it home and divide it.

The next day the fox heaved a sigh. "Oi oi," said he.

"What, what?" said the wolf.

"My godparent is asking me to a baptism," said the fox,
"and I must be on my way." So off he went, and it seems that
he took a good part of the butter that was in the tub. When he
returned home in the evening the wolf asked him what name
they had given the person they were baptizing.

"Under the Lip, Under the Lip," replied the fox.

So they retired that night and the next day or the day after
the fox heaved a sigh. "Oi oi," said he.

"What, what?" said the wolf.

"My godparent is asking me to a baptism," replied the fox.
So he set out and when he returned home that evening the
wolf asked him whether they had performed the baptism and
the fox replied that they had.

"And what," asked the wolf, "did you name the person?"

"Under Half, Under Half," replied the fox.

So they retired. But a day or two later, or perhaps on the
following day, the fox heaved another sigh. "Oi oi," said he,
"my godparent is asking me to a baptism."

He set out that day, and when he returned late in the
evening the wolf asked whether they had performed the
baptism and he replied that they had. Now the answer that
Hector MacMullin had to the question of what the name was
was "All Licked Up, All Licked Up." But "Scrape the Bottom,

Scrape the Bottom" was what Anna MacNeil had in her story.

And the following day or the day after the fox and the wolf set out for the place where the butter was hidden, and the container was empty. Now what could have happened to it? The fox expressed surprise over what had happened to the butter, since nobody knew that it was there except for the two of them. Now they would have to try to prove which one of them had eaten the butter, and they decided to do this by building a big fire and sleeping beside the fire. Whoever had eaten the most butter, the butter would come through him one way or another. And there they were stretched out beside the big fire, and of course the fox was the guilty one. But he found butter somewhere and rubbed it on the wolf so that the blame would be transferred to him. And to be sure, a sentence for the crime had been determined – agreed on – beforehand and the fox had said what was to be done to him if he were found guilty. That sentence was not very great anyway, but the sentence passed on the wolf was a heavy one: a good part of his skin was to be flayed off.

So when they awakened the wolf was found guilty, and the sentence was carried out according to their bargain.

But the wolf started travelling around, and one evening when the fox was coming home he caught a fish somewhere; he had gathered up a string of fish that I believe he had stolen from someone. The wolf met him and asked him where he got the fish, and the fox replied that he caught them down at the river. The weather was cold at the time and he said he had put his tail in the river and that the fish started coming up and making for his tail; but he had to remain there for some time. The wolf was hungry so he went down himself; he put his tail into the river and there he remained. Finally his tail froze in the river and he thought there were a large number of fish attached to it, so he gave a yank that was so violent that he took off the end of his own tail.

And that is where the story ended concerning the fox, the wolf, and the butter.

Neil Campbell

Neil Campbell was an outstanding fiddler. He used to tell a few stories and antecdotes that he gave to me. I believe also that he was considered to be as sweet a fiddler as they had in his area for a number of years.

45 *The Journey Boban Saor Made with His Son*

I used to hear various stories about Boban Saor and about his family. A good many people had short stories about them. And I heard a story about Boban Saor and his son, about when he told his son one day that they were going on a journey and to get ready. And his son asked him where they were going and he answered that they were going to travel until they reached the place where water ran uphill.

They started travelling – both of them riding the horse – and they went some distance until they came to a stream. I am sure that the younger man was looking around to see if he could see the place where water ran uphill. But as they came to the stream, Boban Saor told the lad to dismount to let the horse drink. The lad was standing looking at the horse and after a short while he said to his father,

"We can go back now."

"Why can we go back?" replied the father.

"Oh," replied the young man, "we have reached the place where water runs uphill. Look how the water is flowing up the horse's throat."

"That is true," said Boban Saor, and he understood that the lad was very clever.

46   *How Boban Saor's Son Found His Wife*

Now I got a tale from the late Neil Campbell – he recounted how Boban Saor's son found his wife. The old man told the son one day that he had better go with some sheep that he had there and wished to sell. "And you are to call out," said he, "whenever you see anyone at all out there, that you are looking for somebody to buy these sheep – part of the sheep – who will pay for them and give you back the sheep the next morning."

So the lad set out, and whether his journey was long or short, he came to a place where there was a young woman out at the side of the house and she had a tub – a washtub, as they say – up on a bench and she was doing the laundry. Oh, he was calling out that he was looking for somebody who would buy part of the sheep from him today and pay for them and return the sheep to him tomorrow. She called to him, "Drive them into the pen up there and come inside and get some food. I will buy part of the sheep."

So he went inside. He had some food and she bought part of the sheep from him and paid for them. But she said to him that he was to remain there until the next day, that he was too tired to return. So it happened; he stayed there and when he went to sleep she went out and sheared the sheep. And in the morning the sheep were ready for him to take back with him. She had paid for the wool before; she had bought part of the sheep, sure enough.

Anyway, he returned home with the sheep and the old man asked him now he had done, and he told him what happened.

"Very well," said he. "Now you are to set out tomorrow, and when you reach the place where she is you are to give her a marriage offer. And I hope that she will marry you."

And so it happened. Boban Saor's son set out and he reached the place where the young woman was. He gave her a marriage offer which she accepted willingly enough. And they prepared to marry. They returned home and there was a big wedding, and that's how he got the clever woman.

47   *Boban Saor: The Chalk Line*

When the son's wife and Boban Saor's wife were inside doing
housework, they were, I'm sure, spinning and carding, as
women were accustomed to do. The men were outside hewing
lumber. Perhaps they were going to build a ship or some such
work. But the old woman was twisting thread, and she threw
the spindle across the floor and the young woman rose and she
caught the thread.

"I think," said she, "if something like that were stretched
tight out on the top of the board with some kind of colouring
on it, they could snap it and strike the board with it and it
would make a straight line that they could see, instead of
their having to walk back and forth as I see them doing now
looking at the lumber as they hew it."

So the old woman called to her spouse to come inside, and
Boban Saor came in and she told him what the young woman
had said. And that was what they decided. They were to use a
string with some kind of blacking on it. And from this came
the work with a line which today is called in English "the
chalk line." And that is the story about the line.

Dan MacNeil

Dan MacNeil (Dòmhnall Nìll Eoghainn Mhóir 'ic Ìomhair) lived in Sydney. From him I heard part of the story that I have here about Boban Saor, as well as many more short stories.

48   *Boban Saor: Barley Bread and Milk*

I heard a tale or two about Boban Saor. And it seems that a son of his was married and that son's wife did not know Boban Saor at all – one of the sons was married and living some distance away from the old home. So Boban Saor came to the house when his son was not home. And it seems he complained that he was hungry and the young wife told him that she did not have any food to give him that was much good; she had only barley bread and milk. But he said that this food was good enough for him: there was yeast in the barley and honey in the milk. So she gave him the food and he went on his way.

According to the story as told by Kate Kennedy, Boban Saor was bending back and forth the way wheat or barley bends in the field as he talked to the woman. And when the son came home and his wife told him about the man, he understood who it was.

The story that Dan MacNeil tells has an additional part to it. When Boban Saor was travelling there was a small trickle of a stream and he made a trail in it with a stick – in a stream or a little pool. And then when he was walking past the horse he said to the horse, "You are now as you were last year."

And when he was going down past the field where the barley or wheat was, there was a small breeze blowing and the ears were bending this way and that and he was going with them the way they were bending. To be sure, the wife was taking this in, and when her husband came home she told him everything that had happened and he understood that it had to be his own father. So he went off down the road after him and caught up with him and they were talking and he was questioning him about the things he had done. And he asked what he had meant when he made a trail in the water with a stick. Oh, he replied that it was the same as a man who came to a place where there was no one inside but the woman of the house – that it might be very difficult for the man of the house when he returned home to know what had passed – and that was like the trail that he made in the stream; it was covered over. The son asked him then what he had meant when he said to the horse that the horse was as it had been the year before.

"Oh," replied his father, "I was speaking to the gelding. The gelding was as he was the year before. He didn't have a foal last year and he didn't have one this year."

The son then asked him what he had meant by bending this way and that just like the barley and wheat in the field.

"Oh," he replied, "that is how people are who cannot be relied on. They go this way or that way according to the story. They will give you one story now but then they can so easily switch over and give you a different story."

Roderick MacNeil

Now I should give an account of Roderick MacNeil (Ruairidh Iain 'ic Ruairidh Ruaidh). His mother was a Cameron, a daughter of Alexander (Alasdair Sheumais). Roderick was an extremely amiable, sociable man and he loved to listen to songs. He could tell stories, both short little ones and some that were fairly long. And he could hold forth on poetry. He knew things that the bards had said and was acquainted with some of the things that were found in the long tales, such as events in the Fenian tales. Now the call the Fenians used was known as the *Iolach Mhór*, and he used to say that he heard the *Iolach Mhór* from his wife when it was time for them to go to dinner.[1]

He was very accomplished at telling and remembering funny stories; he was exceptional.

49 *The Tub That Boban Saor Built*

This brings to mind another story about Boban Saor – he used to work at every kind of carpentry and he used to build tubs; he used to work at coopering. He put a tub down at the side of the road one day over a small hollow and hid underneath it, or concealed himself close by. When he had been there a short while, two men came down the road and stopped to look at the tub. One of them said that he had never seen a tub more neatly made than that, and the other said that it was very good indeed.

"I would say," said the first man, "if he were around at all, that it was Boban Saor that built it."

"I would say so too," agreed the other. "But it is a little too high – too deep."

And they continued down the road and out of sight. Boban Saor took the tub inside and cut a piece off the staves; he left the tub perhaps two inches lower. Then he put the tub back outside where it was before and concealed himself under it or close by. Soon two men came down the road and they were looking at the tub and praising it. One of them said what a fine tub it was.

"Indeed," said he, "I would say if he were around at all that it was Boban Saor who built the tub."

"Yes indeed," said the other. "Certainly enough. But don't you think that it is a little too low? I would say it is an inch too low."

"Perhaps it is," said the second man, and they kept on down the road. Boban Saor arose from his hiding-place. He took the tub inside the shop and went at the hoops with a hatchet, bursting them and letting the staves fall to the ground.

"It is only foolishness," he said, "for a man to think that he can do something which pleases everybody."

50   *Crazy Archie and the Hen*

It seems that Crazy Archie was a notorious character and a wanderer who was not wholly to be trusted. And I believe that he used to play bad tricks and good tricks according to his whim.

Anyway he may have been a little bit hungry one time when he arrived at a place and the man in the house – the man of the house – was sick in bed. And what was the woman of the house doing but cooking a hen at the time. So he entered the house and asked her what she had cooking in the pot. She replied that she was cooking a hen and that she intended to give part of it to her husband, that he was sick.

"Well," said Crazy Archie, "I am a doctor."

And he went over and examined the sick man.

"Cook the hen and give it to me," he said. "Don't give that to your husband at all if you wish him to remain alive."

So she gave him the hen. He ate his fill and said to her then,

"Well," said he, "the calf that is with the cow over there in the barn – kill the calf and skin it and put its hide over the man and let him out with the cattle. And if the cattle suffer him to be with them he will be cured."

And she caught on I am sure that he was playing a trick but anyway Crazy Archie went off. He returned to the sick man's house the following day or perhaps a little while after that with a huge bundle of biscuits and sweets and delicacies.

And that is the story from Roderick MacNeil about Crazy Archie.

Anonymous

51 *Crazy Archie and the Minister Souter*

There was a minister in the region called the Minister Souter, and it seems that people use to tease him. So one day Crazy Archie went to the Minister Souter's place and told him that he wanted money to obtain a pair of shoes. The minister went over and got a pen and paper and wrote down an order for him to take to the cobbler.

"Here," said he. "Take this letter to the cobbler and he will give you shoes."

Crazy Archie looked at him. "Oh," said he, "put your letter in a place I won't mention. Give me the money for the shoes."

The minister went over and pulled out a little box from a drawer there and brought back the price of the shoes. Perhaps they cost only two shillings or a little more at the time, but he gave him the money anyway. Crazy Archie thanked him and put it in his pocket saying, "The letter will get me the shoes and the money will get me some whisky to drink."

And there was nothing that the minister could do except to let him go.

Another time Crazy Archie came late one evening to the Minister Souter's place and he said that he required a bed for the night. The minister said to him – I am sure by then he was growing tired of his antics – that he would give him a place up in the loft, in a byre outside or some little outbuilding, whether it was a byre or a barn. That was good enough for Crazy Archie and he said to the minister as bedtime drew near – the minister praised the bed that he was to have, saying how good it was – Crazy Archie said to him if he was a gentleman he would show the bed to the guest. So the minister went and climbed up the ladder to show to Crazy Archie the bed which he was going to occupy, and when he had the minister up above Crazy Archie took away the ladder.

"Since the bed is as good as you say it is," said he, "shouldn't you be the one to sleep in it? And I will sleep in your own bed."

And that is how he got ahead of the Minister Souter.

52   *The Farmer's Big Lad*

I heard this tale many years ago. I don't remember at all whom I heard it from, but I do remember hearing it. Later I found it in English in a book, and it came back to me when I saw it. And when I read the story in English I recalled hearing it a long time ago in Gaelic, but I could not remember whom I heard it from. So I have made some effort to translate it from the English that was in the book and to put it back into the Gaelic as I heard it before, or approximately so anyway.

It seems that a certain farmer had a number of people working outside. One day a certain big lad came along who it seems was rather clumsy. He went back home to fetch a large pot of porridge to feed those who were working – the labourers – there and he was so clumsy that he spilled the contents of the pot on his way back so that they were without food for the whole day. When they returned home in the evening and the farmer asked how they had gotten along, they said only very badly, that they had been hungry. And that was when it became known that the lad had spilled the food he was bringing to them.

So it turned out that he had to leave; the farmer was not going to keep him any longer. He was only a liability because he could not get his work done. And so it was decided that he would go out to seek his fortune.

But the lad told his father that he required a big stick or staff to be fashioned out of iron or steel which he could take with him on his travels to defend himself. So his father went to the smith to get the staff made and the smith fashioned it for him. It weighed a stone, that is, fourteen pounds.

So when the father returned home he went to the lad with it. The lad gave it a shake and it broke, and he said that it would not do. His father returned to the smith and got the smith to make another big staff which weighed two stone. He returned with that to the big lad, but when the big lad gave it a shake it broke. Oh, he said, that would not do at all. The farmer had to go a third time to the smith, and this time the smith fashioned a big staff weighing three stone. When the farmer returned to the lad with that, he tested it and gave it a terrible shake but he only bent it well over. The lad said that he would not put his father to any more trouble sending him again to the smith; he thought that this would do. So he twisted the staff and straightened it out again and it was as good as could be. And he set off with that; off he went to seek his fortune.

But however long a time he was travelling and whatever distance he covered, he arrived at a king's or a gentleman's residence; and they greeted each other. The man asked him who he was and he said that he was a young lad seeking employment; he was looking for a master. And the other man inquired whether he would be willing to hire on as a herds-man and he said he would, that was the calling he most pre-ferred. The gentleman said he was pleased to see such a person coming around at that time; he was just setting off to look for a herdsman since he could not keep herdsmen on the place who would look after the cattle. The giants were taking them away – taking one of the cattle – and the herdsmen were leaving because of this.

He asked the lad what wage he would require and the lad replied that he would require ten guineas a year, and a half-boll of meal per week with whatever milk he would require for the porridge that he would make from the meal, and a little house for himself with a good, quiet bed. The gentleman said that that was a high wage indeed, but since he was in such great need of a herdsman, if the lad would tend his herds, it was worthwhile to give him the wage he required. So they settled on that.

The lad retired that night and on the next day he set out with the cattle. He kept on with them and entered the giant's realm. He drove the cattle in and they had excellent grazing there. He himself went up to the woods and began gathering sticks to build a fire. He intended to kindle a fire to cook his food. But then he heard a terrible sound like a storm and the trees were almost bending over with all the noise, and a big, fearsome giant approached and went right up to the cattle. And the giant began to scold the lad, demanding to know what brought him here, invading his own realm with the cattle.

"You do," said the lad, "frighten me. Take the pick of the herd and be on your way. You frighten me greatly."

The giant went over among the herd and selected the biggest and fattest and knocked her down and bound her feet. Then he called to the lad to come over and help him.

"I won't go," said the lad. "I am afraid of you. You frighten me."

"Don't worry," said the giant. "I won't touch you. Come over and give me some help."

So the lad went over to him and said to the giant, "Put your head there between the cow's feet where she is tied and I will help you get her on your back."

When he got the giant in that position he cut his head off with a sweep of his great staff. He simply hung the head on a tree and dragged the giant's body down and buried it in a pit. I am sure he covered it with leaves and weeds and various things, and late in the evening he returned home with the cattle.

When he arrived at the house with the cattle the king was there to meet him and inquired whether he had any news. And he noticed at the time that the lad had all of the cattle when he came home. Oh, the lad replied that he had no news at all; where would he get news and how could he have any to give? But he would not tell anything of what happened or what he had seen or the like and went right up to retire. And indeed there was plenty of milk from the cows that evening.

The next day he set off with the cattle, but he was not satisfied to remain where he had been the day before. He decided to take them further on, so they went another distance to the giant's domain. They were there for a while and the lad went up to the forest and began to break up sticks intending to make a fire to cook food for himself. And he heard a big, loud, frightful sound like a storm; the great trees were nearly bent over, and a big giant came in and went over to the cattle. The giant scolded him, saying what caused him to put the cows inside a place like this and asking him whether he had seen his brother the day before.

"I have not seen him," replied the lad. "I was never here before today. You frighten me. Take the pick of the cattle and be on your way."

So the giant took hold of the best cow in the herd and threw her to the ground. He bound her feet and asked the lad to come over to help him. But the big lad said that he would not, that he was afraid to go before him.

"Oh, do not worry," said the giant. "I will do you no harm at all."

So the lad went over and said to the giant, "Put your head inside under the cow's feet where they are tied and I will help put her up on your back."

The giant did so and when the lad had the advantage he took a swipe and took the head off the giant. And he just hung the head there on one of the trees and dragged the giant's body down and buried it in a ditch somewhere.

Late that evening he returned with the cattle, and the king was there to meet him as usual, asking him whether he had seen anything that day or had heard any news. No, he had not seen anything and what news would he get anyway? All he had seen was the forest. So off he went to his resting place as usual; he would not give the king any news at all. But the king was very pleased that all the cattle had returned and that evening they gave more milk than usual.

So the lad set out the next day with the cattle as usual, but he had grown a little greedy, so he kept on. He reached the domain of the third giant and put the cattle into the meadow and indeed there was real grazing for them there. He himself went up to the woods and began to gather sticks to make the fire to cook his food. He had not been there long when an extraordinary sound began: storm and mayhem. No such sound had ever been heard before around there, I am sure, or at

least for a good many years. And the giant appeared. And if the
other two were frightful and horrible, this one was really big
and rough. And he scolded the lad, saying to him, "You must
be the one who did away with my brothers."

"I have never been here before today," replied the lad. "But
you frighten me. Take the best cow there and be on your way."

The giant began walking around and the biggest and the
fattest cow that was picked before was the one that he got. I'm
sure the cow was growing tired of all that to-do – being thrown
on the ground and bound. But anyway he asked the lad to help
him put the cow up on his shoulder and the lad replied that he
would not go near to him at all; he was too frightened.

"Do not worry," said the giant. "I will not touch you."

So the lad went over and told the giant, as he had told the
others, to put his head in where the cow's feet were bound and
he would put the cow up on his back. When the giant did he
got his chance and took a swipe at the giant and took off his
head. He just hung the head on a tree and dragged the corpse
down and put it into a pit as he had done with the others and
covered it over with leaves and weeds.

Late that evening he returned home with the cattle as usual
and the king was there to meet him. The king inquired whether
he had any news today.

"No indeed," said the lad. "Where would I get news? From
whom would I get it unless it was the trees and the heather
and the grass? From whom else would I get any news?"

And the king asked him whether he had seen anything to
surprise or astonish him.

"I have not seen anything that would surprise me at all,"
replied the lad.

And the lad retired. He would not tell the king anything of
what was going on.

The next day he went off as usual with the cattle. He got the
cattle into a meadow there where they were grazing, and he
went off to find little sticks in order to build a fire. And then
he heard an extraordinary sound and he looked around and
there was a big, frightful old hag coming, and if the giants
looked tough she looked even tougher.

"Well, well," said the old hag, "you are the impudent one who did away with my three sons."

And she did not approach the cattle – she did not think of going over to them – but came over to the lad and the fight began. And what a fight it was! It must have been terrific. As they used to say,

> They turned the bog into a rocky place,
> And the rocky place into a bog.

And they continued that for some time. But finally the lad got his chance and broke her arms and broke her shins and she fell to the ground.

"Death is above you," said he. "What is your ransom for taking you out of your misery?"

"No small thing," she replied. "There is a chest of gold and a chest of silver and a chest of jewels belonging to me."

"Where are they?" asked the lad.

"They are," she replied, "under the base of the threshold to the hut at the cave where we live."

"Well then," said the lad, "I will put you out of your misery now." And he dispatched the old hag.

That evening he returned home. And when he did the king was not there to meet him as usual; things looked so strange there. He asked what was wrong and was told that there was a big giant with five heads coming out of a cave in the mountain. He was coming down and any time that he did one of the maidens in the kingdom had to be fetched for him and this time he wanted the king's daughter. If he did not get her he would come down in a day or two and destroy the kingdom.

Now it was hard for the king to part with his daughter but he preferred that to having the giant descend and harm the subjects of the kingdom, and so he agreed that the daughter should go. The big lad asked if there was anyone who would go to save her and the king replied that there was none save for one man – the Red Cook – who was going up to try to rescue her. He added that whoever could save her would have her hand in marriage, but gave the lad to understand that indeed he was not at all eager for the Red Cook to have her.

So the lad set out, tired as he was. He set out and climbed until he reached the giant's abode in the crag somewhere out on the mountain. When he arrived there the king's daughter was sitting on a flat stone, and she was very sorrowful. He asked if there was anyone there at all to guard her. She replied that someone had come with her to protect her, but that he was hiding somewhere behind a hillock; she was sorry that the lad had come after her for she knew he was tired and she liked him very much – although she had never shown it – from the first day that he had arrived; she very much enjoyed having him around.

It was not long before the giant came out of the cave and the big lad attacked him and finished him off. But if he did, he himself was wounded – I am sure he fell and a pointed rock caught him – and his arm was badly torn and he collapsed. He was so tired that he fell right to the ground. The princess tore a strip from the bottom hem of her cloak and bound up his arm and then she was forced to return home with the Red Cook. I believe that he took the heads that had been struck off the giant, but she had to keep quiet; at least she had to go along with whatever he said.

When they reached the king's abode, the king was very pleased that she was safe, although he had no use for the Red Cook. The Red Cook was in great haste for a marriage to be arranged – he wanted it to be performed immediately – and he was busy calling for a clergyman in order to perform the ceremony. But that could not be done; they had to take their time and put on a celebration and get things ready. So she told her father that it was not Red Cook who had saved her at all from the giant. But nothing could be done because they did not believe her and the Red Cook had made it all sound so true.

But there was a delay and she said she had a sign by which she could recognize the man who had saved her from the giant and that she had proof of this. The subjects of the kingdom began to gather but no sign appeared of the man who had

performed the deed. At last someone noticed that the big lad –
the herdsman – had not come at all, so he was sent for and
arrived – he was not at all happy but he came anyway – and
she was very hopeful that he would rescue her from those
straits as he had rescued her before.

Anyway, when he arrived they examined his arm. And the
strip that was tied around his arm, when it was taken off,
fitted the bottom of the princess' gown and there was the
proof that he was the one.

I am certain that the Red Cook was sent far away, unless he
was put to death. He had nothing to say anyway. And when
his fate was settled the marriage agreement was made,
followed by a big wedding and a celebration. They used to say
that the wedding lasted nine days and nine nights and that the
last day was the best of all.

And when that was over and settled the lad intended to take
the king over to show him how things were. They arrived and
he showed the king the three giants that had been put in the
pits, and the old hag, and he went over to the trees and got the
heads that were on them. Then he brought the king over to
the cave or the hut where the giants had dwelt, and underneath the threshold there was a chest full of gold and a chest
full of silver and a chest full of jewels. They took those back
with them to the king's domain.

And they were well-off and happy then; they were wealthy
enough. If the king was not rich in the first place he certainly
had wealth enough now. And that is what happened to the
Farmer's Big Lad; clumsy as he was, he did well in the end.

Part Three

WIT, LORE, AND PASTIMES

Repartee and Ready Wit

Dermot MacKenzie (Diarmaid Eòin)

There was a man called Dermot MacKenzie (Diarmaid Eòin 'ic Iain 'ic Alasdair) who was very, very witty with words. He had answers for anything at all that you might say to him. One day he went towards town[1] and as he was going by he stopped in to see a man who used to buy cattle; he had a heifer to sell him so he told the man how good the heifer was. You can believe that he praised it highly and, when the man came to his place to look at the heifer, it was standing over in a field. And the man went up to look at it and he said to Dermot that the heifer was not at all as good as Dermot had said it was.

"Oh, never mind," said Dermot, "you're only seeing the one side of it."

Another time he and his brother-in-law had a falling out due to some misunderstanding that arose between them and they stopped visiting each other. He wouldn't come to see Dermot and Dermot would not go to see him. But anyway that continued for some time until Dermot heard that his brother-in-law was sick – that he was extremely ill – so he went over to see him. And when he entered the house his brother-in-law was indeed happy to see him.

"God bless you, Dermot. What a long time it is since you darkened my door."

"Never mind, John," said Dermot. "Your own tether was just a short one."

They had a large field of oats and somebody set a fire outside. It must have been in the autumn – probably very late in the autumn and things must have been quite dry, or drier than one would think – and the fire raced over and kept on until it burnt the field of oats belonging to Dermot. Most of it was spoiled anyway. And somebody was asking him about the field, remarking that it was a great loss for the field to be burnt. Well, Dermot replied that that could not be helped; the fire was so fierce that it could not be helped. So the man said to him then, "I wonder if you had shaken some holy water on the field, perhaps that would have stopped the fire."

"Don't worry," replied Dermot. "Even if the whole River Tom were blessed and shaken on it, it would not extinguish it."

There was a man down in Hay Cove by the name of Michael MacNeil (Mìcheal Lachlainn 'ac Chaluim) and he used to tease Dermot to make him say something. But he couldn't get ahead of him. Even though he was a bard he was not witty enough to get one over on Dermot. Michael's face was bare but Dermot had a few wisps of beard. So Michael asked him one day when he met him – I think it was at the church where they met this morning – and he asked him, "Where did you get the bristles, Dermot?"

"Oh," said Dermot, "I got them from the pig. Did you miss them?"

Michael MacDonald (Mìcheal Raonaill 'ac Dhòmhnaill Òig)

There was another man by the name of Michael MacDonald He lived down at Middle Cape and he was very witty at repartee; he had a quick answer ready for anything.

Around the beginning of winter there was a big thaw and then a frost so that there was a crust of ice on much of the ground around. Then there was a little snowfall, only enough to hide the ice and not much more. And Michael was crippled; one of his feet was shorter than the other. But a few days before, they had been at the blacksmith shop with the horses to put sharp shoes on them that would be suitable for the ice in the winter. And now Michael was up on the side of the hill sending down sticks of dry firewood that were up there and what did he do but slip on the ice. And when he fell he didn't manage to get up again until he had slid down and struck the level at the bottom of the rut.

Hector, Hector MacNeil, was going past at the time.

"Well Michael, the day before when you were out at the blacksmith's with me if you had only gotten the smith to put a cleated horseshoe on your good foot, it would have served you well right now."

"If I had a cleated horseshoe on right now, my backside is where I would need it."

Martin MacInnis
(Màrtainn Ruairidh Dhòmhnaill Mhóir)

Martin MacInnis lived in a place called Glengarry at the Rear of Big Pond. Words came easily to him, and if you said something to try to get ahead of him in any way he had an instant answer.

One day he was returning home after being at the stores or, as they used to say, down at the shore, and he stopped at a house to visit. And sure enough he was not in any great hurry that day and he left the mare at the main road. When some time had passed one of the women – one who was always ready to say something anyway – said, "By God's truth, Martin. Do you have any sense at all leaving the mare standing up at the post the whole time that you have been in here?"

"Well," said Martin, "I hope you've noticed that I never taught the mare to sit in any place that I left her."

He and another man from the neighbourhood were talking one day and, however the matter got turned around, this man got ahead of Martin; he managed to get one over on him. But Martin never showed a sign of it. I am sure that he laughed, but he was waiting until he saw his opportunity. But towards the end of spring the breeze used to blow in off the salt water and onto the shore below, close to the shore where we were living, and especially where the road passed close to the shore at Big Pond. And Martin came into one of the stores and the other man was inside, the man who had given him the short answer some time previously. And Martin said, "I see," said he, "that you don't have much snow in here at all but there is quite a bit out where we live."

"Oh," said the other man, "that is how it always is. The snow always leaves sooner here where we are than it does out where you live."

"Oh, where we live the snow never leaves at all," replied Martin. "It melts on the ground."

Alexander MacIsaac (Sandaidh 'Illeasbu' Mhóir)

In days past some people used to go to market; they used to take a load of produce that they raised on their farms such as lambs and sheep and sometimes butter. Those were the items they would take to market, and they were very well acquainted with the people they saw on the way. They knew them so well; they used to pass so often. And there was a man by the name of Angus MacDonald (Aonghus Dhòmhnaill Aonghuis Mhóir); he was going past on his way to town one day and whom did he meet but Alexander. But we used to call him Sandy, the son of Gilleasbuig Mór. Anyway Sandy met Angus, and after they spent some time in conversation he looked over.

"Well," said he, "I never saw this horse of yours before until today."

"Oh," replied Angus, "that's a horse we raised ourselves."

"Indeed," said Sandy, "he's a very good one. But the horses that we always had on our own place, we never had to raise them. They used to get up on their own."

Angus MacIsaac (Aonghus 'Illeasbu' Mhóir)

When Angus had the forge down at Murdock's Point – it was to the east of Murdock's Point, Saint Andrew's Channel was the name we had for the place – people used to drop in on their way to town. And at the beginning of the winter there was a man going to town, Angus MacDonald, whom I mentioned before. There were soft spots on the road and the horses were putting their feet down into pot-holes, and whether it was a horse or a mare that he had it caught the heel of its shoe on the other shoe and pulled the horseshoe off and it was bent badly out of shape. So he stopped at the blacksmith's in a great hurry and threw the shoe inside the forge to Angus.

"Here," said he. "Hurry up. I am in a rush so you must straighten that shoe for me."

He went over to the wagon and was going over things that he had when he heard a terrible commotion in the forge and vigorous hammering. After a short time Angus came running out of the forge holding the tongs in his hands and a long stick of iron in the tongs. And what was that but the straightened horseshoe.

"Here," said he, "I think that is as about as straight as I can make it."

Angus had a lot of little lumps on his head about half the size of an egg or the size of a hen's egg cut in two. They were about that size and a large number of them on his head, and he used to go to a man that was down at Big Pond to have his hair cut. And one day he went there and asked the man if he would cut his hair. Oh, the man said that he would. That was Dougall MacPhee (Dùghall Mhìcheil Nìll Dhòmhnaill as we used to call him) who used to cut hair. And when Angus sat on the chair he said to him, "Now Dougall," said he, "be sure that you are careful not to rob the nest."

Where he was living down at Big Pond there was not much shelter from the north and northeast wind because he was so close to the shore; the place was so bare that when the lake froze over completely and the snow came it would drift in over the ice. And the place where they would water the mare was so hard to clean out; he would shovel out a place and then a snowdrift would fill it in. Finally the place got piled up so high that a hollow descended steeply to the place where they used to water the mare. One day he was down there, and by that time the place was extremely steep and getting a little narrow, and the mare was not at all willing to go down into the hollow for a drink. And somebody came down the road and came over to talk to him.

"How little sense you have my friend."

"Indeed," replied Angus.

"Aren't you clumsy!" said the man. "Why didn't you put the mare down backwards – back her down – into the hollow?"

"Well," replied Angus, "even if I did, that isn't the end that my mare drinks from."

Another time Angus went to see people he knew, travelling some distance from his home. But the way Angus was, he was at home in any place he happened to be: people were glad to see him; they wanted him to be with them. But he was at a certain house and someone from the neighbourhood came visiting. It was around the beginning of winter, and there was snow on the ground then anyway. And when this man came in he shook Angus's hand and greeted him.

"I believe," said he, "that those were your tracks I saw over on the edge of the clearing." I am sure that Angus had taken a side path up, a short cut.

"Well," said Angus, "no doubt those were mine. I know I left some there anyway."

John MacIsaac (Iain 'Illeasbu' Mhóir)

He and his brother's family were living in a house and they had a sawmill on the place. And whatever misunderstanding arose between himself and the owner of the house – perhaps the owner was a little difficult to please anyway – he was putting them out. And he said to John, "I want you out of this house."

"Certainly," replied John.

"Yes," said the owner. "You will have to leave here Friday."

"And why," said John, "don't you put us out Thursday? It might be raining Friday."

Mrs Roderick MacIsaac (Anna Ruairidh Ailein)

One fine summer's day she was out at the side of the house with a bench and a tub on it doing the wash and someone stopped by. He just left the horse beside the main road and gave him some oats and went down. He was walking down to the house and they had a great, big dog with a fierce bark. But actually the dog was kind and meant no harm. And as he was coming down the path between the main road and the house the dog came up to him and turned around – it was barking and looking down toward the house or the shore or whatever and barking all the while – and the man stopped in his tracks. She looked up and she said, "Keep on coming my friend," said she. "Don't stop at all."

"I am afraid," he replied, "that the dog will catch hold of me, that it will bite me."

"Oh," said she, "keep on down. I don't believe and I am not aware that that dog ever caught anything or bit a man or anything else with the end that is facing you anyway."

When she was sick – she was in her final sickness as they would say, and terribly ill – at the end of it she was not able to get out of bed, unless with some help she was able to spend a short time sitting on the plank at the "mouth" (side) of the bed, as they used to call it. But she needed help to get even that far. One day her husband helped her into a sitting position, and she spent some time that way on the edge of the bed until she began to grow tired. Her legs were so weak – one of her legs was extremely weak at the time – and she called to her husband.

"Come over, Roddie," said she.

"Yes, Anna," he replied. "What do you need now?"

"If you could give me some help," said she, "so that I could get back into bed. I am getting tired sitting."

"Yes indeed," he replied. "I would give you that, Anna. What do you want me to do?" he asked.

"Oh," said she, "I want you to try to lift my leg and help me get back into bed."

"Oh," said he, "I'll do that Anna. Which leg would you like me to lift?"

"Oh," said she, "I think my hind leg."

Neil MacIsaac (Mac do dh'Anna Ruairidh Ailein)

Before the Inverness people and others began to play (Scottish) music over the radio there was other music on the air, and Neil did not think much of it at all. To be sure, when the Scottish music came on that he liked, such as William Lamey and Chisholm and all of the Inverness County people when they began to record music, he enjoyed it very much. But one night we were somewhere and I mentioned a tune or some music that I had heard over the radio a while before that.

"Indeed," I said, "that was a pretty sorry tune."

"Oh," said he, "it was just something like the tune of the fly buzzing in the globe of the lamp."

Roderick MacNeil
(Ruairidh Iain 'ic Ruairidh Ruaidh)

There was a man in Irish Vale, Roderick MacNeil, and he had a pair of shoes — rubber shoes from Eaton's — which he had had for a long time. But they had become a little thin and worn so somebody told him that he had better return them and that he would get another pair in their place. So he sent them away, though he had had them a long time before he returned them, and the company decided that he had been wearing them too long for them to be returned for a refund. But anyway, they were talking about this and the postage on them was more expensive going or coming back: they cost a little more going one way than the other. And somebody remarked to him, "Wasn't it strange, Roderick, that the postage wasn't the same going as it was coming back? Now what would you say to that?"

"Well perhaps," replied Roderick, "one of those ways they were going downhill."

Joe MacNeil (Eòs Nìll Bhig)

I have a short story concerning what happened to me when I was in the hospital some years ago. On a certain evening we were supposed to have soup, chicken soup, and there were two fine characters in beds over on the other side of the wall, and I used to hold conversations with them even though I wasn't able at the time to get out of bed. And when this arrived for us – the chicken soup – there wasn't much stock there. It was only grey, thin water except for a taste that you could assert must be chicken soup. And one of the men over in the bed on the other side of the wall said that the chicken had only put its foot into the bowl that he received, and the man next to him said, laughing, "All he did was stand beside my bowl."

And I had just taken a taste of the chicken soup and it was very thin indeed, so I told them that they must be hard to please or satisfy with their complaining, that they couldn't possibly be as badly off as I was for all their protesting for the chicken had just flown past my bowl on its way over to visit them.

Another time I was in the hospital and as you know in some hospitals a paper comes around in the morning to indicate your choice of food for the next day. And the choice for every meal was to be put down: breakfast and dinner and supper. One particular day it happened that chicken legs were down for our evening meal or our supper as you may prefer to call it. And in the evening when they came in to us with the plate – to me and to my companion who was over in the bed beside me – it happened that his wife and sister-in-law and some of his daughters were in seeing him at the time. And the food that I got, although it was listed as chicken legs, was actually hunks of liver. I would say that perhaps it was beef liver; there were only rough slices of it anyway. I had begun to eat my supper when one of the women beside the other man's bed looked over and asked, "Was it chicken legs you got for your supper?"

And I laughed and I replied, "Whatever I got for my supper, if I were a rooster walking down the street and I saw a chicken sporting legs that looked like the thing on my plate tonight I believe I would stop crowing."

Anonymous

The subject of cold houses in the winter brought back to memory a story or a short anecdote I heard from a man belonging to Cape Breton.

It seems that there was a certain young man people would tease. And perhaps the man who was with him was a little bit on the proud side and thought quite a bit of himself. And according to the way I heard the story, they were going out to the woods on a cold winter's day. It was probably in February or January — the weather was cold anyway — and this man asked the younger man, "Was your house cold last night?"

"Yes," replied the young man. "Any house that was outside last night was cold."

It seems that this young man had a great gift of verbal wit and that answers came to him easily. Perhaps they held him to be some sort of a fool. It often happened that people would regard someone as being a little stupid when he might be a very wise man.

At any rate according to the account I heard, he was going down the road one day and the people working for the railway where the main road crossed over the railway were fixing up the crossing. The wood in the crossing had grown bad and they had to take the wooden part out; all of the ties between the iron tracks had to be taken out and replaced with new wood. So he came by — whatever errand he was on — and stopped to talk to them.

And I am sure that one of the men just wanted to tease him to see what he could make him say, so he asked him, "How many ties do you think a person will need to fill this gap?"

The young man looked. "Oh," he said, "one would do if it were wide enough."

Proverbs

1 The hindmost man will be caught by the beast.
2 He who comes uninvited will sit without being asked.
3 The man who ties his horse most securely will leave most swiftly.
4 The hand that gives is the one that receives.
5 The dry foot cannot fish.
6 The fox has no tricks unknown to the hunter.
7 The happy man would ask only to be born.
8 No one can stretch a leg except as the cloth permits.
9 The grey coat does not suit everyone equally well.
10 Large eggs do not come from wrens' backsides.
11 A piece of advice for the gossip: do not poke into what does not concern you.
12 Wine is sweet to drink but dear to pay for.
13 Early to the loch, late to the river, and any time of the day to the stream.
14 Do not shame or slight or injure me; when the fun is greatest is the time to stop.
15 How easy it is to bake when the meal is handy.
16 When Black John arises, the minister lies down.
17 When the hand ceases to receive, the mouth ceases its praise.
18 When the day arrives, so will the advice.
19 "What is not mine I will not pull on," as the woman said about the blanket.
20 The slow horse will reach the mill but the fast horse that breaks a leg will not.
21 The cow is milked from its head.
22 Castles are built from scattered stones.
23 Sickness comes in sudden waves but health arrives little by little.

24 It is hard to take away what the hand practises.
25 It's hard to chew meal and blow on the fire.
26 Envy will do the plowing.
27 The quiet pig is the one that eats the most.
28 Each person feels most acutely the pain in his own head.
29 The eye is what keeps possessions.
30 Better a small fire that warms than a big fire that consumes.
31 Two heads are better than one.
32 A thin kneading is better than being completely destitute.
33 A small fish is better than no fish at all.
34 It is better to cease than to crack.
35 It is better to turn back than to drown.
36 The porridge is better for the spoon.
37 Pity the person who will do for evil whatever he can.
38 How often a man has had permission to release his dog without a dog to his name.
39 Associate with a fool and he will stay the night, associate with him again and he will stay for three.
40 They say that the blind man can see his mouth.
41 Hunger comes more than once.
42 A man who can read will understand half a word.

Expressions

1 Long horns on the cattle in Ireland until you reach them.
2 The fox herding the hens.
3 The lamb as white as its mother and its mother as white as snow.
   (Said of people talking about somebody and pretty much sharing the same opinions.)
4 A poor opinion: the badger's opinion of his own backside.
5 A mouth without a button.
   (Said of someone prone to talk about things that do not concern him or her.)
6 He was seven years old twice.
7 A small blow at the end of the horseshoe.
   (If someone had begun something and saw it was easy enough to do, another might say, "Never mind. This is only just a small blow at the end of the horseshoe.")
8 Neither waves nor bow will break on them.
   (I used to hear this from a man no longer living down in our part of the country when he spoke about people who had left and who in his opinion were going to be well off. And the sense I would take from it was that a wave breaking over them was a wave coming into the boat and even though it wouldn't drown them would cause them some trouble. And if they were hunting and happened to break a bow, although that would not do much damage they would lose game because of it.)
9 I am not preventing you from speaking.
10 He's not one to sell his hen on a wet day.
    (Said about a man who would be very careful about items that he was selling.)
11 That's not a tune under his fingers.

12 As empty as the hen coming from the cook.
13 As bare as a kitten's belly.
14 Whoever saw or heard of it: a lapse in the deceit of the fox.
    (Said of people who were not as smart as others – they
    would do something that was a little bit unsuitable – and
    who ought to have more sense about what they did.)
15 Put the fragrance of your own sixpence beneath your nose.
    (Said to someone who was acting silly.)
16 The twisty lad's tune: he prefers everything that's new.
    (Said of people who would jump at something new or
    novel.)
17 Telling it to the grey stones.
18 A report of good health on him.
    (Used when talking of people who were some distance
    away. This meant that the speaker was praying for another's
    good health when he was being spoken of.)
19 The hen pouncing on the spittle.
    (Said of someone who would enter into a bargain or make
    a deal without thinking it over or looking ahead.)
20 As the ram said concerning milking, "It doesn't worry
    me."
21 Neighbourliness without generosity.
    (Said for people who did not often go out visiting.)
22 When he has a dozen irons at the hearth.
23 When that one arrives the mice over the door will hear him.
    (Said of somebody who speaks extremely loudly.)
24 The egg-water came down on them from the white-haired
    man to the infant.
25 Many a change is caused by death and the love of women.
    (When things quite unexpected would happen such as
    people moving or going around.)
26 The passage of the cat over the waterfall.
    (Said of something that was going that people did not want
    to return at all.)
27 A cudgel in the hand of a foolish woman.
28 The lazy tailor's long thread.
29 I like the old man's bread but I don't like the old man's
    breath.

(It was fine enough as long as people were getting a good profit from someone, but when that ran out there wasn't much interest.)

30 There are two sides to every hill.
31 It looks as if the cats have gone off to eat the cheese.
32 He has a good lad waiting outside.

Children's Rhymes

1   *The Rainbow*

I heard this rhyme about the rainbow from a man by the name of John MacNeil (Mac do Dhòmhnall Dhòmhnaill 'ic Iain 'ic Iain). When you saw a rainbow up above, you would act as if you were addressing it, saying

> Rainbow, rainbow,
> Fly away, fly away.
> Your father and your mother are at the gallows
> And they will be hanged before you reach them.

And the rainbow was supposed to disappear when it heard this.

2   *Will You Go to Play?*

Here is a strange rhyme, most of which I got from Alexander Kennedy, the son of Archie Kennedy from whom I heard the old tales. And I got a few words of it also from another man, Donald MacIsaac, who is now away; he's somewhere up in the province of Ontario at this time. And this is how the rhyme went.

> Will you go to play?
> What game?
> To play shinty.
> What shinty?
> A yew shinty.

What yew?
A yew of sky.
What sky?
A sky of birds.
And what bird?
A bird of feathers.
And what feather?
A sprig of heather.
And what heather?
Heather of the wood.
And what wood?
The nut wood.

And the end that he – MacIsaac – had to the rhyme was, when you would say, "And what nut?" he would say, "A nut (or plug) of tobacco!"

Traditional Games

They used to play games in the houses and some of these were fairly difficult. For instance, when a man would sit on a round bottle placed on the floor and put his heel on top of the other foot and would try to thread a needle while sitting on the bottle; that was difficult to do. And they used to make fun of the man: "Why don't you stay still?" He would go back and forth. But when you were used to the game you would get so accustomed to it that the thread would be in one hand and the needle in the other and you could bring them together. And if you were quick enough when you hit the needle you could get the thread into the eye – it was a big needle – and when you let go of the thread it would stay in there. And the next time you swung back you could get hold of the thread and pull it. It was difficult; you would have to try quite often.

Other people used to place a pin in the floor and an empty bottle on the top of their heads and they were able to bend down and take the pin out of the floor with their teeth and stand back up still with the bottle on the top of their heads without upsetting it. It was rare man who could do it: you had to be so supple and go so gently when the bottle was on your head. You had to to put the bottle back so that it would be in the same position as it was when you were taking the pin out of the floor. Getting down to the floor was the difficult part.

Robbing the Old Man was a difficult game. You held two fairly rough pins of wood carved to a sharp point at the ends, one in each hand. And people would balance horizontally on the tips of their toes with their hands on the floor and would have to go along slowly. There was a sewing pin fixed in the floor at some distance so that you could reach it. However long the measured distance was, the pin was fixed there and you had to talk as you were going toward it. Somebody would ask, "Where are you going, my poor man?" "I am going to rob the old man." "And are you sure that you will?" "By that ear I will." You had to keep yourself on the ends of your feet and your weight on one hand while you touched the ear: "By that ear I will." Then you had to go forward another distance. "Where are you going my poor man?" "I am going to rob the old man." "Are you certain that you will?" "By that ear I will." Unless you were level your body would roll over. And then you might be asked a second time on your return journey. You had to go from ear to ear and once you went along and got the pin out of the floor with your teeth, you would begin to come back. "Where were you my poor man?" "I was robbing the old man." "And are you certain that you did?" "By that ear I did." And when that was asked again you had two chances to answer that way before you managed to return and assume a standing position. There was a lot of work involved in the game.

As for the rest of the games that they played there was the Salmon's Leap. You would go along the floor and then you would make a leap.[1] You lifted the tips of your feet from the floor and struck your hands together as you were above the floor. And when you came down the tips of your feet and your two hands struck the floor in the same position as before. You could do that as often as you wished. If you could do it once that was enough. But for anyone who was able to do it even once it wasn't easy, getting up off the floor and clapping your hands together. And I believe that they used to strike their two heels together; when they went up they would strike their two heels together and their two hands. Then they would come back down onto the floor in the position that they were in before. It was not at all easy.

Marriage Premonitions

People used to have a large number of beliefs about the new moon. There was one belief about the first sight of the new moon and a rhyme people would recite to it. I heard the rhyme from Elizabeth Kennedy, a daughter of Archie Kennedy.[1] And you had to look over your left shoulder and pick up whatever was under your foot – a clod or a stick or whatever it was – and recite while you looked at the moon.

> New moon and moon of truth,
> Tell me without falsehood in what direction my love lies.
> The clothes that he wears
> And the colour of his hair.

And as you were reciting the rhyme you would bend down and pick up whatever was under your foot and take it home and put it under your head and sleep on it. And according to the belief you would see your future love in a dream.

There was another game in which people would go outside – they used to go out backwards – and pick up a clod or a piece of earth or some such thing.[2] They would pick something off the ground and bring it inside and then it would be broken up and taken apart to see if they could find a hair in it: any human hair or animal's fur. If they found a hair, even if it came from some animal – as was most likely – they used to think that that was the hair colour of their future lover. They would take the hair with them carefully. They would take it home and put it under a pillow and dream on it; they would have a dream and they would see their lover in the dream.

I heard a story about one man when people were in a house on Halloween night. The man went outside to find a clod and while he was outside someone else plucked a hair from the dog's back and held on to it. When the man came inside with the clod, it had to be divided – a piece given to everyone – and a piece of the clod was given to the other man along with everyone else.

"Here," said he, "is the hair that I found in the clod."

And the first man didn't know what had happened. He didn't know anything about it. He had no idea that a trick had been played on him. And he told me around the time that he married – I don't remember whether he was married or whether he was just ready to be married at the time – he told me the story about that Halloween night. They got a hair from the clod and he said that he put the hair under the pillow and he saw a certain woman. He didn't know her at all, but he saw her. And the first time that he saw her at a dance some time later he recognized her, and that was the one he married. Even though the hair came from the dog's back it worked out for them. Things were so mysterious that way.

People had many signs and ways of accounting for things.[3] They used to throw a shoe over the top of the roof of the house. I think that they turned their back to the house; or if you threw a pebble with your right hand then you would have to throw the shoe with your left hand. They had to throw it over and whatever direction the toe of the shoe was pointing when it landed was the direction in which one's lover was to be found.

And there were other games, such as dipping the ring in a glass of water.[4] That was common enough and anyone could do that; it wasn't difficult to do. They used to get a human hair and put it through a wedding ring. And then they let the ring down three times into the glass of water (holding it by the hair). The glass was not completely full: there was a part left empty so that the ring would not touch the water. And when the ring was lifted out of the water it would swing back and forth and strike each side of the glass. Every time that it struck was counted. If it struck three times it meant three years before the man married for whom they were dipping the ring. In many cases the ring wouldn't move at all. It would swing back and forth and would not go far enough to strike the glass, so that man wasn't going to marry.

There was another game that they had, taking water from a boundary stream, a stream that ran between two properties.[5] You would go down to the stream and you would take up a mouthful of water. And whatever house you were going to visit on Halloween night, you would stand outside at the window or the door where you could hear the conversation going on inside. They would call out some name inside and whatever name they called was the name of the man or the woman that the person was going to marry.

Well, the people believed in it – at least according to the story that I heard. And the account was true of what happened, because I knew a group of men who went to a house and only one of them had been able to keep the water in his mouth after the three of them had gone down to the boundary stream and each had taken a mouthful from the stream. When one of them was taking his mouthful, something such as flotsam coming down with the current went into his mouth and he expelled it from his mouth. And when the other was climbing up the bank to the road he hit a slippery place, on a rock or something, and let the water out of his mouth. But the third man continued on and to be sure he did not talk at all with water in his mouth, and when they came to the house they all remained quiet. They knew that he had the water in his mouth and they all remained silent as they went on up. And a woman was called for while they were playing cards at the table; somebody called her by name. Whatever the reason was she called out her name, and they all heard but none of them had water in his mouth but that one alone. And the name that was called out was the first name of the woman that the man married. One of the people along with us told us the story; he was also present in the house at the time the mother of the lad who told us the story said to the man in question, "Oh," said she, "I am sure that is the name the woman will have whom you marry."

And that was her name, for that was the first name they heard.

I heard a story from another woman about three people – three girls – who went down to the stream and took up water. The three of them took a mouthful of water from the stream and proceeded stealthily toward the house. And someone at the table called out to someone else who was playing cards at the time, and the name called out there was the first name of their future husbands. And all those women married, and married a man by that name. All their husbands had the same name. They did not all marry at the same time – they travelled back and forth in those days – but all the husbands turned out to have the same name. And for that reason it seems that these things used to happen, whether people believed in it or whether it was thought to be by chance.

Signs, Superstitions, and Second Sight

I believe that many of the events that people related amounted to no more than superstitions. Yet I also believe that there was some substance to people's beliefs and some events of this kind did actually take place. Whether they were true or not people believed they occurred and perhaps those who believed did so because they were so observant; there must have been portents that many people did not notice. There are many today who do not take account of such happenings because circumstances have changed so much; life is not going on the way it did in those times. For that reason people today will claim that experiences of that sort never existed – that it was only people's imagination – and these experiences pass them by without their knowing. Perhaps there was a sign this morning that such an event was going to happen to a person, but he didn't see it and passed the day and these things happened to him and he had no knowledge of them until they occurred. But if he had had some warning, and had believed in such warnings and been attentive, perhaps he would have seen what might happen.

It is no different from attempts to predict the weather. When they see certain signs in the sky and account for the winds, how the wind changes the direction it blows, some people can make a good guess at the weather in store. And it is the same with people who possess what are called *giseagan* "superstitions" – who believe in such things – and as a result of that they work for these people. That is my own opinion on the matter because I have had some of that experience myself. And on account of that I must believe; I don't particularly want to believe but if it must be there is no way to avoid it.

Along with all the proverbs, expressions, prayers and so on that there used to be, people had a sort of a belief in certain signs that would occur, things that they used to see and hear. And there was one which they called an augury, which consisted of two wood chips crossed over each other on the floor. If a person happened to be walking where there were sticks on the floor and knocked them with his foot without meaning to or intending to, or perhaps the dog or the cat would hit a chip of wood on the floor as they were going over them, he or she would put them over each other in the form of a cross and people would say, "Do you not see the fine augury on the floor? It won't be long before you get a letter." And I believe when they saw it they would expect good news according to how good the augury looked.[1]

There was also what people used to call the cap of luck (caul).[2] They used to say, "There is a man born with a cap of luck"; how lucky he was and how well he got on in every way.

I was talking about the good luck and bad luck that people would experience.[3] Now there were other signs they had regarding occurrences. Somebody would say, rubbing his lips, "Indeed, I feel the itch of a kiss (or the itch of a dram) today." And there was indeed an itch on his lips at the time. And somebody else would say, "Indeed, I am going to shake the hand of a stranger today." "And how do you mean that?" "Oh, there is an itch in the palm of my right hand." Or someone might say, "Surely I am going to receive some money in a short time. There is an itch in my left palm." And another man would say, "And what does it mean when a person's eye is quivering?" It was good news if it was the right eye and it was poor news – not so good at all – if it was the left eye. And another might say, "Lord how hot my ear is! It's almost on fire with the warmth in it. Someone is talking about me." People would ask the man, "Is it your right ear or your left ear?" "Oh, my left ear." "Oh, well then, that's good enough." "And what is the reason for that?" He would say that without knowing. But some old woman or old man would be talking to him. "Well, when the heat is in your right ear they are making a lot of talk about you and indeed it is probably not very good.

But when that great heat is in your left ear, they are making excuses for you."

And people might hear a sound as if somebody were on the threshold.[4] They weren't hitting the door at all, you understand; there was no knock on the door but you would hear the stamping as if somebody put his foot on the threshold though no one was there. And they would say, "It won't be long before a stranger comes to the house. Did you hear the footfall?"

Like many other things they believed in, they believed that when the rooster crowed at the threshold of the door it was a sign that a stranger was coming, that he was going to come to the house. And when they heard a shrill sound like a bagpipe in their ear they used to say that they were going to get news of death.[5]

Among all the things – signs and things of that sort that they used to talk about – I heard them talking about the *dreag*.[6] It seems that it was like stars – as they say a shooting star – except that it passed very low. They would see the light going past and it would look as if there were sparks or a tail of light following in its trail. The longer it was – the more light there was behind it – that would be a teacher or that would be a clergyman. It might be a priest or a teaching minister and since the congregation would follow him to the funeral, that accounted for the *dreag* of one of them being longer. It would be drawn out longer in the firmament or the sky than that of a lay person. I never saw the *dreag* but I heard it being described quite often.

People would talk about birds, particularly when a small bird entered the house.[7] It was a bad sign for a small bird such as a robin or wren or any of those to enter. And if any of these entered using only one foot, it was a very bad sign indeed. People were always extremely frightened if the man of the house was on a journey or anybody at all belonging to the household was away on a journey and a bird came inside. They would be very, very concerned until he returned home for fear that bad news was going to arrive about him, that something had happened to him. And if they had the chance at all, they would catch the bird to see whether it had two feet.

They used to talk also about unlucky people coming around where they were working.[8] If they were working with tools of any kind, whether it was a mill or whatever kind of gear, when things would begin to go wrong – as often happened – they would order a certain man in the neighbourhood to journey over. They believed strongly that everything would be in order again – that they would be lucky. But they took it as a very bad sign altogether if that same man met them on the road when they were starting a journey to town or to market or anything. They did not at all like the man to meet them on a road even though he was so good when he came to the mill.

The first person to meet anyone starting out on any particular journey, they thought would either bring them luck or not.[9] This is what happened to a man whose wife died and who married again and had one daughter from the first marriage. The daughter and the stepmother did not get along very well at all. They were not very friendly. And one day as her stepmother was going to the store or somewhere the daughter met her at the door and she said to the daughter, "Won't it be too bad for you unless I have good luck, since you are the first one that I met on my journey."

The daughter replied, "They don't consider me lucky for anybody to meet."

"Indeed," replied her stepmother.

"Oh yes indeed," said the daughter. "I was the first one to meet my father the day that he was going to fetch you, and indeed, he was not lucky."

While we are on this subject, I am going to describe the kinds of *giseagan* "superstitions" that people held.[10] If they were going to start out on a journey – whether they were going hunting or to find sheep that had strayed – if you threw an old shoe after them they considered it lucky. As for returning, they did not consider it good luck at all if a man was starting out on a journey and forgot a small detail and had to return inside to fetch something that he had left and should have taken; it was indeed very bad luck for him to have to go back to get that. If a person was going out hunting or fishing they would prevent anyone from calling out to find out where he was going or anything of the kind.

I have one account of people who were said to be able to sink a ship.[11] And Michael MacLean (Mìcheal Iain Chaluim Òig 'ic Iain 'ic Lachlainn Ghobha) used to tell me the story. It came down from oral recitation certainly enough for he was unlettered. He used to tell about a certain woman who they said could practise witchcraft, could sink a ship. And whether it was her father or whoever called it into question, she was asked to prove it. So she asked for an egg, and she put the egg inside a shoe and kept rocking the shoe back and forth according to the story he gave me. And there was a ship out on the ocean and when they looked, the ship, it seems, was rocking back and forth in the waves just as she was working the shoe. And they made her stop. I don't remember what MacLean said was done with her, whether she was done away with or whether she was just made to cease from the deed that she was committing. But it seems to me if that account came over such a great distance there must have been something to it.

On the subject of beliefs that people held – strange little beliefs that they followed – they used to say, if you found a snake-skin (finding it in the spring was better than finding it in the fall) and kept it inside the house, the house would never burn, it would never catch fire.[12] Perhaps people believed in that because the house in which it was kept never caught fire. But then it was never meant to anyway. If the house was going to take fire I don't believe the skin would prevent it even if the snake itself were inside.

They once had a dance in a certain house where there was a Campbell and his wife living up in Johnstown Parish.[13] And it happened on this particular winter's night that they had a dance or, as they used to call it, a frolic. And the dance was held in the sitting room; it was the biggest place and they had the space to do the big reel. And when part of that reel was over and they were standing and resting, one of the men there said to somebody who was in the dance with him and who was sitting or standing over next to the window, "Don't stand there at all. Come over from there."

And the other man came over and they stood. And they were there in the middle of the floor and talking and somebody asked the man about it a little bit later, perhaps the next day or sometime.

"What," said he, "was wrong when you asked that man to stand over beside you and not to stand at the window?"

"Oh," he replied, "a coffin was at the window."

And a short while later – perhaps a month after that – the Campbell's wife died and they placed the coffin over there at the foot of the window. He foresaw this some time before she died.

Apparently a number of people believe that some had the gift of premonition and that they could see things that were about to happen.[14] It seems that they were especially adept at seeing a funeral. I don't know now whether they saw much else – probably they did. But anyway they could see a funeral; that's what was told to me.

Someone was telling me that a certain man had said that he saw his own funeral. As I heard the story, it was Malcolm MacLean (Calum Gobha), the grandfather of Joe Allan. It was himself or Joe's father. Anyway it doesn't matter, I'm sure. In the story he told them that he saw his own funeral. And how would he know that it was his own funeral? Well, he said he recognized everyone at the funeral and he was the only one who was not present. And why wasn't he at the funeral along with everybody else if it were somebody else? And he said that he would tell them the sort of horse that was going to draw the coffin and the horse was not in the surrounding area.

"It is not at all," said he, "in the area yet, the horse that will be pulling the coffin" – whether it would be with a wheeled carriage or a sleigh. But he described the horse, and it seems that the horse had four white legs; and that those horses were very rare in the surrounding area. And apparently around that locality – in that certain piece of country – there were no horses of this kind until one man made a trade and obtained a horse with four white legs. He got a horse of this size and this colour – everything. And when MacLean died that was the horse that drew his coffin to the graveyard. So he must have seen the funeral clearly enough.

I think that some of those people saw a funeral and had an idea whose it was but would not say. They would see coffins and the like, but they would not tell at all whose they were. And that's how things went for them.

Speaking of premonitions and things that happened before a funeral, a mysterious thing happened to me which I believe came true enough.[15] I felt a shaking coming into my arms at the elbows, and the shaking was so bad that it nearly caused me to scream. It only lasted for a few minutes and then it passed and nothing like it ever returned. Time passed and I'm sure it was at least a number of months before I was at a funeral. I was one of the pallbearers: there was a man at the head and at the foot of the coffin and a man on each side at the middle and it happened that I was at the middle. And on the way down to the graveyard, toward the grave, there were places where the ground was quite high. We were walking over high, rounded places – graves that were made years ago which were low on each side with a high place in the middle – and I was standing there on a high place and the others were in a low place on each side of me. You could say that I was up on the hill and the others were in the valley and the weight of the coffin bore down on me and the shaking came into my arms at the elbow when the entire weight of the coffin bore down on me. The woman whose body was in the coffin was a big, heavy woman, and when all the weight came on me I had to support it and I felt the same shaking in my arms then that I had experienced a number of months before.

And I am sure whether or not I believed it before that I had to accept it as true, because I had heard people saying when their arms shook, "I am going to be lifting a dead man's coffin. My arms feel terribly heavy."

Ghosts and Apparitions

It seems that many people had the custom, when they had been to a wake-house and were leaving, of putting their hand on the hand of the person who was dead in the coffin or on the person's forehead.[1] It didn't matter whether they put their hand on forehead or hand – the hands used to be folded on the breast. And the reason that people had, the way in which they believed in this, was that if the spirit of the man should meet you again, you would not fear him in a way that would create any difficulty for you.

I heard an account of a man who died in the country and in those days they used to make coffins and were often short of materials. They would go around the countryside gathering them in various places to get ready to make the coffin. And the storekeepers themselves used to run short of things sometimes; often they would run out of stock until they got other wares in. And apparently in this case everything was ready for the coffin they intended to make except that they had no nails, and there was no one in the neighbourhood who had them. And whether the storekeeper was too far away from them at the time, or whether he had run short of suitable nails, there were women inside who were cooking food to be given to those present at the wake. The people who were making the coffin had to be fed at least, and for those who were going to remain at the wake there had to be food. And, anyhow, most of those who came to the wake to pay their last respects to the deceased also had to be fed. And if they were present at mealtime, supper would also be given to them. And because they were cooking, one of the women was going somewhere to fetch meal or flour or whatever she was going to get, and there was a trunk there and she saw the spirit of the dead man who was on the boards. She saw him bending over the trunk, a trunk in which things were stored. And she told somebody about what she had seen – I am sure she came in a little frightened. And when she related the thing that she had seen, somebody went out and lifted up the cover on top of the trunk and there was a little package down in the corner of the storage trunk containing nails, nails suitable to make the man's coffin. And perhaps the story was true enough that a sign was given to her to show them where they would find the nails.

I am going to tell you a short story that I heard from Angus MacMullin (Aonghus Alasdair 'ic Nìll 'ic Iain 'ic Mhurchaidh 'ac Dhòmhnaill) about the ghost of Beech Hill.[2]

The place called Beech Hill is up on the mainland in Antigonish County. It seems that they always used to see or hear a ghost there. I don't know that they saw anything but, whatever ghost was there, it seems it frightened some people so much that they did not use a certain road at all. People did not travel on that road. And on this particular occasion it seems that the bishop was returning from somewhere late at night on horseback and this was the road that he chose; it must have been the shortest way home for him. So he took that road and the ghost met him on Beech Hill. And when the horse reared up to do battle with the ghost, the bishop fell to the ground. He was there in the mud and I am sure he was well splashed while the horse was attacking with its feet. And it seems that went on until the cock crowed, at which time the battle stopped.

And people were questioning the bishop when they saw the condition of his clothes – his clothes were covered in mud or mire – and he was asked about what happened.

"Oh," said he, "if the grey horse were able to talk he would be the one to tell you. I cannot tell you because I did not experience it all. But they will hear no more of that on the hill anyway."

And that is the story I heard about Beech Hill.

And it was said that a horse would side with you to help you in spite of anything, but there was a great danger that a mare would turn against you, that she would side with your enemy and would harm you when a ghost met you.[3] But it was also said that if a rope were put around her neck – or even if it were nothing but a thread of woollen yarn tied around her neck – that she would side with you and she would fight as fiercely, or perhaps even more effectively, against the spectre.

A dog was considered very good for you, but, according to the accounts they told, you had to be certain that you didn't call the dog's name. There was a danger that if you called the dog's name the dog would turn against you, the spectre would catch hold of the dog's name and would turn the dog against you. And for that reason it was not considered at all fitting to utter the dog's name. But it was said that though a dog was fierce in fighting on your side, a dog didn't amount to any help compared with a bitch; but there was a very great danger that she could turn against you. And it was related that if you let some blood from her ear she would tear the spectre apart even if it were Satan who met up with you; she was so dangerous that she would tear him apart.

On the subject of dogs, I often heard people caution you; they would say, "Don't loose a dog at night and don't restrain him."

By that they meant, setting a dog as you might set it after farm animals or people or wild animals. You were not supposed by rights to loose or to restrain your dog at night. I often heard them discouraging that.

Music and Dance

Fiddlers

Here are the names of a number of fiddlers that I heard some years ago: a Neil Campbell (Niall Eachainn 'ac Dhunnachaidh); and James Campbell (Seumas Pheadair 'ic Eachainn); Murdock MacMullin (Murchadh Dhòmhnaill 'ic Nìll 'ic Iain 'ic Mhurchaidh 'ac Nìll 'ac Dhòmhnaill); Big John MacDonald (Iain Mór Aonghuis Nìll Ruaidh); and John MacNeil (Iain mac Dhòmhnaill Mór Nìll Mhóir); and Neil MacPhee (Niall Alasdair a' Phìobaire); Hector MacNeil (Eachann Aonghuis Phosta); Michael MacPhee (Mìcheal Mhìcheil Nìll Dhòmhnaill); and Neil MacIsaac (Niall Iain 'ic Iosaìg); Roderick MacIsaac (Ruairidh Iain Ruairidh); and Michael MacInnis (Mìcheal Ruairidh Dhòmhnaill Mhóir); and Finlay MacDonald (Mac Iain Nìll 'ic Iain Òig); and Donald MacDonald (Dòmhnall Steaphainn Phàdruig). Of those I heard, the two greatest fiddlers were another John MacNeil (Mac Dhòmhnaill Dhòmhnaill) and Michael MacPhee (Mac Mhìcheil Nìll Dhòmhnaill). And I believe that their music was very similar to the music still played by dance players but that the dancing itself has changed. I don't believe that there is much difference in the music between the fiddlers mentioned above and fiddlers here today who are fairly up in years.

Some of the fiddlers named here used to play certain tunes on the high bass. Finlay MacDonald would almost never play the fiddle without playing one or two tunes on the high bass. John MacNeill (Mac Dhòmhnaill Mór Nìll) also played tunes on the high bass. *Uisdean Friseal* was a tune for which many fiddlers would put the fiddle up to the high bass and the fiddle made a very nice sound when it was tuned to the high bass for that piece.

Neil Campbell, the fiddler mentioned on page 165, used to say that their music did not originate on the Campbell side, but rather on the side of the MacMullins. MacMullin's wife was one of the piping MacNeils – the pipers over in Piper's Cove in Christmas Island Parish – and he claimed that their music came more from that side than from the MacMullins, though at the same time the MacMullins themselves were good musicians.

Now Peter was the best fiddler in the family. And then it seems that Michael, although he did not go out anywhere at all to play, was a particularly good fiddler and could play the pipes. John was also considered an accomplished player. People used to say that Neil had the least talent of all for fiddle playing, and being as good a player as he was, the rest of them must have been surpassingly good.

They used to live close to the place called Hay Cove, out in the rear. There were numerous offspring of the Campbells there including a large number of Duncan's children. It seems that Duncan was a drummer in the army in his time. There were Duncan's sons: Donald, John, Alexander, Andrew, and Hector. Many of these Campbells came over to stay and settled in that place. I read that when the first of them came over he settled on a place and then found out that his brother was down about five miles on the lower side and had acquired land there. They had already planted the potatoes in the ground, as I understand, and had planted them only a few days before he found this out. And they used to relate that he dug up his potatoes out of the ground and gathered them and took them with him. They went down to find a place as close to his brother as they could and he settled down near him. He had to go a little more than a half mile away because the land had already been claimed there, I believe, by MacKenzies.

I was only nineteen years old when I heard him and did not have much of an understanding of music. I did not have the most discerning ear for music at the time. But over the many times since then that I have thought about the music they were able to play, I think that he could put a very Gaelic flavour on the tunes and that he had them very correctly. I think he put something into the tune called *Gun do Dhiùlt am Bodach Fodar Dhomh* that I have not heard anywhere at all since.[1]

And one old musician said to me, and he was an extremely accomplished musician himself on the pipes and fiddle, "No one ever danced a reel – it was the foursome reel that was going then to be sure – and certainly no one will ever dance one," said he, "which could be compared to that tune when he plays it: Niall Eachainn 'ac Dhunnachaidh playing the *Gioban Hirteach*."

Here is a short story that I heard from Neil Campbell. He was telling us a story about a man by the name of Donald Campbell. He was not of the same Campbells as was Neil Campbell himself, but he was an outstanding fiddler and it seems that he was as fine a player as lived in Cape Breton in his time. And it was related that they got their gift from the fairy hill. According to the account that Neil had, Donald Campbell's father was coming home after playing at a wedding, and when he was passing a certain place it seems that there was a fairy woman there milking a cow. And when he saw her she told him that, if he would keep the story quiet and not tell anybody that he had seen her, he would acquire the gift of fiddling for his own and it would be passed on to his son and grandson and that it would never be taken from them no matter where they played. And it is said that he got a bow from the fairy mound.[2]

When he was an extremely old man and had grown blind – I heard this account from Hector MacMullin – it seems that some of the fiddlers visited Donald Campbell's place and his son Angus, who was keeping house for him at the time, was also a fiddler. And of course when a bunch of fiddlers gathered in a house each one of them would spend some time playing. Apparently they were down in the room playing and Angus came down to the other end of the house where his father was.

His father asked him who was playing now and he said that it was Little Malcolm.

"Oh," said he, "isn't it a pity that he does not have his little finger. What a fine fiddler he would be if he still had it!"

And his son Angus asked him, "Are you saying that he doesn't have the use of his little finger?"

"Oh, no," Donald replied, "he does not at all."

And when they went down the man had stopped playing and Angus Campbell asked him whether there was anything wrong with his little finger.

"Yes," he replied, "there is. My little finger was broken years ago and I no longer have the use of it. I have to get by with three fingers."

And that's the story I heard about how discerning an ear for music Donald Campbell had.

There were some fiddlers whose names I have heard but whom I have never heard playing. There was a Neil Mac-Donald (Niall Mhìcheil Alasdair), and Michael Campbell (Mìcheal Eachainn 'ac Dhunnachaidh), and John Campbell (Iain Eachainn 'ac Dhunnachaidh), and Peter Campbell (Peadar Eachainn 'ac Dhunnachaidh), Alexander (Mac Ailein) Mac-Dougall, and there was a Donald Cash, and Tom Cash, and Donald MacNeil (Dòmhnall mac Nìll 'ic Iain 'ic Mhurchaidh), and his sons Roderick (Ruairidh Dhòmhnaill 'ic Nìll) and a Roderick Allister MacNeil (Ruairidh Alasdair 'ic Nìll), and Stephen MacNeil (Steaphainn Alasdair 'ic Nìll); and a Malcolm MacMullin (Calum Iain 'ic Nìll 'ic Iain 'ic Mhurchaidh) who was considered to be one of the fiddlers as good as was up in the neighbourhood where he was living at the time.

Pipers

In an account of the pipers that I have heard, I should mention Jack MacDonald – we used to call him Black Jack and he was a very good piper – and George Sutherland, son of William Sutherland, and the late Anthony MacDonald – I heard his

playing and he was very good. And Donald Austin, the father
of Anthony, was also a piper although I only heard him play
once; and Neil MacIsaac, whom I heard quite often; and Peter
MacKinnon; Joseph MacMullin (Eòs Iain an Tàilleir); and Joe
MacIsaac (Mac Mhàrtainn Dhòmhnaill 'ac Iosaig) was also a
very fine piper; and Peter Morrison was also good. Peter is still
living, as is George Sutherland. There was a Donald MacLeod
who was fairly good and Donald MacDonald, son of Charles
MacDonald (Tearlach a' Mhonaidh) who was a very accomplished piper. And Joe MacAdam: I think he was as good as
any I ever heard. I heard all these pipers playing and they had a
good touch.

But now I will return to Neil MacIsaac because he was the
one with whom I was best acquainted and a remarkable man.
He had the names to the tunes and he knew so many tunes by
heart. He could name hundreds of tunes and tell you in which
books they could be found. And he learned many tunes from
his father. His father was full of tunes; he also played the
pipes and he had a great store of fiddle tunes and pipe tunes –
the size of his repertoire was astounding. Now when people
went to Neil MacIsaac intending to learn to play the pipes, he
would test them carefully. He would ask them innumerable
questions, to the point where he had to see the fingers on their
hands and feel them to find whether or not they would be
good at playing the pipes. And if there was anything wrong in
their people or their parents, such as asthma or consumption
or anything of the sort, he would not at all be willing to teach
them. He was extremely careful about the people who were
going to learn music. And as for those who spent a little time
going to him and acquiring the tunes, I think you can recognize these people as having been with him at one time or another
because you find they have a way with music that gives it a
(special) flavour. I believe, at least, that they put a special
flavour into the music.

I believe that the small pipes could have been played here at
some time in the past. People used to dance a lot to pipe
music. I never saw very much of that done but I know that
MacIsaac used to do a tremendous lot of pipe playing. But he

played the big pipes; they were always his instrument. But they must have had the small pipes to play because the big pipes would make so much noise inside a house. I never saw the small pipes being played at all, but I do believe that I saw one of them with the piper MacIsaac as he was fixing it or making some adjustment on it. But he would not be interested in playing it anyway. He always stayed with the big pipes for playing and it would not bother him much at all to play them however big they were. He was very happy playing and it would be no effort for him to play most of the night throughout the winter playing at a dance.

Dances

Many of the dances were customarily held in dwelling-houses. They also used to hold them in schoolhouses, but that would only be perhaps once or twice a year. They would hold a dance there during the summer when school was out and before the next term started. They would make a little money that way to help with things in the school. Square dances were the dances they had there: the square sets. Eight people went out onto the floor: four men and four women. And people paid to get out onto the floor to dance. There were five figures to it altogether. When the first figure was played and danced the dancers would rest a little time and then start back again and they would keep on that way until the fifth figure was over. The they would stay on the dance floor for another turn or "set," as they call it in English. Then people paid again – the men would pay – and would find women to dance with them. In those days every man who went on the dance floor would pay ten cents and they would get five figures for the ten cents. But if they liked the music and the night was fairly cool, or if they were near to a window they would stay until perhaps three of the sets were over. And that would mean doing fifteen circuits of good tunes played for them before they left the floor.

The dances that they used to hold in the dwelling-houses

were called frolics. Often people would be there to cut firewood or to plow or mow or some such work. In particular, widows and women who had no helpers around used to put on these dances in their houses. And then again they had something they called a raffle. They would sell tickets on something with a number on every ticket and when they were all sold so many copies were put in a hat and somebody would pull one out and whatever number was on it was the number that won the prize.

And lastly, the youth would gather somewhere, particularly in the dwelling-houses. They would not be altogether so enthusiastic about attending dances held in the schoolhouses. Men used to take fairly young girls dancing so that they could learn. They would volunteer to take them there so that they could learn the dance and become accomplished dancers, and some of the young girls were very good. They were very light and lively on the dance floor and it would give great pleasure to those at the dances to escort them.

The foursome reel, to my memory, was never danced. I never saw a foursome reel danced unless they danced it in a place where they were presenting a program of entertainment. As far as that's concerned I saw one group dancing the Reel of Tulloch and that is all I ever saw of it, but that was only a demonstration for people to show how it went.

One man gave an account of an outstanding dancer who was able to snuff out candles at each end of the room. Whether this was true or not, he said that this man would put a small glass of water in the crown of his hat and was able to dance so lightly up and down from end to end of the room that he could snuff out the candles with his heels and keep the glass of water in the crease in the top of his hat. As long as it was in the crease in the hat, it wouldn't jump out, it wouldn't spill, and it wouldn't fall out. He would have to be extremely light and extremely accurate. It wouldn't do for him just to come close, to approach the candles and hit them with his heels without passing over them, nor could he break the candle or knock it over, but just hit it. But he could put out the candles.

And speaking of places where people used to dance, I saw

dancing on a bridge when a group of young people gathered in the evening and someone was there to play fiddle. They used to give the bridge a sort of a sweeping; if there was gravel on it or anything they would prepare it and spend some time dancing. They would do perhaps three or four dance sets there. There was not much traffic in those days so it did not interfere.

Notes

The following abbreviations and shortened references have been used in the notes. Full references are found in the Select Bibliography. Numbers and dates refer to field-recordings made by the editor and deposited in the Gaelic Folklore Project Tape Collection at St Francis Xavier University, Antigonish, Nova Scotia. Numbers preceded by AT and followed by a title correspond to the Aarne-Thompson folktale classification system as given in Antti Aarne and Stith Thompson, *The Types of the Folktale* and listed on page 269.

C.B. Mag.	*Cape Breton's Magazine.* Wreck Cove 1973–
CG	Alexander Carmichael, *Carmina Gadelica.*
GWSU	Allan McDonald, *Gaelic Words and Expressions from South Uist and Eriskay*
LNF	John Francis Campbell, *Leabhar na Féinne*
LSIC	Séamus Ó Duilearga, *Leabhar Sheáin Í Chonaill*
MWHT	John Francis Campbell, *More West Highland Tales*
SD	K.C. Craig, *Sgialachdan Dhunnchaidh*
SGS	*Scottish Gaelic Studies.* Oxford 1926–
SS	*Scottish Studies.* Edinburgh 1957–
SSU	Angus MacLellan, *Stories from South Uist*
Superstitions	John Gregorson Campbell, *Superstitions of the Highlands and Islands of Scotland*
TGSI	*Transactions of the Gaelic Society of Inverness.* Inverness 1871–
W&S	*Waifs and Strays of Celtic Tradition.* Argyleshire Series 5 vols. Volumes cited are:
	2 MacInnes, *Folk and Hero Tales*
	3 MacDougall, *Folk and Hero Tales*
	4 Campbell, *The Fians*
WHT	John Francis Campbell, *Popular Tales of the West Highlands*

INTRODUCTION

1 A North Uist reciter, Pàdruig Moireasdan, also literate in Gaelic,

recently contributed a collection of traditional material learned entirely from oral sources. See Moireasdan, *Ugam agus Bhuam*.

2 For this reason little reference has been made to the rich and varied stock of songs (of which Joe Neil, though not an active singer, knows scores) that were regularly enjoyed in the neighbourhood; or the more than one hundred *puirt-a-beul* (mouth-music) sets of words to tunes that Joe Neil has recited for us, not to mention the immense store of lore concerning religion, weather, folk-medicine, annual festivals, farming, fishing, and material culture that still lives on in the memories of the older natives of his parish.

3 See Delargy, "Gaelic Storyteller"; Dégh, *Folktales and Society*.

4 Campbell was acquainted with Kate Patterson of Rear Christmas Island, Cape Breton County, who was a well-known singer and a proficient story-teller. See J.L. Campbell and Collinson, *Hebridean Folksongs* 2: 6.

5 Dunn, "Gaelic in Cape Breton," mentions that at that time the folktale was "virtually extinct" and supplies a listing of the rare but interesting examples recorded by himself and the Reverend P.J. Nicholson of St Francis Xavier University, or recited by the Reverend J.D. Nelson MacDonald. Of particular interest here is Dunn's observation (p. 7) regarding the paucity and abased status of the folktale as compared with Gaelic song: "The principal reason must be that in a changing society new forms of entertainment have taken its place. The *seanachaidh* has no role in this new society; his office as public entertainer is no longer desired or needed." For a translation of a further Cape Breton folktale noted down that year by the same collector, see Dunn, *Highland Settler*, 45-6.

6 Edited by P.J. Nicholson, *The Casket*, 12 August 1943, 8; 19 August 1943, 8; 2 September 1943, 7.

7 Jackson, "Notes on the Gaelic of Port Hood," 179–83, 186.

8 MacDonnell and MacKinnon, "Cath nan Eun."

9 The magazine, edited by Ronald Caplan and published in Wreck Cove, Victoria County, Cape Breton, began in 1973.

10 Hector Campbell, *Luirgean Eachainn Nill*.

11 See Dillon, ed., *Early Irish Society*, 13. That a peripheral area such as Cape Breton should prove to contain material of such value and interest to the collector of Gaelic folklore would seem to run counter to the thesis advanced by folklorist C.W. von Sydow that folk wanderings lead to a mass extinction of folk tradition. See von Sydow, "Geography and Folk-Tale Ecotypes," 354.

12 C18 A1 2/76, printed in *C.B. Mag.* 16 (June 1977): 24–32; 17 (August

1977): 30–9; Ronald Caplan, ed., *Down North: The Book of Cape Breton's Magazine* (Toronto: Doubleday Canada 1980), 83–96.

13 Delargy "Gaelic Storyteller," 188. Such has not always been the case for every collector. See Hyde, *Beside the Fire*, xlv–xlvii.

14 See Donald Archie MacDonald, "Collecting Oral Literature," 424.

15 Delargy, "Irish Tales and Story-Tellers," 65.

16 Sayers, *Peig*, vii.

17 Delargy, "Gaelic Storyteller," 181.

18 For descriptions of *céilidhs* held in the nineteenth century, see *WHT* 3: 158–9; *CG* 1: xii–xiv; *W&S* 2: ix–x; Delargy, "Irish Tales," 71.

19 Delargy, "Gaelic Storyteller," 194; Calum Maclean, "Hebridean Storytellers," 125 (evidence cited from Barra); *WHT* 1: 224–5.

20 For hero-tales see Delargy, "Gaelic Storyteller," 181; for wonder-tales see Delargy, "Irish Tales," 71.

21 Carmichael, *Deirdire*, 5–6; Delargy, "Gaelic Storyteller," 198; Dégh, *Folktales and Society*, 118.

22 Maclean, *The Highlands*, xv; Maclean, "Hebridean Storytellers," 129; Delargy, "Gaelic Storyteller," 181. For similar practice in Hungary see Dégh, *Folktales and Society*, 92.

23 321 A10 16/4/81.

24 77A8–78A1 10/5/78.

25 From a conversation (22/1/81) with Dan Joe ("The Sailor") MacNeil, a native of Deepdale, Inverness County.

26 *W&S* 4: xi–xii; Christiansen, *The Vikings*, 66. See also Dégh, *Folktales and Society*, 75.

27 Dunn, *Highland Settler*, 52. Alexander Maclean Sinclair in gently ironic tones had already called attention to the obvious educational function of recited Gaelic lore in Nova Scotia before the turn of the century: see *Mac-Talla* (Sydney), 9 September 1893, 5.

28 The effects of story-telling on the psychic development of children in traditional rural societies should receive serious study while it is still possible; suffice it to suggest here that folktales may have provided a major source for the unusual degree of serenity and clarity of mind that can still be observed among the island's older Gaelic-speakers. An innovative and psychologically insightful interpretation of a folktale noted down from a nineteenth-century Irish Gaelic reciter is given by Heinrich Zimmer in *The King and the Corpse*, 26–66. See also Charlotte Bühler and Josephine Bilz, *Das Märchen und die Phantasie des Kindes* (Munich, 1958). For a psychoanalytic study of children and folktales in urban Europe, see Bruno Bettelheim, *The Use of Enchantment: The Meaning and Importance of Fairy Tales* (New York: Random House 1977).

23018

29 Dégh, *Folktales and Society*, 85. For an interesting parallel with the Scottish Gaelic waulking-song tradition, see J.L. Campbell and Collinson, *Hebridean Folksongs* 2: 2n1.
30 Delargy, "Gaelic Storyteller," 180.
31 Ibid., 210.
32 Ibid., 181.
33 Recorded (24/10/80) from Dougall MacDonald of Troy, Inverness County (297 A4); Maclean, *The Highlands*, 67.
34 38A2 15/3/78; 42A8–43A1 22/3/78. Recorded from Dan Angus Beaton, Blackstone, Inverness County; Maclean, *The Highlands*, 91–4.
35 Archie Dan MacLellan and family (C2A4 15/11/77). See *CG* 2: 352–3.
36 Bruford, *Gaelic Folk-Tales*, 240. For information on this bard, see *Smeòrach nan Cnoc 's nan Gleann*, ed. Hector MacDougall (Glasgow: Alexander MacLaren & Sons 1939), 113–22.
37 *Aiseirigh Cadail Lachlainn*, J. Shaw Coll. C14 A1 2/76, printed with translation in *C.B. Mag.* 23 (August 1979): 18-32.
38 Delargy, "Gaelic Storyteller," 195–6.
39 *TGSI* 25 (1901–3): 179–265. See Delargy, "Three Men of Islay."
40 *WHT* 1: 1.
41 Maclean, "Aonghus agus Donnchadh," 173. According to Maclean, *Alasdair Mac a' Cheird* may be "the longest story that has ever been recorded in the history of folklore recording"; see *Tocher* 31 (Summer 1979): 64.
42 Delargy, "Gaelic Storyteller," 206; Murphy, *Saga and Myth*, 5–6.
43 *SD.*
44 *WeS* 4, xxxvii; Delargy, "Gaelic Storyteller," 191; Christiansen, *The Vikings*, 69.
45 *WeS* 4: 31; Christiansen, *The Vikings*, 67; *LNF* 218.
46 Christiansen, *The Vikings*, 71.
47 *WHT* 1: xxv.
48 Jackson, "International Folktale," 183–4, 188, reports the Fenian dialogue; see *An Teangadóir* 3, no 15 (1955): 42 for the Antigonish County native's repertoire; Hector Campbell, *Luirgean*, 53–68.
49 From a conversation with Alec Goldie of Irish Vale, Cape Breton County (19/7/79).
50 See Part 2, no 1, and Hector Campbell, *Luirgean*, 57. For a general discussion of runs in Scottish and Irish tales see Bruford, *Gaelic Folk-Tales*, 183–209; Hyde, *Beside the Fire*, xxvii–xxix; *WeS* 2: 448–51.
51 AT 953 may well have been the model from which the convention of in-tales in Gaelic story-telling spread. See Murphy, *Ossianic Lore*, 52.

The text and translation of *Conall Ruadh nan Car* (J. Shaw Coll. 5 A3 [1964]) are printed in *C.B. Mag.* 21 (December 1978): 13–21.

52 "And great is the blindness and darkness of sin and ignorance and design of those who teach and write and cultivate Gaelic, that they are more desirous, and more accustomed, to compose vain, seductive, lying and worldly tales about the Tuatha De Danann and the Sons of Mil and the heros and Finn MacCoul and his warriors and to cultivate and piece together much else which I will not enumerate or tell here, for the purpose of winning for themselves the vain rewards of the world, rather than write and teach and cultivate the true words of God and the pure ways of truth." Bishop Carswell's introduction to his Gaelic translation of the Prayer Book (1567), quoted in Donald Archie MacDonald, "Collecting Oral Literature," 414. The original Gaelic passage is printed in R.L. Thomson, ed., *Foirm na n-Urrnuidheadh* (Edinburgh: Oliver & Boyd 1970), 11.

53 *CG* 1: xxv–xxvi; *WHT* 1: iv.

54 Information from a conversation with Angus MacKinnon and field-notes (11/3/78).

55 Delargy, "Gaelic Storyteller," 181; Ó Súilleabháin and Christiansen, "Types of Irish Folk-Tale," 6. In the rare instances when a Gaelic reciter is called upon to recite in English, the result, as Dutch folklorist Maartje Draak described from her meeting with Duncan MacDonald of South Uist (*Fabula* 1 [1958]: 47–58), is more a laboured translation than a lively rendition.

56 Maclean, "Aonghus agus Donnchadh," 173, and "Hebridean Story-tellers," 126–7.

57 Maclean, *The Highlands*, xiii, and "Hebridean Storytellers," 124.

58 *WHT* 1: xxi–xxiii; Delargy, "Three Men of Islay," 126–33.

59 *CG* 2: 352.

60 Angus MacLellan, *The Furrow behind Me*, and see also the introduction to Angus MacLellan, *Stories from South Uist*; Donald Archie Mac-Donald, "Donald Alasdair Johnson – a storyteller from South Uist"; Moireasdan, *Ugam agus Bhuam*. For a successful and widely read folklore autobiography by Tomás Ó Crohan, an Irish informant from the Blasket Islands, see *The Islandman*, trans. Robin Flower (Oxford: Oxford University Press 1985). The Irish original first appeared in 1929.

61 Delargy, "Irish Tales," 79.

62 Cf. Delargy, "Gaelic Storyteller," 198–200. For Hungarian parallels see Dégh, *Folktales and Society*, 79.

63 See Maclean, *The Highlands*, 123–32; R. David Clement and Hamish

Henderson, "Alasdair Stewart ('Brian')," *Tocher*, 29 (Autumn 1978):
265–301.

64 *WHT* 1: vi, li–lii.

65 In some instances the challenge of recording for a collector, along with
the resulting attention within the locality, has turned passive tradition-
bearers into active reciters. See Delargy, "Gaelic Storyteller," 189.

66 Delargy, "Gaelic Storyteller," 188.

67 Matheson, "Duncan MacDonald," 2.

68 Maclean, "Hebridean Storytellers," 126–7.

69 Curtin, *Irish Folk-Tales*, 169.

70 When Joe Neil was eighteen or nineteen, Anna NicNeacail (Bean
Mhìcheil 'ic 'Illemhaoil), then an old woman and perhaps more
perceptive than the rest, counselled him with these words: *Cuimhnich
gura h-i a' Ghàidhlig ite as àirde tha 'nad churrac. Agus na dean thusa
dìochuimhn' air cuimhn' a chumail oirre agus a bhith dìleas dhi.*
"Remember your Gaelic is the highest feather in your cap. Don't forget
to retain it in your memory and to be loyal to it." (225 A3 27/6/79)

71 Matheson, "Duncan MacDonald," 4.

72 Delargy, "Irish Tales," 79; Maclean, "Hebridean Storytellers," 126.

73 Delargy, "Gaelic Storyteller," 196; Matheson, "Duncan MacDonald,"
3–4; Maclean, "Hebridean Storytellers," 128.

74 Maclean, "Hebridean Storytellers," 125; Delargy, "Gaelic Storyteller,"
185.

75 Dégh, *Folktales and Society*, 88.

76 Moireasdan, *Ugam agus Bhuam*, xx. According to folktale researchers
as experienced as von Sydow ("Geography," 347, 379) and Delargy
("Gaelic Storyteller," 208) the number of accomplished reciters
("traditors") in a given community is invariably limited to only a few
per thousand people. While an examination of the lists of South Uist
and Barra reciters from the 1860s and 1870s in J.F. Campbell of Islay
and Alexander Carmichael's works is inconclusive in this regard,
information from reciters active in our own time would tend to make
this number conservative for Scottish Gaelic areas.

77 *CG* 1: xxiv. Reidar Christiansen's anecdote concerning the return of a
collector forty years later to hear a young man recite a tale "in exactly
the same words and manner as he had got it from an old man in the
same house forty years before" (Christiansen, *Vikings*, 70) is a
misquotation from a letter to J.F. Campbell of Islay from his collaborator
John Dewar printed in *WHT* 1: li–liii. Dewar did come across the same
tale recited by a younger man, but "about therty miles distante from
where I had heard it told forty years before that; and the man which

told me the tale could not tell me the meaning of some of the old
Gaelic words that was in it" (p. lii). This would be an ordinary enough
experience for any collector.

78 302 A10–304 A1 4/12/80; 305 A7–306 A1 5/1/81.
79 See Delargy, "Gaelic Storyteller," 189–90, for Irish examples.
80 Draak, "Duncan MacDonald of South Uist," 52–3.
81 Bruford, *Gaelic Folk-Tales*, 55, 64–5.
82 Delargy, "Gaelic Storyteller," 200.
83 Bruford, *Gaelic Folk-Tales*, 60, 238.
84 Hyde, *Beside the Fire*, xix; see Bruford, *Gaelic Folk-Tales*, 60.
85 Christiansen, *Vikings*, 75; *WHT* 1: xxv.
86 Delargy, "Irish Tales," 80.
87 Christiansen, *Vikings*, 72–3; Bruford, "A Lost MacMhuirich Manu-
    script," see bibliography; J.L. Campbell and Thomson, *Edward Lhuyd*,
    39–41.
88 The manuscript employs a system of abbreviations, later filled in, which
    is certain evidence of its being taken down from oral recitation. The
    collector, James (Seumas Beag Sheumais Dhòmhnaill Mhurchaidh)
    MacNeil, a native of Irish Vale, Cape Breton County, later became the
    editor of *Teachdaire nan Gàidheal*; see Dunn, *Highland Settler*, 88–9.
    The tale, titled *An t-Each Dubh* "The Black Horse," may well be the
    tale of the same name collected by Hector MacLean from Roderick
    MacNeill of Mingulay, mentioned above, and listed by J.F. Campbell
    in *WHT* 4: 422–3. See James MacNeil's papers, 1930–42, MG 6/24,
    deposited with the Beaton Institute, University College of Cape Breton
    (Sydney, N.S.).
89 Delargy, "Gaelic Storyteller," 201; Murphy, *Ossianic Lore*, 60.
90 *WHT* 1: xli; *Mac-Talla* (Sydney), 10 (6 June 1902) – 12 (21 August
    1903).
91 For the English version see Curtin, *Myths and Folklore*, 92–113.
92 Hyde, *Beside the Fire*, xxiv. See also Delargy, "Gaelic Storyteller," 194.
93 Delargy, "Irish Tales," 67.
94 Lord, *Singer of Tales*, 29; Dégh, *Folktales and Society*, 83, 85.
95 Donald Archie MacDonald, "Collecting Oral Literature," 425–6; Joe
    Neil recalls the term "raiment of the tale" being used by Michael
    MacPhee of Big Pond referring to the story-telling of Donald (Dòmhnall
    Bàn) MacNeil mentioned on p. 14, Part 1.
96 Maclean, "Aonghus agus Donnchadh," 173.
97 Bruford (*Gaelic Folk-Tales*, 240) suspects that MacNeill's lengthy
    version was a "deliberate compilation," possibly with the help of
    transcriber Hector MacLean. J.F. Campbell notes in his diaries (Delargy,

"Three Men of Islay," 126–7) that during the process of transcription in a small "public" in Paisley both men were "rather screwed. Hector the worse."

98 Maclean, "Aonghus agus Donnchadh," 173; Delargy, "Gaelic Story-teller," 206–7.

99 Angus MacLellan, *Saoghal an Treobhaiche*, 3, 214.

100 See Maclean, "Hebridean Storytellers," 124; and Delargey, "Gaelic Storyteller," 186, and "Irish Tales," 65.

101 See Part 1, pp. 19–20 and Part 2, p. 96.

102 Maclean, "Hebridean Storytellers," 124.

103 Maclean, "Aonghus agus Donnchadh," 171–2. See also Matheson, "Duncan MacDonald," 1–32.

104 See *SSU*, passim; J.L. Campbell, "Angus MacLellan," 193–7.

105 *LSIC, passim*; Delargy, "Gaelic Storyteller," 189–90.

106 See Robinson, *Satirists and Enchanters*, 117; J.L. Campbell and Collinson, *Hebridean Folksongs* 2: 112–21.

107 See Roger D. Abrams. "Proverbs and Proverbial Expressions," in *Folklore and Folklife*, ed. R.M. Dorson, 117–28.

108 J.L. Campbell, "Proverbs from Barra."

109 Maclean, "Death Divination," 57.

110 *CG* 5: 286–97.

111 From Lauchie MacLellan, Dunvegan, Inverness County.

112 See MacDonnell and Shaw, "Raonall Mac Ailein Òig."

113 Carmichael (*CG* 1: xxix–xxxiii) gives a memorable description of the effects of the suppression of traditional music and song in some districts of the Scottish *Gàidhealtachd* during the nineteenth century.

114 J.F. and T.M. Flett, "Some Hebridean Folk Dances."

115 Maclean, "Hebridean Storytellers," 121.

PART ONE: THE WORLD OF THE STORY-TELLER

Middle Cape

17A3 20/1/78; 17A4–18A1 20/1/78; 135A2–138A1 23/11/78; 138A2–139A1 23/11/78; 226A6 30/6/79.

1 Joe Neil was born 23 February 1908 at Reserve Mines, Cape Breton County, and was adopted and raised by Neil (Niall Beag) MacNeil and his wife, both of Barra descent.

2 The period immediately before World War ı marked the decline of

Gaelic-speaking monoglots in the rural areas of the island along with the first appearance of non-Gaelic-speaking children among Highland farming families. The last monoglot Gaelic-speaker in Cape Breton known to us, Mary Rankin of Broadcove Banks, Inverness County, died in 1976 aged about ninety-five.

3 The exclusion of Gaelic in any form from the classroom has, until the last decade, been the rule in all of the schools serving Cape Breton's Gaelic-speaking districts. Although such ends were generally achieved through various forms of social pressure, including ridicule, incidents of physical punishment for the use of Gaelic are still vividly recalled by informants living today. See D. Campbell and R.A. MacLean, *Beyond the Atlantic Roar: A Study of the Nova Scotia Scots* (Toronto: McClelland and Stewart 1974), 131.

4 See p. xxx.

5 The fish referred to is smelt (*morghadan*) and the river (actually a stream), known as *Allt Ruairidh Bhric*, is close to the reciter's boyhood home.

6 In the rural areas people of Joe Neil's generation show a marked reticence concerning what would be termed idle gossip, particularly where it concerns local personalities. When such references do occur in conversation they are seldom direct, frequently tinged with humour, and always quotable. Here, as in Gaelic Scotland, the acceptable outlet for social comment and speculation was through the more formal device of satirical songs. Although there are now few bards of note left in the region, large numbers of satirical songs survive in all Highland communities (see Dunn, *Highland Settler*, 69–70).

7 See p. 120. Joe Neil and Hector know each other from early manhood.

8 A Gaelic newspaper edited by Jonathan G. MacKinnon and published in Sydney from 1892 to 1904; see Dunn, *Highland Settler*, 83–9.

9 *Sar-Obair nam Bard Gaelach*, ed. John MacKenzie. For a partial list of the various editions, see Donald MacLean, *Typographia Scoto-Gadelica* (Edinburgh 1915), 245–9.

10 A. Maclean Sinclair, ed., *Clàrsach na Coille* (Glasgow 1881).

11 *Teachdaire nan Gàidheal* was published in Sydney from 1925 and appeared intermittently for more than ten years; see Dunn, *Highland Settler*, pp. 88–9.

12 The *Casket* was founded in 1852.

Story-tellers

139A2–143A1 23/11/78.

1 AT 2030. See *WHT* 1: 161–7; D.A. MacDonald and Bruford, *Scottish Traditional Tales*, 1–3. This is a formula tale for children, undoubtedly the most universally recognized Gaelic story in Cape Breton.

2 Anna MacNeil ("Tannag") was by all accounts highly respected as both a tradition-bearer and a personality and was especially beloved of children. Around 1920, when she was over eighty and too infirm to make her rounds, she was sent to the asylum in Sydney (there being no poor-house at the time), and she died there a few years later.

3 Cf. *Gairm* 109 (An Geamhradh 1979–80): 49.

4 Compare the account of a story-telling session in the Isle of Barra in the summer of 1859 from the collector Hector MacLean (*WHT* 1: v): "They speak of the Ossianic heroes with as much feeling, sympathy, and belief in their existence and reality as the readers of the newspapers do of the exploits of the British army in the Crimea or in India ..."

5 This reference is not known to the editor from printed Fenian literature

6 A Fenian lay well known in Scottish Gaelic which seems to have no Irish counterpart. For printed versions, see *W&S* 4: 130–3; *WHT* 3: 136–60; *LNF*, 68–71; *Gillies' Collections* (Perth, 1786), 69–77. The above versions agree in giving *frithealadh* "dealing with" for *fighe* "weaving."

7 This is confirmed by the editor's experience with leading Cape Breton story-tellers such as Hughie Dan MacDonnell (Deepdale, Inverness County, d. 1976), Lauchie MacLellan (Dunvegan, Inverness County), Hector Campbell (Hillsdale, Inverness County, d. 1975), Joe Allan MacLean (Rear Christmas Island, Cape Breton County, d. 1984), and Joe Neil. The famous South Uist story-teller, Angus (Aonghus Beag) Mac-Lellan, recited a short tale to the editor in 1961 in which gestures were not used; Duncan MacDonald of South Uist was observed by Maartje Draak ("Duncan MacDonald of South Uist," 48) reciting tales with his hands on his knees. With these reciters, peripheral dramatic effects seem to be achieved through the voice, ranging from imitations of various story characters to a dry, understated tone for humorous descriptions and an accelerated near singsong peculiar to the longer tales. Such observations contrast partially with Calum Maclean's description of Seumas MacKinnon, the last great story-teller in Barra ("Hebridean Storytellers," 124), and more markedly with Delargy's poignant image of Kerry story-teller Seán Ó Conaill practising his stories "using the gesticulations and the emphasis, and all the other tricks of narration" ("The Gaelic Storyteller," 186).

PART TWO: THE RECITERS AND THE TALES

The Kennedys

269A2 13/5/80; 140A1 23/11/78.

1 Murdock Kennedy's grandson Alexander (d. 1985 aged about eighty)
   informed us that Murdock was born on the Isle of Canna, Inner
   Hebrides.
2 Archie Kennedy was born in 1852 and died in 1936.
3 Von Sydow ("Geography," 348) notes the importance of a regular
   audience of "passive tradition carriers" to the maintenance of the
   story-teller's skill: "They know the traditor's repertoire and encour-
   age him to tell his tales. So they act as a kind of sounding-board for the
   tale. It is often due to their presence and insistence that the traditor
   consents to function; and if he moves from the district and no longer
   has their insistence, he often ceases to be active."

1 *The Man in the Light Grey Coat*

J. Shaw Coll. C21A1 2/76 From Archie Kennedy.

This tale is printed in *C.B. Mag.* 22 (June 1979): 30–6. A closely related
Cape Breton version was recorded ca 1960 from Neil MacIntyre of
Benacadie Pond, Cape Breton County, by C.I.N. MacLeod and published in *Sgeulachdan à Albainn Nuaidh*, 94–101. The version also
appears in *Gairm* 15 (An t-Earrach 1956): 243–8.
    A number of versions noted down from oral sources in Scotland in
the last century have been published: *W&S* 2: 32–67; *W&S* 3: 27–55;
MWHT 2: 68–77; *TGSI* 25 (1901–3): 185, 247; *WHT* 2: 209–31 (titled
Murachadh Mac Brian). The tale is mentioned in J.F. Campbell's lists
of tales (*WHT* 4: 389, 406) with an English summary in vol. 18, p. 118
of the collector's manuscripts, now held at the National Library of
Scotland, Edinburgh (Bruford, *Gaelic Folk-Tales*, 253, 261). In his comparison of the Scottish and Irish variants, Bruford (pp. 129, 252–3) suggests that the origin of the various Irish oral and manuscript variants
may lie in an earlier Scottish folk-tale.
1 See *W&S* 3: 35, 48; *W&S* 4: 160; *LNF*, 177 verse 25. Thomas F.
   O'Rahilly, *Early Irish History and Mythology* (Dublin: Dublin Insti-

tute for Advanced Studies 1964), 334–6, cites Irish parallels containing the formula *cuir do mheur fo d' dheud fios.*

2 A virtually identical tableau involving the pursuit of a deer by Caoilte, the use of the *deud-fios* "tooth of knowledge," and seven summer seats is to be found in a Fenian tale from Barra titled *An Gruagach Bàn, Mac Rìgh Eireann* (*WHT* 2: 430–1, 443–4).

3 See *TGSI* 25: 247–8.

4 This bewitching run is common in the repertoire of Gaelic reciters in Scotland and is the only run to have been recorded in Cape Breton in more than fragmentary form. See *SSU*, 34, 212; *SD*, 34; *MWHT* 1: 230, 236; *WHT* 2: 440; Hector Campbell, *Luirgean*, 93.

5 Cf. *W&S* 2: 450. This formula, like a number of others from Cape Breton reciters, may be a fragment of an earlier, lengthier travelling run: compare the formula in Hughie Dan MacDonnell's rendition of the romantic tale AT 953 (*C.B. Mag.* 21 [December 1978]: 14) with the travelling runs in *WHT* 1: 9, 17: *MWHT* 1, 42.

6 A formless monster-adversary.

7 See *W&S* 2: 42; *W&S* 3: 267.

8 Joe Neil understands the Son of the King of the Golden Pillars to be *Ceudach Mac Rìgh nan Collachan Òir,* known also as *Mac Rìgh nan Collach* (Hector Campbell, *Luirgean*, 87–8; Bruford, *Gaelic Folk-Tales*, 124). For the association of the present tale with the *Ceudach* tales, see Bruford, *Gaelic Folk-Tales*, 129, 132 n41; *W&S* 4: 273, 276, where *Rìgh nan Collach* is a brother to Fionn's father Cumhal.

9 A common counter-geas (retaliatory spell or prohibition). See *MWHT* 1: 430.

2 *O Cròileagan of the Horses*

41A8–42A1 16/3/78 From Archie Kennedy.

The tale of which this is a short fragment, *Leigheas Coise Céin* "The Healing of Cian's Leg,' originally consisted of over twenty parts, including a large number of in-tales, and took several nights to recite (*CG* 1: xxiii–xxiv; *W&S* 2: 464). The Reverend Donald MacNicol, in an instructive passage on Gaelic folk tradition in the Highlands, singles out the tale as an example of the advanced state of story-telling: "One of those, in particular, is long enough to furnish subject of amusement for several nights running. It is called *Scialachd Choise Ce* or Cian O Cathan's Tale; and though *Scialachies*, or tellers of tales by profession, are not now retained by our great families, as formerly, there are many

still living, who can repeat it from end to end, very accurately"
(*Remarks on Dr. Samuel Johnson's Journey to the Hebrides* [London:
T. Caddell 1779], 322). See also *TGSI* 25 (1901–8): 179.

The oldest written record is in a late fifteenth-century Irish manuscript (Egerton 1781; British Museum, Irish MSS, edited and translated
by S.H. O'Grady, *Silva Gadelica*, vol. 1 [London, 1892], 296); however,
the nineteenth-century Scottish Gaelic oral versions, listed below, are
more coherent and detailed and seem to derive from an oral tradition
that antedates the manuscript versions, according to Bruford, *Gaelic
Folk-Tales*, 135, 262; and Gerard Murphy, *Ossianic Lore*, 61. For the
Scottish Gaelic oral versions, see *TGSI* 14 (1887–8): 78–100 (Tiree);
TGSI 25: 262–4; *W&S* 2: 206–77. None of the published versions have
been taken down from reciters in the Outer Hebrides.

1 See Bruford, *Gaelic Folk-Tales*, 144 n5.
2 CF. *Ghlaodh e còmhrag* (*W&S* 2: 274).
3 For a possible origin of this name see Bruford, *Gaelic Folk-Tales*, 168.
4 *Iall Greugach*; cf. *WHT* 2: 183, 194.
5 *Fear Diad mac Daimhein*, Cù Chulainn's comrade-in-arms. See
Calum Maclean, "Táin Bó Cúailnge" 168.

3 Ìseadal Son of the King of the Hunts, Fionn's Foster-Son

38A4–39A1 16/3/78 From Archie Kennedy.

The above is a fragment of *An Bhruidhean Chaorthainn* "The Rowan
Mansion," a Fenian tale in which Fionn and his retainers are trapped
and later rescued after a number of battles by Diarmaid and other
members of the band. Scottish oral versions, which are rare, are printed
in *WHT* 2: 181–202; *SSU*, 27–8; D.A. MacDonald and Bruford, *Scottish Traditional Tales*, 53–4. Tale no 8, *Diarmaid agus Bean Chaol a'
Chòt' Uaine* "Diarmaid and the Slim Woman in the Green Coat" may
have belonged to the same tale in Archie Kennedy's repertoire, or to one
of the other tales of the *bruidhean* type circulating in Scotland and
Ireland. The earliest manuscript version of the tale (ca 1600) is Scottish. See Bruford, *Gaelic Folk-Tales*, 47, 115–18, 251; Murphy,
Ossianic Lore, 52–4; Murphy, *Duanaire Finn*, pt. 3, 26. For a folk
retelling of the tale in Ireland, see Murphy, *Duannaire Finn*, pt. 3, xxv;
Mac Róigh, *Bruidhean Chaorthainn*.

1 The motif of stringing a withe (a flexible willow stick) with heads
occurs in two of the Scottish oral versions of the Death of Cù Chulainn
(see notes to 13). See Calum Maclean, "Táin Bó Cúailnge," 181; *TGSI*

2: 38; MacLeod, "Maoim Chruachan and Cuchullin." *Baoth Maol a' Chruachain* may echo *Maoim a' Chruachain*, the Queen Medb of the Ulster Cycle in these nineteenth-century versions.

4 *How Oscar Got His Name*

41A2 16/3/78 From Archie Kennedy.

1 The same punning question is asked in another Fenian tale; see *W&S* 4: 29; cf. Mod. Ir. *oscar* "agility in plying the limbs."

5 *Oscar and Mac a' Luin*

29A2 8/4/78 From Archie Kennedy

1 *Deud-fios*: see above p. 237 n1 for references to the tooth of knowledge.
2 Cf. *WHT* 3: 354, 360.

6 *Fionn and the Strange Adversaries*

39A3 16/3/78 From Archie Kennedy.

7 *How Conan Got His Name*

40A7 16/3/78 From Archie Kennedy.

A South Uist version of this tale is printed in *SSU*, 20. For a description of Conan, see *W&S* 4: 73–4.
1 Cf. *W&S* 4: 73; *WHT* 4: 233.

8 *Diarmaid and the Slim Woman in the Green Coat*

145A4 24/11/78 From Archie Kennedy.

The events described in this fragment involving the Slim Woman (*Bean Chaol*) are commonly incorporated in the *bruidhean* tales. The Fenian warrior who remained stuck to the floor was Conan (*W&S* 3: 71–2). *Bean Chaol* is mentioned elsewhere in J.L. Campbell, *Sia Sgeulachdan*, 40; *WHT* 2: 90, 424–49.
1 Cf. *W&S* 4: 74.

9 *The Death of Diarmaid*

145A7–146A1 24/11/78 From Archie Kennedy.

For other versions of this tale, see *WHT* 3: 49–102; *W&S* 4: 54–63; *SSU*, 29–32; *Tocher* 18 (summer 1975): 62–5; *LNF*, 158–64.

10 *The Amhas Òrmanach*

146A6 24/11/78 From Archie Kennedy.

AT 326 The Youth Who Wanted to Learn What Fear Is.

A tale resembling this type is printed in *WHT* 2: 290–9. For Irish variants, see *Béaloideas* 1: 398, 4:50, 4: 230, 10: 188, 19: 29; *Folklore* 47 (1936): 286. The long tale *Echtra Chonaill Ghulban* contains references to an *Amhus Òr-aramach* with various meaningless variants on the name (Bruford, *Gaelic Folk-Tales*, 168).

11 *Jack and the Master*

J. Shaw Coll. C17A1 Feb. 1976. Heard from Archie Kennedy and later reinforced by a printed version.
AT 1000 Bargain Not to Become Angry, combined with types 1005, 1006.

A Scottish version of this tale transcribed in 1860 is printed in *WHT* 2: 318–43. Some Irish versions bear a striking similarity to this rendition. For possible (partial) written sources, see Patrick Kennedy, *The Fireside Stories of Ireland* (Dublin: M'Glashan and Gill 1870), 74–80; Joseph Jacobs, *Celtic Fairy Tales* (London: David Nutt 1892), 182–91. See also *Béaloideas* 5: 44–7, and 10: 178–80.
1 *Bonnach* is a round, flat kind of bread or cake.

12 *Great Brìd of the Horses*

17A1 20/1/78 From Murdock Kennedy.

This is a surprisingly coherent fragment of the Middle Irish literary tale *Tromdamh Guaire* "Guaire's Troublesome Guests," which exists in its oldest form in a fifteenth-century manuscript version from the Book of Lismore and contains elements from earlier traditions (see Maud Joynt, ed., *Tromdamh Guaire* [Dublin: The Stationery Office 1931]; Seán O Coileáin, "The Making of Tromdamh Guaire"). During a visit to South Uist in 1871 J.F. Campbell took down a summary in English of the tale from an oral source based on a version contained in a lost manuscript belonging to the MacMhuirich family (Bruford, "Mac-Mhuirich Manuscript," 158–9). See also W.J. Watson, "Cliar Sheanchain," *The Celtic Review* 4 (1907–8): 80–8; Robinson, *Satirists and Enchanters*, 96, 125–7; *W&S* 2: 465–7. In the Middle Irish version the bards' demands for blackberries in January, a boar, and to be mounted on a special steed are included among other seemingly impossible requests. The counter-demand for the *cronán snagach* is made by King Guaire's brother Marbhán. That oral versions of the story were once widespread and popular in Scotland is clear from numerous references; see *W&S* 2: 206 (where reference to the *Cliath-sheanachair* is contained in an introduction to *Leigheas Coise Céin*, no 2 above); Angus Macleod, ed., *The Songs of Duncan Ban MacIntyre* (Edinburgh: Oliver & Boyd 1952), 455–6; *CG* 2: 270; J.L. Campbell, ed. *A Collection of Highland Rites*, 55–6.

A fragment of another tale, known as *Smeuran Dubha 'san Fhaoilleach* "Blackberries in January" and incorporating the task mentioned here (H. 1023.3) was supplied by Mary Anne MacKenzie of Washabuck, Victoria County (237A8 16/11/79). Compare the version of AT 953 by the same title in *MWHT* 2: 410–36. An allusion to this task is further preserved in a proverb; see Nicholson, *Proverbs*, 51, 349; see also *Tocher* 14 (Summer 1974): 235–8.

13 The Death of Cù Chulainn

38A3 16/3/78 From Murdock Kennedy.

A more complete version of this fragment of the Ulster Cycle epic, *Táin Bó Cúailnge* "The Cattle Raid of Cooley," was recorded in 1959 from the South Uist reciter Angus MacLellan by Dr Calum Maclean for the School of Scottish Studies; see Maclean, "Táin Bó Cúailnge," 160–81 (includes extensive manuscript references from Irish tradition along with a discussion of the oral variants from Scotland); *Gairm* 29 (Am Foghar 1959): 67–73. The two previously published Scottish Gaelic folk variants were collected during the last century, one by Alexander Carmichael in Iochdar, South Uist, in 1872 (*TGSI* 2 [1872]: 25–42) and the other from an Eigg informant by Kenneth MacLeod and published in translation (MacLeod, "Hero Tales," 512–16). All of the Scottish variants agree with the present version in citing a prohibition against proclaiming Cù Chulainn's death aloud (Maclean, 174; Carmichael, 38; MacLeod, 516). Bruford (*Gaelic Folk-Tales*, 95, 104 n4) notes that there were a number of manuscripts of the Táin and other Cù Chulainn tales in Scotland about 1700; one was in the possession of the Reverend John Beaton of Mull, and the MacMhuirichs held another manuscript, also now lost, from which the Uist oral versions may have derived. See note 87 to the introduction above. For an older, possibly related literary version, see Whitley Stokes, "Cuchulainn's Death," *Revue celtique* 3(1876–8): 175–85. The proper name *Fitheach* "raven" given here originated with the raven that appeared, according to Scottish Gaelic tradition, signifying the death of Cú Chulainn (MacLeod, 515–16; W&)S 4: 8). For other Cù Chulainn stories in Scottish Gaelic, see *WHT* 3: 194–9. The reference in the fragment to the Rock of Big Fergus (*Clach Fhearghuis Mhóir*) is unparalleled in Cù Chulainn tales elsewhere. The stone, traditionally belonging to Fergus Mór mac Eirc, the first of the Dàl Riata kings to rule in Scotland, is the only surviving symbol of Scottish sovereignty. Its Irish counterpart, *Lia Fáil*, situated at the royal seat of Tara also bore the name *Bod Fhearghuis* (R.A.S. MacAllister, *Tara, a Pagan Sanctuary in Ireland* [London: Charles Scribners & Sons 1931], 112) and was said to cry out under one destined for the kingship (Alwyn Rees and Brynley Rees, *Celtic Heritage* [London: Thames & Hudson 1961], 146). Joe Neil recalls vaguely from the tale that the stone was approached by those seeking to benefit from its power of prophecy, but the thread of the story is lost. Probably the association between this tradition and the Cù Chulainn stories is secondary.

14 *The King and the Foal*

128A2–129A1 21/11/78 From Kate Kennedy.

AT 875 The Clever Peasant Girl.

Cape Breton versions have been recorded from Sandy William MacDonald of Glencoe, Inverness County (59A2 9/4/78); Hector Campbell of Hillsdale, Inverness County (Hector Campbell, *Luirgean*, 73–6), and Dan MacKenzie (Dòmhnall Sheònaidh Iain Fhionnlaigh) of Benacadie Pond, Cape Breton County (31A8 20/2/78). See also Dunn, *Highland Settler*, 45–6. A version from Scotland is given in translation in D.A. MacDonald and Bruford, *Scottish Traditional Tales*, 80–4. This type is more common in Ireland; *Béaloideas* 1: 156–7, no 2; 11: 150–1, no 32.

15 *The Castle that Boban Saor Built*

15A3–16A1 20/1/78 From Kate Kennedy.

This is the most popular of many stories told in Scotland and Ireland concerning Boban (or Goban) Saor, a carpenter of legendary skill. In Cape Breton, versions were recorded from Joe Allan MacLean (70A1

28/4/78) of Rear Christmas Island, Cape Breton County, and Sandy William MacDonald (109A12 – 110A1 20/10/78). A Scottish version from Angus MacLellan is printed in *SSU*, 45–7; Irish versions appear in *LSIC* 5: 264–5; Murphy, *Tales from Ireland*, 84–7; Kennedy, *Legendary Fictions*, 70–2.

16 *Working with the Adze*

16A3 20/1/78 From Kate Kennedy.

Compare the version from Angus MacLellan in *SSU*, 45.

17 *Did You Ever See the Like of Me*

163A3–164A1 29/11/78 From Alexander Kennedy.

The Scottish versions of the tale, known also as *A' Chailleach Bheurr*, have been gathered and examined by J.G. MacKay in a lengthy study ("Comh-abartachd eadar Cas-shiubhal-an-t-Sléibhe agus a' Chailleach Bheurr," *SGS* 3 [1931]: 10-51). The name *Uilleam Dean Suidhe* "William Sit Down" occurs here as a ploy in the battle of wits between the *cailleach* and her protagonist; it is also listed as a story-title in J.F. Campbell's lists of tales (*WHT* 4: 398).

The MacLeans

271A2–272A1 13/5/80.

18 *Duanach the Widow's Son*

129A2–130A1 21/11/78 From Donald (Mac Chaluim Iain) MacLean.

AT 1049 The Heavy Axe, 1088 The Eating Contest.

A similar version of the tale was recorded by Sister Margaret MacDonell (14/8/68) from Hector Campbell at Hillsdale, Inverness County (Hector Campbell, *Luirgean*, 1–10). Angus MacKinnon of St Margaret's Village, Victoria County, recited an outline of the same tale, titled *Reamhrachan a' Chraicinn Chaorach*, that he had often heard from his grandfather Sandy MacKinnon of neighbouring Lowlands, Inverness County (11/3/78). For Irish versions, see *Béaloideas* 4: 228–9 no. 6; 17: 211–13.

19 *The Man with the Long Tales*

120A3–121A1 22/11/78 From Donald (Mac Chaluim Iain) MacLean.

AT 2301A Making the King Lose Patience.

20 *The Strong Woodsman's Son*

C17A1 2/76 From Donald (Mac Chaluim Iain) MacLean with later reference to an unidentified printed version.

AT 650A Strong John.

Regarding MacLean's oral version, Joe Neil adds (220A3 31/6/79): *Nuair a bha mi 'nam ghille òg, chuala mi 'n sgeulachd aig fear 'ga h-aithris, fear ris an abramaid Dòmhnall Mac'Illeain ... Co-dhiubh, leis cho coltach 's a bha 'n naidheachd "Gille Làidir na Coilleadh" nuair a chunna mi ann a' leabhar i ris a' naidheachd a chuala mi aig Mac'Illeain aon uair 'ga h-innse, smaointich mi gum biodh e iomchaidh gu leòr dhomh a h-ionnsachadh; agus bho 'n a bha i cho coltach gun cuirinn sios i 's gum biodh i air chuimhne. Ach ma's math mo chuimhne air a' ghnothach, 's e tarbh mór a bh' aigesan air ainmeachas ann an aon dhe na h-euchdan móra a bha ri dheanamh – a bha a' dol a chuir as dha 'n ghille mhór làidir. Agus cha n-eil beachd agam ro mhath mun chòrr, ach gu robh e air ainmeachas fuamhaire na duine mór fiadhaich làidir air choireiginn a bh' aige ri dhol a shabaid ris. Agus chaidh aige air cuir as dha 'n duine mhór a bha sin agus chaidh aige air cuir as dha 'n tarbh fhiadhaich cuideachd. Cha d' rinn e ach breith air adhairc air agus chuir e suaineadh 'na amhaich agus bha e marbh. Agus dh'fhoighneachd e c'àite robh a' bhéist mhór a bha iad a' dol 'ga chuir-san dha'n bheinn 'ga ghlacadh agus thuirt iad ris gum b'e siod a bh' ann. O, thuirt e nach robh 'n siod ach creutair beag suarach: gum faodadh duine sam bith a ghlacadh 's cuir as dha. Ach co-dhiubh mar a thuirt mi, leis cho coltach 's a bha suidheachadh na sgeulachd ris a' rud a dh'innis Mac'Illeain, ghabh mi spéis dhi. Agus cha tug esan cunntais as an fhìor-thoiseach idir: thòisich esan aig nuair a bha Mac na Banndraich aig aois bliadhna air fhichead agus a thuirt a mhàthair ris gu robh an t-am aige bhith falbh a nist amach 'ga chosnadh. Ach bha cuid mhór dhe 'n sgeulachd as an toiseach nach do thòisich e oirre. Tha mi creidsinn gu robh cabhag air as an am agus 's cinnteach gu robh a' chuid mhór dhi aige oir bha e math gu innse sgeulachdan, an duine bha seo, ged nach maireann e 'n diugh.*

When I was a small boy I heard the tale recited by a man we used to call

Donald MacLean ... And when I saw the story "The Strong Lad of the Wood" in a book, it resembled so closely the story I heard MacLean telling on one occasion, I thought it would be appropriate to learn it; since it was so similar I could record it sometime so that it would be remembered. But if I recall things correctly, MacLean mentioned a big bull in one of the great feats that was to be performed – it was going to do away with the big, strong lad. I don't remember the rest very clearly, except that a giant or a big, strong, wild man was mentioned that the lad had to fight. He succeeded in vanquishing the big man and the fierce bull as well. He just seized its horns and twisted its neck until it was dead. Then he asked where the great monster was that they were sending him to the mountain to catch and they replied that that was it. Oh, the lad answered, that was just a puny, insignificant creature; anyone could catch it and kill it. Anyway, as I mentioned, the setting of the tale was so close to MacLean's rendition that it caught my interest. But MacLean did not recount the very beginning of the tale; he began where the Widow's Son was twenty-one years old and his mother told him that it was time to go out and support himself. There was a good deal in the beginning that he did not start on. I believe he was rushed at the time, but certainly he knew most of it because this man was a good story-teller, though he is not living today.

A detailed version of the tale recorded from Dan MacKenzie of Benacadie Pond, Cape Breton County (81A6–82A1 18/5/78) titled *Laghaiste Mór mac Iain Garaidh* includes the opening part omitted by Donald MacLean and closely parallels Joe Neil's rendition. See *W&S* 3: 187–215. A large number of variants have been collected in Ireland; see *Béaloideas* 2: 148–55, 156 (bibl.); 7: 66, 68, 154–5 no. 3.

1 *W&S* 3: 197, 211 (Muileann Leacain).

21 *The Woman Who Was Awarded a Pair of Shoes by the Devil*

178A3 3/12/78 From Michael MacLean.

AT 1353 The Old Woman as Trouble Maker.

One other Cape Breton version, *A' Chailleach a Bheat an Deamhan* "The Old Woman Who Beat the Devil," was recorded from Dan MacKenzie of Benacadie Pond, Cape Breton County (242A2 15/12/79). See also *Béaloideas* 2: 206–7; 9: 66–7 no 2; 18: 144–5 no 1.

22 *The Three Knots*

225A4 28/6/79 From Michael MacLean and Hector MacNeil.

The story was recorded from Joe Allan MacLean of Rear Christmas Island, Cape Breton County (245A6–246A1 24/1/80) and John Rannie MacKeigan of Marion Bridge, Cape Breton County (320A6 27/3/81). Scottish versions are published in translation in D.A. MacDonald and Bruford, *Scottish Traditional Tales*, 131–2; J.G. Campbell, *Witchcraft*, 19. For an interesting Donegal parallel, see Ó hEochaidh *et al.*, *Síscéalta Ó Thír Chonaill*, 132–3.

23 *How the Fairy Suitor Was Tricked*

224A3 27/6/79 From Michael MacLean.

A variant was recited by Joe Allan MacLean (245A5 24/11/80) and the story is well known in the Highlands: *Tocher* 20 (Winter 1975): 128–9; D.A. MacDonald and Bruford, *Scottish Traditional Tales*, 125; *Tocher* 1 (Spring 1971): 12–13. For fairy suitors, see *CG* 5: 132–63.

24 *The Night It Rained Porridge*

178A2 3/12/78 From Mrs Michael MacLean.

AT 1600 The Fool as Murderer and AT 1381B The Sausage Rain.

The tale was recorded from Joe Allan MacLean (199A3 9/3/79) with the title *Dòmhnall Dona Mac na Banndraich* "Bad Donald the Widow's Son." Scottish versions are given in *Gairm* 11 (An t-Earrach 1955): 254–5 (Barra); *Tocher* 6 (Summer 1972): 172–5.

25 *Stirling Castle*

222A6–223A1 22/6/79 From Donald (Chaluim Nill Mhóir) MacLean.

26 *The Miser and the Tailor*

172A8–173A1 1/12/78 From Donald (Chaluim Nill Mhóir) MacLean.

For Irish versions see Pádraig Ó Siochfhradha, *An Seanchaidhe Muimhneach* (Baile Átha Cliath: Institúid Béaloideasa Éireann 1932), 246–7; *Béaloideas* 3 (1932): 93.

27 *The Two Misers*

173A2 1/2/78 (C15A2 2/76) From John MacLean.

AT 1704 Anecdotes about Absurdly Stingy Persons.

The MacIsaacs

270A5–271A1 13/5/80.

28 *Jack Fury*

91B4–92A1 16/6/78 From John MacIsaac.

AT 1535 The Rich and the Poor Peasant.

   Among the Scottish versions assembled by J.F. Campbell (*WHT* 2: 232–52) this rendition most closely resembles that from Barra. Irish versions are given in *LSIC*, 160–70; *Béaloideas* 4: 236, and 8: 31ff. For additional bibliographic material, see *Béaloideas* 10: 202; Jackson, "International Folktale," 291.

29 *The Man Who Received the Three Counsels*

178A4–179A1 3/12/78 From John MacIsaac and Angus MacMullin.

AT 910B The Servant's Good Counsels.

   See Moireasdan, *Ugam agus Bhuam*, 31–6; *MWHT* 1: 74–83 (with references); D.A. MacDonald and Bruford, *Scottish Traditional Tales*, 11–13; *Béaloideas* 2: 47–50 (bibl.), 8: 25–8, 9: 86–8, 132 (bibl.), 10: 180–1; Jackson, "International Folktale," 289 (bibl.). This *exemplum* type was recorded in Irish literature as early as the twelfth-century manuscript *Merugud Ulix* "The Wandering of Ulysses": see Murphy, *Ossianic Lore*, 17.

30 *The Forgetful Minister*

161A3–162A1 28/11/78 From John MacIsaac.

AT 1775 The Hungry Parson (Guided by a Rope [X431]).

31 *Monday, Tuesday*

224A5–225A1 27/6/79 From John MacIsaac and Angus MacMullin.

AT 503 The Gifts of the Little People.

   The numerous Gaelic versions of this widespread international folktale are unique in Scottish Gaelic fairy-lore in having no air associated with the song. See *Tocher* 26 (Autumn 1977): 107–9 (Barra). Irish versions: *Béaloideas* 1: 65–6, 2: 16 (bibl., 23), 6: 169ff. no 161, 7: 62; for further references see Jackson, "International Folktale," 287.

32 *Angus MacIsaac's Trip to the Moon*

161A2 28/11/78 From Angus MacIsaac.

AT 1881 The Man Carried Through the Air by Geese and AT 1894 The Man Shoots a Ramrod Full of Ducks.

Tall tales involving hunting are particularly popular throughout North America. See Aarne and Thompson, *Types of Folktale*, 509–10; and Thompson, *The Folktale*, 214. A similar hunting tale was recorded at Mabou Harbour, Inverness County, from Angus Gillis (301A8 1/12/80).

33 *The Big Pig*

162A2 29/11/78 From Angus MacIsaac.

AT 1960 The Great Animal or Great Object.

The MacMullins

270A3–A4 13/5/80.

1 Joking references among Gaels to the traditional tales as *breugan* "lies" are so widespread and frequent as to be worthy of notice. The allusion calls to mind the Icelandic term *lygisögur* "lying tales," which Delargy ("Gaelic Storyteller," 221–2) observed to be "the nearest parallel to these late Gaelic romantic or hero-tales." For a further parallel between Icelandic and Gaelic story-telling traditions, see John MacInnes, "Gaelic Poetry and Historical Tradition," *The Middle Ages in the Highlands* (Inverness: The Inverness Field Club 1981), 142.

34 *The King of Egypt's Daughter*

57A4–59A1 8/4/78 From Angus MacMullin and Alexander MacLean.

AT 506 The Rescued Princess.

WHT 2: 121–40 (Barra); *Béaloideas* 4: 293–8 (bibl.). For Irish versions, see O'Sullivan and Christiansen, "Types of Irish Folk-Tale," 104 (bibl.); *Béaloideas* 1: 46, 167, 180. A comparative study of the tale type was published by Sven Liljenblad (*Die Tobiasgeschichte und andere Märchen mit Toten Helfern* [Lund 1927]).

35 *The Fair-haired Doctor*

222A4 22/6/79 From Angus MacMullin.

This is the most popular of many tales known in the Western Isles concerning *An t-Ollamh Muileach*. See *Tocher* 25 (Spring 1977): 50–2; D.A. MacDonald and Bruford, *Scottish Traditional Tales*, 135; *WHT* 2: 382; *Tocher* 24 (Winter 1976–7): 295. The name refers to various of the Beatons, who were hereditary physicians and shenachies throughout the Highlands and Islands from the thirteenth century (J.L. Campbell and Thomson, *Edward Lhuyd*, 12–22).

36 *The Bad Mother's Daughter*

119A7–120A1 30/10/78 From Angus MacMullin.

AT 901 The Taming of the Shrew.

One additional Cape Breton version was recorded from Dan Mac-Kenzie of Benacadie Pond, Cape Breton County (242A3–243A1 15/12/79). Angus MacLellan's closely corresponding South Uist version appears in *SSU*, 65–9. Irish versions are published in *LSIC*, 153–6 (bibl., 423); Jackson, "International Folktale," 289 (bibl.); *Béaloideas* 1: 345–8 (bibl.).

37 *The Lad, the Girl in the Cradle, and the Ring*

223A17 27/6/79 From Angus MacMullin.

AT 930D Fated Bride's Ring in the Sea.

MWHT 1: 292, 307; Aarne and Thompson, *Types of Folktale*, 328.

38 *The Widow's Son and the Robbers*

127A2–128A1 20/11/78 From Hector MacMullin.

AT 304 The Hunter.

This type is rare both in Scottish and Irish Gaelic, although the incorporated type AT 956 (Robbers' Heads Cut Off One by One as They

Enter the House) is known in both traditions. Cape Breton: AT 956B recorded from Peter (Pàdraig Aonghuis Sìne) MacEachern, Glendale, Inverness County (J. Shaw Coll. C1B11 7/63); Ireland: *Béaloideas* 4: 62–3 no 35; Jackson, "International Folktale," 290 (bibl.).

39 *The Golden Bird*

124A4–127A1 20/11/78 From Hector MacMullin, reinforced from a written source.

AT 550 Search for the Golden Bird.

Seumas MacManus's collection of Irish folktales, *In Chimney Corners* (New York 1919), 37ff contains a version of the tale, and is mentioned by Joe Neil as one of the books of tales that came into his possession during the 1930s. However the tale is well documented in Highland tradition (*WHT* 2: 344–76). For Irish manuscript and printed versions, see O'Sullivan and Christiansen, "Types of Irish Folk-Tale," 116–17.

1 The rest of the story suggests that the youngest son rescues his other brother, presumably in a house where he spent more than one night.

Angus MacKenzie (Aonghus Sheumais Mhurchaidh Bhàin)

273A2 13/5/80.

40 *The Soldier Who Was Refused a Drink of Water*

159A2–160A1 28/11/78 From Angus MacKenzie.

AT 1536A The Woman in the Chest (K2321, K2151).

An additional Cape Breton version was recited by John K. MacNeil of Iona, Victoria County (210A10–211A1 2/5/79). One Scottish Gaelic version is printed in *WHT* 1: 237–43. The tale is popular in Ireland; see *LSIC*, 171–4, 424 (bibl.).

Joe MacLean (Eòs Pheadair Chaluim Ghobha)

272A2 13/5/80.

41 *The Shirt of the Man without Worries*

119A6 30/10/78 From Joe MacLean.

AT 844 The Luck-Bringing Shirt.

The story is printed in *C.B. Mag.* 1 (1973): 10. See also *Mac-Talla*, 31 August 1900, 67, 70–1.

John MacNeil (Mac do Dhòmhnall Dhòmhnaill 'ic Iain 'ic Iain)

308A14 26/1/81.

42 *The Young Lad Who Quit School*

153A28 27/1/78 From John MacNeil (1922).

For an Irish version, see *LSIC*, 192–3, 425–6 (bibl.).
1 The Gaelic word is pronounced *meoghlan* which is Uist for *meanglan* "branch"; see *GWSU*, 178, and below, s.v. *miar* for semantic parallel.
2 For the Gaelic word, *tùic*, see *GWSU*, 244, s.v. *tòichd* "a large, bulky thing."

Mrs Michael MacNeil (Anna Nighean Dhòmhnaill Iain Dhiarmaid)

272A3 13/5/80.

43 *The Little Old Man with the Grains*

225A2 27/6/79 From Mrs Michael MacNeil.

AT 1655 The Profitable Exchange.

A Barra version of this children's tale is printed by Christiansen in his wide-ranging study (*Béaloideas* 3: 107–20). See also *Tocher* 3 (Autumn 1979): 98–9; D.A. MacDonald and Bruford, *Scottish Traditional Tales*, 4; *Tocher* 20 (Winter 1975): 124–7. Irish variants subsequent to Christiansen's study are printed in *Béaloideas* 4: 96.

44 *The Fox, the Wolf, and the Butter*

224A4 27/6/79 Mrs Michael MacNeil, Hector MacMullin.

AT 15 The Theft of Butter (Honey) by Playing Godfather and AT 2 The Tail-Fisher.

Scottish versions of AT 15 are found in *WHT* 3: 108–12, 116-18 (Barra);

Storey, *Bha Siod Ann Reimhid*, 26-30 (Barra); *Tocher* 30 (Winter 1978–9): 359–60 (Shetland). Irish versions are in *Béaloideas* 2: 339 ff. (bibl.); Aarne and Thompson, *Types of Folktale*, 25. A Scottish version of AT 2 is given in *WHT* 1: 280–1, and an Irish in *Béaloideas* 3: 240, 255 (bibl.).

1 In Cape Breton Gaelic *sionnach* and *madadh ruadh* are both used for fox. *Madadh alladh* is the usual word for wolf.

Neil Campbell (Niall Eachainn 'ac Dhunnachaidh)

269A3–270A1 13/5/80.

45 *The Journey Boban Saor Made with His Son*

15A1 20/1/78 From Neil Campbell.

This story was also recorded from Joe Allan MacLean of Rear Christmas Island, Cape Breton County (69A3 28/4/78). For an Irish version, see Murphy, *Tales from Ireland*, 84–7.

46 *How Boban Saor's Son Found His Wife*

15A2 20/1/78 From Neil Campbell.

See *SSU*, 44–5. Irish versions are printed in Murphy, *Tales from Ireland*, 83–4; Kennedy, *Legendary Fictions*, 68–79.

47 *The Chalk Line*

16A2 20/1/78 From Neil Campbell.

Dan MacNeil (Dòmhnall Nìll Eoghainn Mhóir 'ic Ìomhair)

270A2 13/5/80.

48 *Boban Saor: Barley Bread and Milk*

16A4 20/1/78; 268A5 13/5/80 From Kate Kennedy and Dan MacNeil.

A fragment was recorded from Joe Allan MacLean (298A5 21/10/80).

Roderick MacNeil (Ruairidh Iain 'ic Ruairidh Ruaidh)

308A15 26/1/81.

1 This is not among the various names for the Fenian band's rallying call listed by Bruford, *Gaelic Folk-Tales*, 120–1 n 4.

49 *The Tub That Boban Saor Built*

16A5 20/1/78 From Roderick MacNeil.

50 *Crazy Archie and the Hen*

297A2 23/10/80 From Roderick MacNeil.

The character of Gilleasbuig Aotrom "Crazy Archie," a trickster given to caustic wit, is celebrated in many Scottish Gaelic communities, both Protestant and Catholic, in short anecdotes such as these.

Anonymous

51 *Crazy Archie and the Minister Souter*

221A5 22/6/79 Oral source not recalled.

52 *The Farmer's Big Lad*

196A7–197A1 8/3/79 From an unidentified reciter and reinforced by a written version.

AT 300 The Dragon-Slayer.

Joe Neil's version of the hero-tale was once widely enjoyed in Cape Breton; it is alluded to by the singer and story-teller Lauchie MacLellan of Dunvegan, Inverness County (J. Shaw Coll. C13A10 2/76) who heard it from his paternal grandfather, Neil MacLellan, with the title *Sgeulachd a' Chamain Iaruinn* "The Tale of the Iron Shinty-Club: *"Bha 'n sin Sgeulachd a' Chamain Iaruinn aige, Sgeulachd na h-Ubhaill Òir, Rìgh Tullach Uaine ... O Dhia seall oirnn mar a bha a leithid dhiubh aige. 'He had The Tale of the Iron Shinty-Club, The Tale of the Golden Apple, The King of Green Hill ... O God look down upon us, the like he had of them. If I had him here for one day I'd get* him to go through all of them ... I'd eat every one of them.'" Another longer version, also in Joe's repertoire, is discussed on p. xvi. The present rendition corresponds closely to that printed in *W&S* 2: 72–104, especially the synopses of variants, 95–103. The tale has enjoyed immense popularity in Ireland; see O'Sullivan and Christiansen, "Types of Irish Folk-Tale," 59–62; *Béaloideas* 7: 9 (bibl.).

PART THREE: WIT, LORE, AND PASTIMES

Repartee and Ready Wit

Dermot Mackenzie (Diarmaid Eòin)

154A17, A23; 155A1, A2 28/11/78.

1 *Sios* "down" refers to a northerly direction, as from Middle Cape to Sydney.

Michael MacDonald (Mìcheal Raonaill 'ac Dhòmhnuill Òig)

155A11 28/11/78.

Martin MacInnis (Màrtainn Ruairidh Dhòmhnaill Mhóir)

156A1, A6 28/11/78.

Alexander MacIsaac (Sandaidh 'Illeasbu' Mhóir)

156A11 28/11/78.

Angus MacIsaac (Aonghus 'Illeasbu' Mhóir)

157A2, A4, A5, A10 28/11/78.

John MacIsaac (Iain 'Illeasbu' Mhóir)

157A12 28/11/78.

Mrs Roderick MacIsaac (Anna Ruairidh Ailein)

158A6–A7 28/11/78.

Neil MacIsaac (Mac do dh'Anna Ruairidh Ailein)

158A11 28/11/78.

Roderick MacNeil (Ruairidh Iain 'ic Ruairidh Ruaidh)

158A13 28/11/78.

Joe MacNeil (Eòs Nìll Bhig)

221A2–A3 31/6/79.

Anonymous

306A1–A2 9/1/81.

Proverbs

134 22/11/78; 151 27/11/78; 231 31/8/79.

Items not given a recording number here were supplied by Joe Neil in a written list.

See Nicholson, *Proverbs*; J.L. Campbell, "Proverbs from Barra," 178–208; Charles W. Dunn, "Gaelic Proverbs in Nova Scotia," *Journal of American Folklore* (reprint, n.p., n.d.); J.L. Campbell, *Sean fhocail agus Comhadan* (Glasgow: An Comunn Gaidhealach 1968).

1 151A7.
2 151A2.
3 151A6.
4 231A21 From Michael MacLean (Mìcheal Iain Chaluim).
5 231A25 From Michael MacNeil (Mìcheal Ruairidh 'ic Iain 'ic Eachainn).
6 From Neil MacNeil (Niall Ruairidh 'ic Iain 'ic Eachainn).
7 231A15 From Roderick MacNeil (Ruairidh Sheumais Ruairidh Ruaidh neo Ruairidh Ealasaid).
8 231A12 From Mrs Neil MacNeil (Bean Nìll Ruairidh 'ic Iain 'ic Eachainn) and Michael MacNeil.
9 231A11 From Mrs Neil MacNeil and Mrs Roderick MacNeil.
10 231A6 From Michael MacLean.
11 151A4 A popular saying in the Hebrides. See *GWSU*, 45.

12 151A2 From Mrs James MacDonald (Bean Sheumais Aonghuis Ruairidh 'ic Aonghuis).
13 151A2 From James Smith.
14 134A9 From Michael MacLean.
17 231A13 From Michael MacLean.
18 231A8 From James Smith; Michael MacLean; Mrs Michael MacPhee.
20 151A2.
21 134A5.
22 231A3.
23 134A4.
24 231A26 From Donald MacPhee (Dòmhnall Nìll Dhòmhnaill).
38 From Malcolm J. MacLean (Calum Iain).
41 154A15 From Donald MacLellan and Mrs Donald Campbell (Bean Dhanaidh Iain Dhòmhnaill), Big Pond.
42 From Joseph MacLean.

Expressions

134 22/11/78; 151 27/11/78; 154 28/11/78; 231 31/8/79; 232 31/8/79.

1 232A2.
2 231A33 From Donald MacPhee.
3 154A13 From Donald MacPhee.
4 From Dougall MacPhee (Dùghall Mhìcheil Nìll Dhòmhnaill).
5 231A35 From Neil MacNeil.
6 From Neil MacNeil. See *GWSU*, 43, given in this reference as applying to a person who is very wide awake.
7 From Neil MacNeil.
8 134A3.
    Gaelic *bogha* "a bow for archery" is the word understood and given by the reciter. More likely intended here is the homonymous nautical term *bodha* "submerged rock" from Old Norse *boði* (cas. obl. *boða*) "a breaker (on hidden rocks)." See Carl Hj. Borgstrom, *The Dialects of the Outer Hebrides* (Oslo: Norwegian Universities Press 1940), 31, 137.
9 See *GWSU*, 64, used when introducing a subject foreign to a conversation.
10 154A2.
11 231A16 From Michael MacNeil and Mrs Neil MacNeil.
12 231A24.
13 232A7.

14 154A14 From Michael MacPhee (Mìcheal Mhìcheil Nìll Dhòmhnaill);
    231A7.
15 151A4.
16 154A8 From Donald MacPhee.
17 From Murdock Kennedy (Murchadh Sheumais Mhurchaidh).
18 231A14 From Alex MacLean (Alasdair Nìll Chaluim).
19 231A23 From Michael MacPherson (Mìcheal Nìll Ruairidh).
20 231A4 From Donald MacPhee.
21 231A9 From Neil MacNeil.
23 154A12.
24 *Uisge nan uighean* "egg-water" is associated in popular belief with bad
    luck.
25 154A10 From Donald MacPhee.
26 231A18 From Mrs Michael MacDonald (Bean Mhìcheil Dhòmhnaill
    'ac Dhòmhnaill Òig).
27 231A17 From Mrs Anna MacNeil (Bean Mhìcheil Ruairidh 'ic Iain 'ic
    Eachainn). See *GWSU*, 196, where the expression was used to prevent
    one child from striking another with a stick.
28 231A36 From Mrs Michael MacLean (Bean Mhìcheil Iain Chaluim).
29 231A30 From Michael MacLean (Mìcheal Iain Chaluim).
30 231A32 From Mrs Neil MacNeil.
31 154A11.
32 231A31 From Mrs William MacDonald, Big Pond.

Children's Rhymes

1 *The Rainbow*

134A12 22/11/78 From John MacNeil.

2 *Will You Go to Play.*

135A1 22/11/78 From Archie Kennedy.

One Cape Breton version was recorded from Dougall MacDonald,
Troy, Inverness County (279A1 24/10/80). See also the Scottish Council for Research in Education, *Aithris is Oideas*, 89.

Traditional Games

21A2 16/6/78.

1 Lauchie MacLellan, Dunvegan, Iverness County, has supplied a fur-

ther description of *Leum a' Bhradain* "The Salmon's Leap" (319A5 26/3/81); see *GWSU*, 263. The player begins in a horizontal position supported by his hands and the tips of his toes.

Marriage Premonitions

See *Tocher* 26 (Autumn 1977): 87–8; J.G. Campbell, *Witchcraft*, 147–8 for parallels.

1 14A5 16/3/78. The same belief is attested in the Highlands cf. J.G. Campbell, *Witchcraft*, 305. For invocations to the moon, see *CG* 3: 274–305.
2 91B1 16/6/78.
3 91A2 16/6/78.
4 91A2 16/6/78.
5 91B1 16/6/78. For other magical properties of boundary streams, see *CG* 4: 144, 147, 155.

Signs, Superstitions and Second Sight

176A2 1/12/78.

1 144A1 23/11/78.
   Cf. *CG* 2: 158–9; *CG* 5: 286–97; *GWSU*, 131.
2 144A1 23/11/78.
   Cf. *CG* 2: 344–5; *CG* 6: 57 s.v. *currac-rath*; *GWSU*, 93.
3 144A1 23/11/78.
   GWSU, 74, 216.
4 144A1 23/11/78.
5 144A1 23/11/78.
6 144A1 23/11/78.
   J.G. Campbell, *Witchcraft*, 111; *GWSU*, 104.
7 144A1 23/11/78.
   For birds as death-omens, see J.G. Campbell, *Witchcraft*, 110; *CG* 6: 148 s.v. *tàsg*.
8 147A7 24/11/78.
   Such persons were referred to as *droch-chòmhalaichean*. See J.G. Campbell, *Superstitions*, 253; *GWSU*, 80; *LSIC*, 320.
9 147A7 24/11/78. Presumably according to subsequent events on the journey. This could be the basis on which *droch-chòmhlaichean* were identified. Joe Neil believes that the anecdote used to illustrate this belief may be derived from his reading.

10 151A3 27/11/78.
    J.G. Campbell, *Superstitions*, 255, *GWSU*, 113, s.v. *éigheach*.
11 148A5 24/11/78.
    Cf. J.G. Campbell, *Witchcraft*, 23.
12 148A5 24/11/78.
13 41A3 16/3/78.
    For a general introduction to the phenomenon of second sight (*dà-shealladh*) in the Highlands, see J.G. Campbell, *Witchcraft*, 120–32.
14 148A1 24/11/78.
15 176A2 1/12/78.
    See J.G. Campbell, *Witchcraft*, 128–9.

Ghosts and Apparitions

 1 175A3–176A1 1/12/78.
    J.G. Campbell, *Witchcraft*, 173–6.
 2 219A3 16/6/79.
    For bòcain "ghosts," see J.G. Campbell, *Witchcraft*, 181–7.
 3 219A4 16/6/79.
    J.G. Campbell, *Witchcraft*, 185.

Music and Dance

Fiddlers

269A3–270A1 13/5/80; 261A2 28/3/80.

For a description of the Gaelic origins of Cape Breton fiddle music see the booklet by William Lamey, John Angus Rankin, and John Shaw accompanying the record *Cape Breton Scottish Fiddle* (London: Topic 12TS354 1978).

1 The tune, known in the collections as Greig's Pipes, is named in the Gaelic manner from the first words of the corresponding *port-à-beul* or mouth-music. It is customarily played by Cape Breton fiddlers using the high bass (*scordatura*) tuning.
2 The acquiring of gifts, particularly music, from a fairy mound is a belief known elsewhere. See *Tocher* 26 (Summer 1977): 108–12; John MacInnes, "Gaelic Poetry and Historical Tradition," *The Middle Ages in the Highlands* (Inverness: The Inverness Field Club 1981), 154.

Pipers

150A5–151A1 27/11/78.

Dances

91B1 6/6/78; 150A4 27/11/78.

The snuffing of candles by dancers as a demonstration of their skill was common in other localities. Johnny Williams of Melford, Inverness County, recalls a verse composed by a local bard, Dougall MacLennan (Dùghall Iain Ruaidh) (10/3/82):

> *Gura h-ann aig Allt 'ic 'IlleMhìcheil*
> *Bha na h-ighneagan bu toil leam.*
> *Dhannsadh iad air ùrlar clàraich*
> *'S smàladh iad le 'n sàil a' choinneal.*
> Carmichael's Brook is where the girls dwelt
> Whom I admired.
> They could dance on the board floor
> Snuffing out the candle with their heels.

Select Bibliography

Works of reference are arranged beginning with those dealing in a general way with folktales, then listing works on shared Gaelic folktale traditions, and finally covering folktales in the various relevant Gaelic-speaking areas.

Folktales

Aarne, Antti, and Stith Thompson. *The Types of the Folktale, a Classification and Bibliography.* Folklore Fellows Communications 184. Helsinki: Academia Scientarium Fennica 1973.

Dégh, Linda. "Folk Narrative." In *Folklore and Folklife: an Introduction,* edited by Richard M. Dorson, 53–83. Chicago: University of Chicago Press 1972.

– *Folktales and Society: Story-Telling in a Hungarian Peasant Community.* Bloomington: Indiana University Press 1965.

Dorson, Richard M., ed. *Folklore and Folklife: an Introduction.* Chicago: University of Chicago Press 1972.

Lord, Albert B. *The Singer of Tales.* Cambridge: Harvard University Press 1964.

Sydow, Carl Wilhelm von. "Geography and Folk-Tale Ecotypes." *Béaloideas* 4(1934): 344–55.

Thompson, Stith. *The Folktale.* New York: Holt, Rinehart and Winston 1946.

Zimmer, Heinrich. *The King and the Corpse.* Princeton: Princeton University Press 1971.

Gaelic Tales and Story-Tellers

1 *Ireland and Scotland*

Bruford, Alan. *Gaelic Folk-Tales and Medieval Romances.* Dublin: The Folklore of Ireland Society 1969.

Christiansen, Reider Th. *The Vikings and Viking Wars in Irish and Gaelic Tradition.* Oslo: Norske Videnskaps-Akademi: 1931.

Delargy, James. "The Gaelic Storyteller." *Proceedings of the British Academy* 31 (1945): 178–221.

Murphy, Gerard. *Ossianic Lore and Romantic Tales of Medieval Ireland.* 1955. Reprint. Cork: The Mercier Press 1971.

2 *Ireland*

Béaloideas. Dublin 1927–   .

Curtin, Jeremiah. *Irish Folk-Tales.* Edited by James Delargy. Dublin: The Talbot Press 1964.

– Myths and Folklore of Ireland. 1890. Reprint. New York: Weathervane Books 1975.

Delargy, James. "Irish Tales and Story-Tellers." In *Märchen, Mythos und Dichtung,* edited by Hugo Kuhn and Kurt Schier, 63–82. Munich: C.H. Beck 1965.

Dillon, Myles, ed. *Early Irish Society.* Dublin: Colm O Lochlainn 1963.

Hyde, Douglas. *Beside the Fire.* London: David Nutt 1910.

Jackson, Kenneth. "The International Folktale in Ireland." *Folk-Lore* 47 (1936): 263–93.

Kennedy, Patrick. *Legendary Fictions of the Irish Celts.* London: Macmillan 1866.

Mac Róigh, Fearghus. *Bruidhean Chaorthainn (Donegal Folk Version).* Dublin 1911.

Murphy, Gerard. *Duanaire Finn.* Part 3. Irish Texts Society 43. Dublin 1953.

– Saga and Myth in Ancient Ireland. Dublin: Colm O Lochlainn 1961.

– Tales from Ireland. Dublin: Browne and Nolan 1946.

Ó Crohan, Tomás. *The Islandman.* Translated by Robin Flower. 1929. Reprint. Oxford: Oxford University Press 1985.

O Coileáin, Seán. "The Making of Tromdam Guaire." *Ériu* 28 (1977): 32–67.

Ó Duilearga, Séamus [Delargy, James]. *Leabhar Sheáin Í Chonaill.* Dublin: The Folklore of Ireland Society 1948.

Ó hEochaidh, Seán, Máire Ní Néill, and Séamas Ó Catháin. *Síscéalta Ó Thír Chonaill/Fairy Legends from Donegal.* Dublin: Comhairle Bhéaloideas Éireann 1977.

O'Sullivan, Sean [Ó Súilleabháin, Seán]. *Folktales of Ireland.* Chicago: University of Chicago Press 1966.

– and Reider Th. Christiansen. "The Types of Irish Folk-Tale." *Folklore Fellows Communications* 188 (1963).

Robinson, Fred Norris. *Satirists and Enchanters in Early Irish Literature.*

1911. Reprints in Irish Series 1, American Committee for Irish Studies. N.p. n.d.

Sayers, Peig. *Peig.* Áth Cliath agus Corcaigh: Comhlucht Oideachais na hÉireann n.d.

3 *Scotland*

Bruford, Alan. "A Lost MacMhuirich Manuscript." *Scottish Gaelic Studies* 10, pt. 1 (1963): 158–62.

Campbell, John Francis (of Islay). *Leabhar na Féinne.* 1872. Reprint. Shannon Ireland: Irish University Press 1972.

– *Popular Tales of the West Highlands.* 2nd ed. 4 vols. 1890–3. Reprint. Detroit: Singing Tree Press 1969.

– *More West Highland Tales.* Edited by J.G. MacKay. 2 vols. Edinburgh: Oliver and Boyd 1940, 1960.

Campbell, John Gregorson. *The Fians.* Waifs and Strays of Celtic Tradition, vol. 4. 1891. Reprint. New York: AMS Press 1973.

– *Superstitions of the Highlands and Islands of Scotland.* Glasgow: James MacLehose and Sons 1900.

– *Witchcraft and Second Sight in the Highlands and Islands of Scotland.* 1902. Reprint. East Ardsley, Yorkshire: E.P. Publishing 1974.

Campbell, John Lorne. *Sia Sgeulachdan.* Edinburgh: T & A Constable 1939.

– "Proverbs from Barra Collected by the Late Neil Sinclair." *Scottish Gaelic Studies* 10, pt. 2 (1965): 178–208.

– "Angus MacLellan M.B.E. ('Aonghus Beag')." *Scottish Studies* 10 (1966): 193–7.

– ed. *A Collection of Highland Rites and Customs.* Cambridge: D.S. Brewer 1975.

– and Francis Collinson. *Hebridean Folksongs.* Vol. 2. Oxford: Oxford University Press 1977.

– and Derick Thomson. *Edward Lhuyd in the Scottish Highlands, 1699–1700.* Oxford: Oxford University Press 1963.

Carmichael, Alexander. "Toirioc na Taine." *Transactions of the Gaelic Society of Inverness* 2 (1872): 25–42.

– *Deirdire.* 1905. Reprint. Inverness: Club Leabhar 1972.

– *Carmina Gadelica.* 6 vols. Edinburgh: Scottish Academic Press 1928–71.

Craig, K.C. *Sgialachdan Dhunnchaidh.* Glasgow: Alasdair Matheson 1944.

Delargy, James. "Three Men of Islay." *Scottish Studies* 4 (1960): 126–33.

Draak, Martje. "Duncan MacDonald of South Uist." *Fabula* 1 (1958): 47–58.

Flett, J. F., and T. M. Flett. "Some Hebridean Folk Dances." *Journal of the English Folk Dance and Song Society* 6, no 2 (1953): 112–27.

Gairm. Glasgow 1952– .

McDonald, Allan. *Gaelic Words and Expressions from South Uist and Eriskay*. Edited by John Lorne Campbell. Dublin: Dublin Institute for Advanced Studies 1958.

MacDonald, Donald Archie. "Collecting Oral Literature." In *Folklore and Folklife* edited by Richard M. Dorson, 407–30. Chicago: University of Chicago Press 1972.

– "Donald Alasdair Johnson – a Storyteller from South Uist." *Tocher* 2 (Summer 1971): 36–7.

– and Alan Bruford. *Scottish Traditional Tales*. Edinburgh: University of Edinburgh, School of Scottish Studies 1974.

MacDougall, James, ed. *Folk and Hero Tales*. Waifs and Strays of Celtic Tradition, vol. 3. 1891. Reprint. New York: AMS Press 1973.

MacInnes, Duncan, ed. *Folk and Hero Tales*. Waifs and Strays of Celtic Tradition, vol. 2. 1890. Reprint. New York: AMS Press 1973.

Maclean, Calum. "Hebridean Storytellers." *Arv* 8 (1952): 120–9.

– "Aonghus agus Donnchadh." *Gairm* 10 (An Geamhradh 1954): 170–4.

– "Death Divination in Scottish Folk Tradition." *Transactions of the Gaelic Society of Inverness* 42 (1953–9): 56–67.

– "A Folk Variant of the Táin Bó Cúailnge from Uist." *Arv* 15 (1959): 160–71.

– *The Highlands*. 1959. Reprint. Inverness: Club Leabhar 1975.

MacLellan, Angus. *Stories from South Uist*. Translated by John Lorne Campbell. London: Routledge & Kegan Paul 1961.

– *The Furrow behind Me*. Translated by John Lorne Campbell. London: Routledge & Kegan Paul 1962.

– *Saoghal an Treobhaiche*. Edited by John Lorne Campbell. Inverness: Club Leabhar 1972.

MacLeod, Kenneth. "Maoim-Chruachan and Cuchulinn." *The Celtic Magazine* 13 (1887–8): 514–16.

Matheson, William. "Duncan MacDonald." *Tocher* 25 (Spring 1977): 1–32.

Moireasdan, Pàdruig. *Ugam agus Bhuam*. Edited by Dòmhnall Eairdsidh Dòmhnallach. Steòrnabhagh: Club Leabhar 1977.

Nicholson, Alexander, ed. *A Collection of Gaelic Proverbs and Familiar Phrases*. 2nd ed. Edinburgh: MacLachlan and Stuart 1882.

Scottish Council for Research in Education. *Aithris is Oideas*. London: University of London Press 1964.

Scottish Gaelic Studies. Oxford 1926– .

Storey, Lisa. *Bha Siod Ann Reimhid*. Inbhirnis: Club Leabhar 1975.

Tocher. Edinburgh 1971– .
Transactions of the Gaelic Society of Inverness. Inverness 1871– .

4 *Nova Scotia (Cape Breton)*

Campbell, Hector. *Luirgean Eachainn Nill.* Edited by Margaret MacDonell and John Shaw. Stornoway: Acair 1981.
Cape Breton's Magazine. Wreck Cove, N.S. 1973– .
Dunn, Charles, W. "Gaelic in Cape Breton." *An Gaidheal* 43 (1948): 143–5; 44 (1948): 6–9.
– *Highland Settler: A Portrait of the Scottish Gael in Nova Scotia.* Toronto: University of Toronto Press 1953.
Jackson, Kenneth. "Notes on the Gaelic of Port Hood." *Scottish Gaelic Studies* 6 (1949): 179–83.
MacDonnell, Hughie Dan, and Kathleen MacKinnon. "Cath nan Eun." *Gairm* 50 (An t-Earrach 1965): 136–50.
– and John Shaw. "Raonall Mac Ailein Òig." *Cape Breton's Magazine* 13 (June 1976): 18–19.
– and Shaw, John. "Conall Ruadh nan Car." *Cape Breton's Magazine* 21 (December 1978): 13–21.
MacLellan, Lauchie, and John Shaw. "Lauchie Tells Lauchie's Dream." *Cape Breton's Magazine* 23 (August 1979): 18–32.
MacLeòid, C.I.M. *Sgeulachdan à Albainn Nuaidh.* Glasgow: Gairm 1960.
MacNeil, Joe Neil, and John Shaw. "Iain Mac an Iasgair Mhóir." *Cape Breton's Magazine* 16 (June 1977): 24–32; 17 (August 1977): 30–9.
Mac-Talla. Sydney, N.S. 1892–1904.

Aarne-Thompson International Folktale Types